THE CRAFT OF PIANO PLAYING

A New Approach to Piano Technique

Alan Fraser

Illustrations by Sonya Ardan

The Scarecrow Press, Inc.
Lanham, Maryland, and Oxford
2003

SCARECROW PRESS, INC.

Published in the United States of America
by Scarecrow Press, Inc.
A Member of the Rowman & Littlefield Publishing Group
4501 Forbes Boulevard, Suite 200, Lanham, Maryland 20706
www.scarecrowpress.com

PO Box 317
Oxford
OX2 9RU, UK

Excerpt from *Awareness Through Movement* by Moshe Feldenkrais in Appendix 1
used by permission of HarperCollins

British Library Cataloguing in Publication Information Available

Library of Congress Cataloging-in-Publication Data

Fraser, Alan, 1955–
  The craft of piano playing : a new approach to piano technique /
Alan Fraser ; illustrations by Sonya Ardan.
    p. cm.
  Includes bibliographical references (p.   ) and index.
  ISBN 0-8108-4591-1 (pbk. : alk. paper)
  1. Piano—Instruction and study. I. Title.
MT220 .F8 2003
786.2'193—dc21

2002190802

☉™ The paper used in this publication meets the minimum requirements of
American National Standard for Information Sciences—Permanence of
Paper for Printed Library Materials, ANSI/NISO Z39.48-1992.
Manufactured in the United States of America.

For Jelena

CONTENTS

SECTION I — THE FOREGROUND PIANISTIC PROBLEMS IN MUSICAL CRAFT

PART I – GETTING STARTED

PART II – GENERAL PRINCIPLES OF MOVEMENT AT THE PIANO

PART III – HAND STRENGTH AND FUNCTION A: PERFECTING LEGATO

PART IV – HAND STRENGTH AND FUNCTION B: THE SPECIAL ROLE OF THE THUMB AND ITS RELATIONSHIP TO THE FOREFINGER

SECTION II — THE MIDDLEGROUND
SOME GENERAL ASPECTS OF MUSICAL CRAFT

PART XI – RHYTHM

PART XII – PHRASING

PART XIII – ORCHESTRATION

SECTION III — THE BACKGROUND
TELL A STORY

PART XIV – EMOTIONAL CONTENT

PART XV – A FEW LAST THOUGHTS

CONTENTS

ILLUSTRATIONS

MUSICAL EXAMPLES

APPLICATIONS

ACKNOWLEDGEMENTS

Not only many valued colleagues and friends helped me in preparing this book, but several people even nearer and dearer to me—bringing the book to press has been largely a family affair. I would like to thank especially my father F. Clarke Fraser for his great help in editing the text. His clarity, insight and constant support helped keep the ball rolling when the task looked insurmountable. And my wife's uncle Zoran Nikolich was an invaluable source in our work on his Serbian translation. Reviewing the entire manuscript sentence by sentence became virtually the preparation of a second edition that has been incorporated into this first. Thanks to another invaluable translator, Meng Qui of Wuhan Conservatory, who fulfilled the daunting task of translating my complex ideas clearly to my Chinese students, and stimulated me to further clarity and exactitude in their expression. Thanks as well to Sonya Ardan for her talent, patience and understanding in preparing the illustrations.

My production team was superb. Warm thanks to Rebecca Massa, Debra Schepp, Beth Easter for her meticulous, insightful proofreading, and my typesetter Nenad Bogdanovich whose patience with me and skill with my materials remain unquantifiable!

Of the many personal friends who leant their valuable support, I would like to single out John Seely and Jerry Karzen—they'll know why.

My debt to all my teachers is too great to be adequately acknowledged. I am especially grateful to Phil Cohen, a pioneer of true vision and genius who provided the seed for many of my key ideas. And warmest thanks to Kemal Gekich, a most highly esteemed colleague and dear friend whose youthful exuberance, personal magnetism, scathing wit, incisive perception, selfless dedication and awesome talent have all left their mark on both me and this book.

Finally, thanks to all my students both past and present, each of who in his or her own way was also my teacher.

SECTION I
THE FOREGROUND

PIANISTIC PROBLEMS IN
MUSICAL CRAFT

I

GETTING STARTED

1 INTRODUCTION

A new approach

This book presents a new approach to the art of piano playing aimed at extending the physical and musical capacities of pianists from the dedicated amateur to top-level professionals. In it I have taken principles movement from Feldenkrais Method[2] and the Eastern martial arts and applied them to the dynamics of piano performance. My book's title pays homage to Heinrich Neuhaus, the celebrated Russian pianist-pedagogue. Published over fifty years ago, Neuhaus' monumental work *The Art of Piano Playing* still stands for many of us as the pianist's bible. Hopefully my work will lead pianists to greater success in implementing his precepts, by showing them more clearly *how*. By filling in a missing link between musical intention and physical execution, this book aims to advance the craft of piano playing.

The process of reforming pianistic habits by means of a written text is not easy, as each pianist presents a unique set of acquired skills and unresolved problems. However, this system of movement physics at the keyboard aims to be comprehensive enough that each pianist may find the way to a fluid, capable untangling of some of the piano's most notorious technical Gordian knots.

Natural, individual and systematic human activity

Moshe Feldenkrais, creator of the method out of which much of my theory arises, cites three successive stages of development in all human activity: the natural, individual and methodical.[3] All our natural activities such as running,

---

[1] 1.1 Fedor Chaliapine, *Ma Vie, traduit du Russe par andre Pierre* (Paris: A. Michel, 1932); 155 (English translation mine).

[2] 1.2 See chapter 46, appendices I, II, III.

[3] 1.3 Moshe Feldenkrais, *Awareness Through Movement* (New York: Harper & Row, 1972); 25-29.

jumping, walking or eating, are a common heritage: they function similarly in everyone. But occasionally an individual finds a special way of doing something, and if it is an improvement over the normal way, this tends to be adopted by those around him. Thus Australian aboriginals throw boomerangs, the Japanese learn judo, and North Americans go snowboarding! In the third stage, somebody observes the specialized activity and systematizes it, so that the process is now carried out according to a specific method as the result of knowledge and instruction, and no longer instinctively.

In the history of the various trades and arts practiced in the civilized world, we can find these three stages almost without exception. In the dawn of humanity people produced wonderful drawings naturally, and Leonardo da Vinci employed elementary principles of perspective, but it was only in the nineteenth century that these were fully defined; since then they have been taught in every school of art.

The simpler and more common an action is, the later will be the development of the third stage. Accepted methods were developed for the weaving of carpets, mapmaking, geometry and mathematics thousands of years ago, yet walking, standing and other basic activities are only now, through systems such as the Alexander Technique and Feldenkrais Method, reaching the third, or systematic stage. Where then does piano playing stand in all this?

Reduced physical prowess has led to homogenized musical expression

A hundred years ago, all Russian conservatory students underwent an exceptionally rigorous technical regime. Rachmaninoff said that scales and arpeggios were the foundation of his technique and that all his life he practiced them religiously. When he graduated from Moscow Conservatory it is said that he could play any Hanon exercise at 220 quarter notes to the minute, transposed to any key! Modern pedagogy scoffs at the 'mindless mechanical drill' of that era, but now we seldom if ever see this kind of physical mastery. To reach the Olympics, an athlete needs to acquire both a set of increasingly refined physical skills and basic strength. And so do aspiring pianists.

Today our main focus tends to be on relaxation, indirect attack on the key for warm tone, and supple arm movements to avoid injury. Unfortunately, this can limit us to a narrower pianistic sound spectrum. A reduced variety of dynamic and tonal range cannot do justice to our musical sophistication, and prevents the piano from doing what it alone can do so well—simulating the sound of an entire orchestra.

I suspect that even many advanced pianists now lack the sheer facility and the resulting power that our most illustrious forebears possessed, and this is one key reason why it is so often difficult to tell one pianist's playing from another's. The problem is not too much focus on technique, but too little. Of course I am not suggesting that the student go off and pump iron or do Charles Atlas exercises to develop bulging muscles. But when I show my students how to organize themselves physically to get good sound, their hand tends to tire very quickly. Their technique hasn't evolved to the point where it would make such great demands on their physical strength. They do not lack musicality, but their technical focus has not been far-reaching enough to manifest that musicality fully.

We have failed to preserve and pass on to following generations crucial knowledge about the most advanced aspects of piano technique. Although some artists have reached unimaginable heights, a full understanding of what they *did* has not yet been incorporated into piano method. Gone for the most part (with a few commendable exceptions) are the freedom and extravagance of expression, 'the grand manner' for which we admire the old boys such as Rachmaninoff, de Pachmann, Friedman, and of course, the one they called 'the last Romantic', Vladimir Horowitz.

These great pianists constituted the second, individual stage of development in piano playing. Each of them brought the art to a new level. Nobody can duplicate their talent, but certain aspects of how they were organized physically *can* be analyzed and systematized. I propose the creation of a new generation of Romantics through an intelligent reconstitution of piano technique in its highest form. A further reaching, more global systematization of piano method can lead to improved physical ability, in turn freeing musical individuality to express itself more fully. This book aims to restore both physical and creative power to the pianist.

Much has been done already to systematize piano playing, but up until now the focus has been more on musical than physical issues. This is not a bad thing; it is the natural way. We conceive a certain sound, phrasing, emotion, and rely to a large extent on an instinctive process somewhere in our sensory-motor system to transform our musical idea into sonic fact. However in the light of new insights into the physics of human movement, we can now educate that instinctive process by recognizing and defining the physical processes involved in implementing our musical intentions.

We cannot expect a revival of the Draconian regime of Moscow 100 years ago. Instead I offer a series of exercises designed to develop hand/arm structure and function both intellectually and physically. If we cannot return to the old, let us invent new paths to pianistic perfection.

Horowitz: a benchmark in ability

One of the prime forces driving me towards my discoveries was the playing of Vladimir Horowitz. It was not only the marvelous music he made but also the way he made it. There was something entirely different going on when he played. He existed in a different state, something akin to the trance state of meditation, but in which he was *doing* the most amazing and complex things. The meditator observes without doing; Horowitz seemed to observe the unfolding of a composition—as understood by his enchanted imagination—even while he was occupied with the myriad complexities involved in actually playing it!

Theoretically it should be possible to play as well as or even better than the master, but imitating him in any habitual way gives superficial results—you are more likely to produce a gross caricature of his mannerisms (many of which were unattractive in any case!) than the ineffable beauty he could create. If you want to approach what he *did*, you must first undertake a profound analysis of all the ingredients of his process, then attempt to acquire them. Our goal is not to play like Horowitz, but as capably as he did. These are two very different things!

Other movement disciplines feed view of piano technique

The more this analytical process encompasses, the better chance it has of bringing relevant new information into the picture—thus my 20-year studies of T'ai Chi Chuan and Feldenkrais Method. It was something about Horowitz's *quality* of movement that led me to consider movement in its own right. The principles I learned away from my instrument allowed me to return to the piano with new insights.

One practical aspect of Horowitz's meditative, trance-like level of awareness was his remarkable economy of movement. Many people thought he was very stiff, but that incredible variety and richness of sound he produced belies the impression. I believe that although he did not appear to move much, internally his movement was exceptionally free, exact and effective.

This quality is exactly what the T'ai Chi master possesses. Studying Feldenkrais Method and T'ai Chi Chuan has allowed me to learn the qualities of precise, effective, meditative movement, and to develop a series of keyboard exercises designed to enhance those qualities in our playing.

Back to movement basics for fundamental, global improvement

In many sports and martial arts, certain basic movements are practiced which later on become the building blocks for more complicated techniques. Moshe Feldenkrais took that process (creating exercises based on the component parts of a complex activity) one step further, returning to the individual components of generic human movements themselves—movements such as bending and straightening, standing, walking—to improve the whole action by fine-tuning each constituent part.

All parts of our body tend not to be equally well represented in the motor cortex, and these more poorly represented parts do not participate in movement as well as they could. Feldenkrais Method uses directed awareness of specific sensations to bring these parts back into full neuro-muscular representation. This is one means by which we can refine the 'building blocks' of the most basic human movements, and bring a new ability and sophistication to the performance of more complex tasks.

In classical piano, the 'basic exercises' have always been scales, arpeggios, double notes and of course etudes. The exercises I present here aim to do for piano what Feldenkrais Method does for human movement. The plan: to examine every detail of the basic movements required to play piano, movements fundamentally defined by the requirements of music and sound, not only of scales and other traditional aspects of technique. The goal: by executing these basic movements with a new level of command, with an understanding that is not only intellectual but sensory— kinesthetic, physical, functional and practical— we bring a new level of physical skill to our playing.

Conscious analysis of normally automatic actions

Most of our actions are automatic, and necessarily so—the thinking mind simply cannot work quickly enough to keep tabs on everything proficiently. If I drove a car trying to observe and analyze every move I made, I would crash in no time. Yet to improve movement patterns learned long ago, or even while learning a new movement, I must undertake exactly that process of 'disassembly' and observation. If I do so intelligently, when I again put the action on automatic pilot I will have a new ability, elegance and ease of execution—a new functionality.

Primary focus on the physical

Some colleagues claim that this book focuses too much on the physical, giving short shrift to musical and philosophical aspects of piano playing. But in my experience, sensing with increased awareness how I produce a sound physically, leads me to perceive that sound with much greater accuracy, and ultimately to consider musical and philosophical aspects of my playing in a new light as well. In any case the starting point of my approach, which I call the background, *is* character, emotional content, the message the composer felt and wanted to convey. Only from this do I proceed to its musical means of expression, the middleground. Yet sooner or later in my work (and more often sooner than later!) I end up back at the foreground, the physical means to achieve musical goals, simply because we don't know enough about the physical realities of keyboard practice! Only the most talented of us can rely on an instinctive process of finding the best physical way. For many of us, starting from the physical can become an effective way to move towards more profound music making.

So this book does concern itself primarily with the foreground, and with good reason. I have tried to create movement patterns that activate a physical organization most useful to the pianist, and then relate these to elements of musicianship—in fact, to synthesize musical and physical issues. I aim to help both pianists who need remedial work in basic strength at the keyboard and those who seek a new dimension of musical understanding and a new path for the development of pianistic skills. I do my best to maintain an eminently practical orientation, avoiding as much as possible the time-consuming presentation of theoretical detail and instead guiding the student through an experiential process.

I have tried my best to transmit this knowledge in the spirit of service— service not so much to you personally, dear reader, as to music itself. I invite you to give your utmost in concentration and dedication, with a true intention to serve something higher. If you succeed in staying with me as I guide you through these investigative processes, we can look forward to a breakthrough in your ability at the piano.

2 How to Use This Book

Be flexible—adapt the book to your own learning style

The main body of this text comprises the lesson transcripts found mostly in section one. It is difficult to communicate the real substance of a lesson through the printed medium, without the benefit of sound, vision and touch. I have tried to make up for this by an exact use of language, doing my best to be both precise and graphically descriptive.

Some of you will want first to familiarize yourselves with part I, *General Principles of Movement at the Piano*, while others will prefer to plunge straight into the more practically oriented sections that follow.

You do not necessarily need to read this book in the set order of chapters. You may very well find it expedient to browse, jump around a bit, get a feel for the material and perhaps happen by chance upon the points most relevant to you. For instance, although I deal first with hand strength and structure, arm function and arm rotation, for many students natural finger shape may be the most desirable starting point, a central locus. You must see what works best for your own particular needs.

Most important, try things out! Don't sit there like a couch potato—get to a piano (or even a table top for some of the exercises) and do the things you are reading about. You will find through experience what feels good for you and what doesn't. Remember the saying, "use it or lose it!" My variant (with apologies to the famous manufacturer of running shoes): Don't eschew it, just *do* it!

This is especially important for pedagogues. There is a danger inherent in attempting to show a student these exercises without having incorporated them thoroughly into one's own system. In the end, the knowledge you can most effectively transmit to others is that gained through your own experience. When I came to Yugoslavia I expressed to Kemal Gekich the desire to become a really great teacher. His response was to tell me to first become a great player. I tried my best to take him at his word, and whether I succeeded or not, without this attempt the book would not exist in its present form.

Listening

Remember that listening never ceases to play a crucial role even in these physically oriented exercises. Your ear should be your guide in everything. You should be constantly training and refining it, to better hear any deficiencies that might exist in your sound, and to evaluate that through the exercises your sound is indeed improving.

Over and over again I see pianists inadvertently sabotaging their own best musical intentions with automatic physical habits learned long ago. They simply don't notice that their hand is acting in *opposition* to the desired musical result. For instance we may have a *forte* legato passage in the bass register to be played in crescendo, yet the arm is overly active on each attack, the fingers strangely inert, the notes not even really joined physically. But the pianist is accustomed to playing like this, and finds the resulting forced, non-legato sound acceptable! He thinks he's doing what he's not! He has lulled himself into a false sense of security because he is doing what he was told, moving his arm in the standard generic manner taught by 'tradition' (but really by default).

How can I help him? First I must call attention to the deficiency in his sound. But then, and perhaps even more useful, I call attention to what he is doing physically to create that deficiency! Monitoring his physical organization may help him notice flaws in his sound that previously escaped his attention. To couch it in terms of Neuro-Linguistic Programming (NLP), the physical sensation creates an *anchor* for the experience of improved hearing. He can better produce the desired musical result when he understands and remembers the physical *feeling* of doing it.

The enriched kinesthetic picture cultivated by the exercises aims to open a whole new dimension of perception, and especially of *hearing*. If the physical is not aligned with the aural, even your most assiduous efforts will be for naught. Remember, your *ear* must be the ultimate judge.

Tendonitis—a cautionary note

I have been told that some of my exercises are actually dangerous and can damage the hand, cause tendonitis, etc. I acknowledge this legitimate concern, and would like to stress that if you are at all worried about tendonitis, approach the hand strength exercises with extreme caution. I developed them with a group of students who were in very good pianistic shape to begin with. If you have had problems, then *do not begin at full power but at 5 percent.* Try to divine and define *function* before you increase power gradually to full strength. Understand the principle before putting it into practice. Experiment, always taking care not necessarily to avoid strain entirely, but to manage it wisely. Your aim is to activate muscles that need to be activated while relieving stress on muscles that do not need it. If done correctly, you will find that in fact, these exercises, through accessing the hand's true strength and function, can both relieve tendonitis and prevent its occurrence.

Tendonitis most often arises from constant, long-term overpressing. Even though theoretically, pressure on the key after it has been struck should have no effect on the sound produced, pianists will insist on maintaining a constant pressure for hours of playing, without adequate finger activity that would evoke intermittent fluctuations in that pressure. This of course can exert a tremendous stress on the mechanism.

Many of my exercises employ very strong pressing, but rarely will you be required to *play* like that. The pressing exercises are designed to improve the kinesthetic representation of certain structural and functional attributes of the hand. The information acquired by pressing should then be incorporated into your normal manner of playing—pressing should not become your normal approach to the keyboard!

If the muscular contraction that produces the sound is maintained only for the minimum time required to achieve the sonic result, there will be no fatigue. Fatigue results from the muscles staying contracted longer than they need to. Here it is even worse because this ongoing contraction also interferes with the free production of the next tone. Much of my text aims to have you produce richer tone through reducing the duration of your muscular impulses to effective lengths. This way of improving your sound also reduces stress on your physical mechanism.

Pain

Once on a bus in New York I saw the most incredible advertisement for the U. S. Marines. A picture of a big, burly man climbing a rope ladder bore the caption, "Pain is just weakness leaving the body"! As a blanket statement nothing could be more ludicrous. Pain generally signals that something is not working properly and that the problem needs to be addressed. In piano playing, most pain anywhere above your wrist falls into this category. In grossly general terms, something below your wrist isn't working as it should—something above is overworking in compensation. However, there are certain types of pain in the hand itself that may signal not a problem but the beginning of its resolution. Certain muscles may be starting to acquire proper function. Muscles that have lain dormant for too long may be finally beginning to do the work they were designed to do. Just like the ache in your calves when you run after a three-month layoff, this type of pain may be not only innocuous but even desirable, if of course you act with moderation and not undue force. Learn to discriminate!

There are of course exceptions to these general guidelines—the bottom line: *proceed with intelligence and caution!*

Performance anxiety

This approach can also serve as an effective antidote to debilitating performance anxiety, which I divide into two types. Positive performance anxiety derives from the knowledge that something wonderful *might* happen between you, the music and the audience in a performance, but there is never a guarantee that it will. It is just as well that there is nothing anybody can do to eradicate this type of nervousness, because it tends to improve rather than impinge upon one's performance. The inrush of energy and excitement it can engender has a great deal to do with the degree of inspiration one brings to one's playing.

Negative performance anxiety derives from a sense of insecurity. If I have a real basis to feel confident then I won't experience that kind of nervousness. But there's the rub: I may *think* I feel sure when in fact an unacknowledged physical or technical insecurity may be the real root of the problem. I have found that the approach presented here can really uproot and resolve this type of performance anxiety. You *will* be emotionally secure when you have created the physical and musical basis for it.

These exercises are preparatory, developmental. Study and do them; incorporate their kinesthetic message into your reflexes, your senses, your physical apparatus, and then leave them. Forget them; just remember the feeling. Just play! With newfound power, ability, discrimination—play, and enjoy.

Anatomical terms

Although I avoid technical jargon, you should be clear about a few terms. The three bones of each finger are called *phalanges*. Thus the finger joints are the *interphalangeal joints*.

The joint closest to your fingertip is the *distal* interphalangeal joint.

The middle joint is the *proximal* interphalangeal joint.

The bones of the hand are called the *metacarpals*. Thus the knuckle that joins your finger to your hand is the *metacarpal-phalangeal joint*. What I call the *metacarpal ridge* is the row of metacarpal-phalangeal joints, the enlarged distal ends of the metacarpals that form your knuckles.

It is interesting that on an x-ray the metacarpals resemble a fourth set of phalanges. There is nothing to indicate that they are bound together, a fixed structure within the flesh of the hand. Cartilage and tendons bind one knuckle to another. If you play around with your hand a bit, massage it this way and that, you will begin to see that the metacarpals are not totally fixed. They do have some degree of flexibility, some capacity for movement up and down. This flexibility could become a useful element of your technique.

The *wrist* is a clever arrangement of eight bones, a double hinge joint that moves most easily in the plane that is vertical when our hand lies flat. Here the range of movement is almost 180 degrees whereas if your hand lying flat swivels horizontally it can cover an arc of only about 90 degrees.

Your *humerus* is the bone connecting your elbow to your shoulder. Your forearm has two bones. The *radius*, closer to your thumb, rotates around the *ulna*, the bone closer to your fifth finger. Rotating your hand to lie palm down is called *pronation*, to lie palm up, *supination*.

Extension means opening the limbs or straightening the joint; *flexion* means closing them or bending the joint.

Your *biceps* is the 'goose egg' muscle on the front of your upper arm. Its function is to flex, closing the elbow joint to fold your arm. It also helps supinate – externally rotate – the forearm (as in turning a screwdriver). The *triceps* joins the back of your elbow to your shoulder. Its function is extension, opening the elbow joint and straightening your arm. It also helps to move the arm towards the body (adduct), and has a crucial function in playing, to stabilize the position of your partially extended arm.

3 Background, Middleground and Foreground: A Plan for Work

The basic layout of this book, contrary to conventional methodology, deals first with physical concerns and only then progresses to musical issues. But remember, the evolution of this approach followed the reverse process. Before we plunge into the nuts and bolts of piano technique, let's touch briefly on some of the key issues that originally impelled me towards my focus on the physical.

The background: tell a story

First and foremost, music must tell a story. If it is to be called art, music must not only communicate the notes but the emotional tone of the tale, the distillation of life experience out of which the work was created. It was through feeling these things that the composer gave birth to his works in the first place, and to do him service we must plunge back into his psychic world, recreating not only his aural constructions but the most significant aspects of his inner life.

Like a great actor, I must not fake the emotions I'm trying to draw out of the music but experience them as I play, letting their very essence flow through me as I recreate. It is my artistic duty to ignite that process in myself even as I observe it. Thus I attempt to discover the program of the work, the composer's poetic or dramatic inspiration, which could be as simple as 'happy' or 'sad', or as complicated as an entire Shakespeare play! The program I ascribe to a work may or may not be what the composer had in mind, but the resulting complex, intense emotional process that fuels my performance may bring me closer to fulfilling music's fundamental purpose: to communicate.

My approach to interpreting a work begins with the *background* conception of music's meaning—its spiritual, programmatic and emotional content which

12

must be expressed, lived in performance. This must be the source, the basis for my decisions about the *middleground*, certain key principles of musical craftsmanship concerning what type of sounds best express that content, and the *foreground*, the specifically pianistic elements of musical craft and their physical realities—how to create those sounds at the piano.

Thus the idea of telling a story should always be the source of our vision, the *why*, the background idea that suffuses all our preoccupations with the details of the middleground and foreground, the *how's* and *what's*. If a pianist attempts to invoke this essential background process before mastering the requisite elements of craftsmanship, the result is chaos, not art. Conversely, perfect craft without this infusion of feeling or empathy remains sterile.

The middleground: some musical craft essentials
1) Strategies of expression in rhetoric

The science of rhetoric, or declamation, is the heart and soul of any musician's art. Making the music speak is what it's all about. It is rhythmic and dynamic inflection that gives life and a speaking quality to melodic line, that makes it tell a story. But little attempt has been made to codify practice in this realm. Are there any indisputable criteria for good phrasing? Can we judge one style of rubato to be better than another, or is it all a question of taste?

Long notes longer, short notes shorter

The term *tempo rubato* literally means 'robbed time'—the stealing of time from one point in the melody and 'paying it back' somewhere else. But rubato is not the only technique used in musical rhetoric, and not even the most important one. We need to clarify the difference between rubato and melodic and harmonic inflection or accentuation, what Heinrich Neuhaus calls melodic intonation. Inflection serves not to impair time and rhythm but rather to bring them into heightened relief. Our signs of notation cannot adequately express the slight lingering or flowing forward of melodic inflection, because it involves literally atomic time values.

The most effective type of rhythmic inflection is lending more of a note's 'length quality' to it, making long notes slightly longer, short notes shorter. This enhances the music's structural quality: proportional relations are preserved and even strengthened rather than distorted into a caricature.

This simple little rule is often not only ignored but contravened! Why do so many pianists employ the opposite strategy? At a recent major piano competition I listened, somewhat appalled, as one young pianist after another, trying their best to be expressive, fell into the trap of rushing through long notes, lingering over short. This destroys the musical proportions so carefully crafted by the composer, leaving an impression of instability, weakness and hysteria rather than emotional depth.

Entasis

The builders of the Parthenon were very shrewd in this regard. They knew that if they made its lines straight, the temple would look pretty good. But if the 'straight' lines were bent imperceptibly into convex curves they would appear even straighter, more perfectly proportioned! This technique of purposeful, almost imperceptible curvature is called *entasis*. They used it knowing that human perception is distorted—our organs of sight, hearing, touch and taste do not transmit visual, auditory and sensory stimuli to us with absolute accuracy. If you look carefully at the Parthenon's floor and frieze, you can see them curving up slightly from the corners to the midpoints. This diagram shows the distortions the architects employed in exaggerated form.

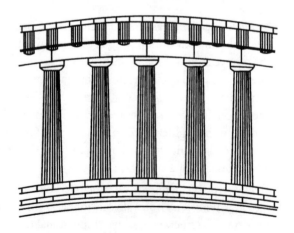

Illustration 3.1: Proportional refinements in the Parthenon, visually exaggerated

To our eyes, which take in visual stimuli through convex lenses, this makes their lines appear to be *more* straight when viewed from a distance, more perfect than actual geometric symmetry would.

Just as entasis renders a visual effect more vivid through distortion, the principle of lengthening long and shortening short actually highlights aural contour, allowing us to feel each unique expressive shape more vividly. I call this *aural entasis*, and it is an essential element of musical rhetoric. To some extent, aural entasis should suffuse every bar of music we play, but that's not the end of the story. In musical rhetoric there are many more tricks to the trade.

Inflecting melodic contour

In addition to inflection of long and short rhythmic values there is also the dynamic inflection of melodic contour. A rudimentary strategy here is to get louder the higher the melody climbs, softer the lower it descends. But it's not so simple: melodic and harmonic structure very often may require diminuendo in climbing or a crescendo in descent.

Still further strategic elements can be found in the practices of a good singer, who for instance combines rhythmic and melodic concerns when stretching the high note of a phrase or taking more time to span larger melodic leaps. The singer may do this for technical purposes (larger leaps are more difficult to sing in tune), and yet there is also an important element of musical expression in this practice that we would do well to emulate.

Inflecting syncopations

Rhythmic displacements should also get special attention. Wait an instant before sounding a syncopation, then lean on it, linger over it, let its musical function be felt, and finally slide ahead out of it back into real time. On the other hand, when melodic structure takes precedence over rhythmic, you might want to flow through a downbeat rather than giving it its normally strong stress.

But the science of melodic inflection is even more than these basic strategies. It is a complex and involved art based on the fact that a melody's expressive content is inherent in its structure. Any alteration from the neutral or mechanical reproduction of a note, any manipulation that is designed to enhance the audibility of musical structure, falls under this rubric.

2) Pulse

Before launching into the complexities of expressive inflection, all good musicians will have done their basic homework, cultivating healthy pulse. Listen analytically to a selection of classical recordings. Do you notice that metronomic regularity is no guarantee of rhythmic vitality, that certain performances seem more 'alive' than others? This is because the basic nature of rhythm is much more than a simple regularity of accented and unaccented beats. *Pulse* ideally suffuses the accented beats, giving them life. In order for rhythm to come truly alive, the player must feel the pulse almost larger than life. In the same way that an informed distortion of note lengths can actually highlight rhythmic contour, intelligent distortion of the flow of pulses can allow them to be felt with more intensity.

This can be done by putting micropauses in front of each pulse note, then using that momentary pause to feel a balance, a 'poised-ness', to feel an *oomph* rising up from somewhere inside and generating an *alive* rhythm. Then, keeping the flow of unaccented attacks leading to the next pulse relatively light, subtle and very even can enhance the power of the pulse even more, without it becoming rough or over-obvious. If this is unfamiliar to you, try listening to a really good jazz group—they tend to do it much better than we classical musicians![1]

At the piano, try feeling as if there is resistance to your hands in the air as you enter the pulse note, or as if your fingers were struggling to flow through some thick liquid like honey in order to strike the key. This keeps you in control. Cultivation of healthy pulse gives tremendous stability, security, accuracy and a wonderful sense of capability. One can *do*, one is not just being 'done'.

3) Basic sound: orchestration

In music, the quality of sound is determined largely by the quality of orchestration and legato. The basic principles of voicing, balancing of parts and control of the melodic line are all common musical knowledge, but over and over again I find pianists fall short of the mark when it comes to putting these ideas into practice.

---

[1] For more on pulse, see *Rhythm* in appendix III.

To orchestrate effectively at the piano, the coloring of contrasting voices through differentiated dynamics must be done in a huge way, far more than you may have imagined, and this takes strength! Take, for instance, the second theme from Chopin's G minor Ballade—a typical cantabile melody in a *p* dynamic.

Example 3.1: Chopin: Ballade in G minor, Op. 23, *mm. 67-73*

Here your melody should actually range from *p* all the way up to a full *f* while your accompaniment never ventures above a *p* and for the most part stays down around ***ppp***! The larger the hall and the better your instrument, the more you need to do this. This is the technique to unlock the heart of a concert instrument—it is the only way to make it really speak! And speak it will—amazingly!

These orchestrational principles also hold in loud chordal passages such as the second appearance, *ff* in A major, of the G minor Ballade's second theme.

Example 3.2: Chopin: Ballade in G minor, Op. 23, *mm. 106-109*

Here, the melody in full chords is the heart of the matter. The underlying harmonies jangle and sing but do not interfere, do not rob the heart-tones of their resonance. Similarly, the bass must provide a healthy, resonating platform without overwhelming the right hand. The bass strings of the piano are so much longer than the descant, it's very easy to overpower. You must give the illusion of bass power without sacrificing treble shine. This knowledge of when, where, and how much to adjust what, is the science of pianistic acoustics.

4) Basic sound: legato

Legato is the 'seamless' joining of one note to another to create an even melodic flow. Instrumentalists try to imitate the sound of the human voice to perfect their legato, yet it doesn't come so easily to singers either. They too must work hard to bring their legato to the highest level. For us pianists, Arnold Schultz puts it so well that I will let him speak for himself:

> The absence of a true legato is *by far the most important factor* in what is popularly designated as bad piano tone. The objection will be raised, no doubt, that such a statement exaggerates the significance of close tonal connection. I think, however, that the matter stands the other way around, that the greatest single point of neglect and inattention in modern [remember, this is 1936!] teaching and playing relates to the manner in which tonal units follow upon one another.

Too often legato is taught as an academic duty owed to a phrase mark rather than as one of the chief joys which a tonal succession, regardless of the instrument producing it, can give to the human ear. The moment of union between two tones of different pitch constitutes a high aesthetic pleasure, an instinctive craving being satisfied when a given vibrational rate is merged with, or—to put it metaphorically—is born out of, another vibrational rate. The singer who failed to connect his tones would rob his audience of much of the pleasure they might otherwise have in the beauty of his tone. He is taught, as a matter of fact, to take consonants, the necessary interruptions of tone, as swiftly and as unobtrusively as possible. The violinist, too, produces some of his most compelling effects as he causes one tone to melt into another. Similarly, at the piano, legato must be employed not merely to conform to a set of musical rules, but rather to produce a vital and highly attractive sensuous beauty.[2]

Without an absolute command of legato, full control of melodic evenness is impossible. But once this physical command of evenness has been instilled in one's system, the ability to control melodic evenness transfers easily to non-legato articulations. Various degrees of portato and staccato can now be employed without unwanted bumps ruining the melodic line. This is why legato is one of the main foundations of not only a pianist's but of any musician's technique.

5) Orchestration and sound image: experience leads to conception, conception to realization

When I tell my students to orchestrate, I very quickly run up against an elementary problem: they simply cannot do it! There are two reasons for this.

For one, they tend not to have the optimal sound image in their ears. If you have never experienced what a piano can *do*, you cannot know it. Often the most effective way to lead someone towards the ability to produce a certain sound is simply to demonstrate. They really *hear* it, perhaps for the first time! With a tangible conception of the sonic goal now in their ears they now at least have some chance of discovering how to produce that sound themselves. And finally the

---

[32] Arnold Schultz, *The Riddle of the Pianist's Finger* (New York: Carl Fischer, 1936); 196-7

moment of enlightenment comes: Oh, yes! *That* sound makes this *emotion*, which
is what the composer wanted.

The foreground—cultivating physical capability

But the enlightenment of a demonstration is not enough—students must be
able to manifest their newfound understanding in practice. And here we run
up against a second major obstacle: they have never subjected their bodies to
such extreme physical demands, and their hands simply have no idea how to
go about it. Both orchestration and legato require much greater hand strength
than we may have suspected. When we first impose these new stresses on our
hands, we don't feel they have the strength. But the strength is actually there,
just waiting to be tapped!

Skeletal alignment to empower hand function

For this, the hand must be activated, galvanized into action so that it becomes a functional entity, a structure that is maintained by the very activity it supports. Ironically, if you acquire the physical organization and strength needed, you can often begin to produce that sound even without having heard it, simply because you are now capable.

This leads us to the foreground: the nuts and bolts, the reality only we pianists have to deal with and the main concern of this book—the mechanics of physical function at the keyboard.

4 WHERE TO START?

Different schools of pianism each have their individual strengths, generally linked to a specific style of expression. Here I attempt to speak in a language that holds across the board. I believe it is possible to improve technique without impinging on the dictates of any one aesthetic, if we take the nature of human movement as our point of departure. The way we move is a fundamental ingredient of any pianistic approach, be it acknowledged or not. Incorporating certain characteristics of human movement into one's methodology can empower any playing style, improving ability while allowing one to remain faithful to and even enhance one's own particular musical aesthetic.

1) Moshe Feldenkrais said that movement is life—life without movement is unthinkable. Thus one measure of our pianistic 'wellness' could be the quality of our movement. Feldenkrais also loved to say, "If you know what you're doing you can do what you want." Here he may seem to belabor the obvious, but in his method we discover a very specific meaning for this. The richer the sensory information being sent to your brain (the actual kinesthetic or proprioceptive images), the better basis you have for organizing movement. In other words, the more you can sense or feel, the more you know what you're doing—the more you have control over your actions.

2) It follows that the less effort involved in an action, the finer your ability to sense and control it. To illustrate: hold a compact disk in the palm of your hand. Now have someone place a fountain pen or similar object on it. You can feel that the pen is there—it is easy to detect the difference in weight. Next try putting five thick books on your hand and then have your friend place the fountain pen there again. Now of course it is impossible to sense the difference—the increased effort needed to hold the books masks the slight change in pressure. Fechner and Weber ascertained that the ratio of effort to sensory ability is 40:1. If your mus-

23

difference of less than one gram.

This demonstrates the efficacy of naturally soft muscle tonus in graphic fashion. Do you see how reduced effort drastically increases your ability to *sense*, to *feel*, and thus eventually to *act* effectively? But how can we reduce effort without reducing efficacy?

3) The more correct the alignment of your skeletal structure, the less effort needed to carry out an action effectively. The forces go through your bones, and so your muscles work less to maintain structural stability. They now have much more power available to do their actual job, locomotion—activation.

This brings us to the point where both traditional schools of piano technique fall short. The finger action school neglected the participation of the arm and other parts of the body, which led to all sorts of physical and tonal problems. The arm weight school over-relaxed, and emasculated the natural power of the fingers (more on that in chapter 8). What we will be aiming for is a cultivation of structural alignments and a quality of movement that respects and uses those alignments, giving us a basis for healthy, effective, elegant movement—movement that makes both us and our music making well.

Bringing the idea of skeletal alignment into the picture leads us to a new vision of human movement, based on structural functionality. Maintaining structural integrity facilitates vastly increased freedom and effectiveness in movement, while effective activity is crucial in generating, rebuilding that very structure (maintaining its alignment). There is a symbiotic relationship between activity and structure.

Now we have an effective basis to remedy

– over moving
– an over-relaxed, powerless approach
– an overly tense approach

Moshe Feldenkrais said that health is "being able to fulfil your unavowed dreams." This for me is a singularly poignant definition. We all have stated goals, yet somewhere inside we cherish those little golden dreams, hopes so precious yet apparently so far from reality. It seems too good to be true that they could manifest! Yet this is just what both Feldenkrais Method and this approach to piano aim to cultivate: a state of wellness that is more than just lack of illness—a capability that is vital and potent.

Thus our plan to enhance physical capability will follow a two-step process:

– develop stability of skeletal structure
– develop its functionality, its ability to move: suffuse that struc-

ture with life, with action.

Elements of the foreground

The foreground of this book will focus mainly on five key elements of piano technique:
- Consolidate hand structure to improve its strength and function (parts II-IV)
- Maximize capability for finger articulation (part V)
- The role of the arm—active and/or passive? (part VI)
- The role of the arm—rotation (part VII)
- Natural finger shape (part VIII)

In practice these are very much interrelated and cannot be separated out into discreet elements. Such arbitrary divisions are a necessary evil, a didactic tool that aims, through elucidation of each separate component, for a synthesis of improved abilities. A general discussion of movement in part I precedes these five central topics. After separate discussion of each element, part IX examines how they can be combined in practice and includes some other technical concerns that elude such straightforward categorization.

The relationship of movement to sound

We first focus on the physical because everything you do while playing, *sounds*. In other words, *all* your movements, both intended and unintentional, affect the sound you produce. Thus the more your physical sensitivity, the greater your control over your sound. The smaller and finer the efforts involved in a movement, the richer the sensory information available. The more you can sense, the better you can monitor and direct your actions. Sensitivity leads both to physical and musical strength.

Another, contrasting, idea is that sometimes an intense *effort* in the correct place is the best path to effective, empowered relaxation. Remember, you should be able to *maintain* sensitivity even while increasing effort to the maximum. This paradox is a key problem confronting pianists.

Our starting point will be to increase the functionality of the fingers in order to clarify, stabilize and activate hand structure. This in turn frees the wrist and all the more central parts of the mechanism (lower arm, upper arm, shoulder, spine, pelvis) to accommodate and follow the movement of the hand in a supportive pelvis) to accommodate and follow the movement of the hand in a supportive way. Once all this is in place we have a dependable foundation of function from which we can broaden our investigation to include other physical elements of musical inflection.

The hand's power derives from function not force

A pianist's hands must have great strength to handle the instrument successfully, yet this strength must not negate the suppleness and sensitivity so much cultivated in modern pedagogy. It must be derived from functionality, not brute force. Most 'banging' one hears stems from an *underuse*, an ineffective use of strength—not overuse.

Avoid injury by maximizing, not reducing, functional options

Activation of the hand's natural strength firms up its structure, and eliminates the weakness of function that leads to tendonitis, carpal tunnel syndrome and the other 'music performance related injuries'. Through development of a stronger, more capable functionality we not only improve our music making but also, hopefully, allow all the music performance injury specialists to focus on maintaining wellness instead of healing injury, as in traditional Chinese medicine where the doctor is embarrassed (and dismissed!) if his patient gets sick.

The most natural way to elicit this strength is to try for a sound that cannot be created without it! For instance the piano can produce a type of electric sound, where you really feel you're 'bonging' the soundboard directly and sending it into un-stifled, free vibration, your finger acting like a drumstick on a drumhead. But for this, everything below your wrist must not even *hint* at collapse. The assembly of bones must be neutral, not stiff, yet so well organized that all the tremendous stress exerted on it doesn't distort its structure. Great power can now be transmitted through your hand, but because it is structurally secure, there is no cramping and damping of the sound. Your hand responds just as that drumstick does, instantaneously ceasing to exert any excess pressure on the key, freeing the sound to vibrate onward in time and space. Your hand maintains its supple, alive, functional, structural integrity—not a mechanically stiff, locked structure.

Active fingers contribute much to this practical implementation of power. A very alive and ultra-supported finger attack does not need to cramp you up. Done well it keeps the structure of your hand building itself, reinventing itself constantly. When you are organized properly, the more power you have in your hand and fingers where you need it, the freer and more responsive can be your wrist, forearm and upper arm.

This quality of movement may be radically different from that which we habitually bring to the keyboard. It is not so easily acquired, and to give ourselves every possible chance of success, I will turn now to a more general discussion—a reconsideration of the very nature of human movement.[1]

---

[1] Further reflections on movement can be found in appendix I.

II

GENERAL PRINCIPLES OF MOVEMENT AT THE PIANO

5 A Meditation on Some Inner Workings of Movement

Stillness in the meditative sense of the word, that which the gurus seek, consists not so much in a lack of visible movement, as in the absence of any muscular contractions that would *hinder* the ordinary functions and activities of human life. Meditative stillness does *not* mean 'dead'—it is an alive quality that can suffuse our muscular activity, changing *its* quality.

The most truly effective quality of movement derives from this stillness. In piano playing, true stillness in the sense of an alive, agile neutrality is a desirable precondition for significant artistic creation.

Habitual contraction as a hindrance to movement

When a muscle is habitually contracted, as many of ours are, something that was originally designed for movement is being used for the opposite purpose. Habitual contraction holds a certain position rather than generating movement. When bones are aligned so that they support their *own* structure, the help they need from the surrounding muscles to maintain position is reduced to a minimum. This frees the muscles to do their real job—activation!

In the case of emotional 'holding' (as in a chronically contracted rib cage, which virtually all of us have to some degree), the muscles originally served to inhibit the expression (by panting, sobbing, etc.) of undesired emotions, emotions that we were not ready to admit into conscious awareness. But if that inhibitory function continues after it is no longer needed, it interferes with normal breathing. It becomes a type of anti-movement.[1]

---

[51] See chapter 67, *Feeling Emotion in Performance.*

The benefits of cultivating effective stillness

Why is it worth spending months, even years, trying to achieve an alive, capable stillness sitting at the piano?

> 1) It improves your **hearing**. When all that habitual contraction, that purposeless effort falls away, the amount of excess brain activity is so diminished that you become far more aware of the sounds you are making. Can you imagine the relief of acquiring a state-of-the-art satellite dish, and after years of watching a snowy, staticky TV screen, finally getting to see a movie theatre quality picture? Reducing habitual muscular contraction can give you the aural equivalent.
>
> 2) It improves your **feeling**, in the sensory meaning of the word. Habitual contractions inhibit the transmission of spatial sensory information to the brain. When they cease, the brain receives an enriched information base and has a better basis for deciding the most appropriate signals to *send* for effective movement.

When (1) and (2) are in place,

> 3) They improve your **feeling and understanding** in the emotional sense. When your sensory motor system is cleared of all that excess static, you play better. The music *sounds*, you can hear it sound, and you are free to perceive it more deeply and accurately, to grasp its emotional essence, to assimilate it on every level. If you are on the ball, you will not allow this emotional understanding to reactivate any superfluous muscle 'activity'. You will remain neutral (not dead, but in a state of neutrality that is capable, sensitive and ready to respond), a channel through which those emotions may manifest themselves in sound.

Reversible movements are free of inhibitory habitual contractions

Another quality cultivated by a meditative stillness is reversibility. In movement, to be capable of reversing the direction at any point you must be in a higher mode of control. There must be a certain sensitivity, a relaxed, aware relatedness to what you're doing. If you can't reverse your movement in the moment, it means you're using too much effort and inadvertently hindering yourself. If to reverse your direction you must first decouple all the extra effort, then cease the actual action, and finally head in the other direction, it's a lengthy and awkward process. To play the piano with command you need choice: to be so in touch with yourself physically that at any point in time you can 'turn on a dime', change instantaneously the direction of your physical motion, your musical thought, your expressive intention.

6 SLOWING THE KEY DOWN

There is a school of thought that sees the remedy for harsh tone in slowing down the speed of the key. This is an experience-oriented or subjective description of a complex functional process. What we perhaps perceive as slowing the key down is in fact reducing the rigidity or convulsiveness of the muscular contraction with which we move the key. Trying to slow the key down is a mental trick, a practical adaptation to the subjective nature of our perception, a way to improve the effective stillness with which you play. It helps you to physically sense your action better and respond more exactly to it. The increased elegance and exactitude of your attack helps you better attenuate the shock of the key hitting the key bed.

However, in objective terms, to increase your orchestrational range you need not only to be able to slow the key down, but also to *vary* the key speed maximally —to slow it down *or* speed it up as much as is required by dynamic differences.

Hidden causes of harsh tone

Harsh tone does not result, as some claim, from overly quick key descent. Greater key speeds are necessary for greater volume. Harsh tone is a result of:

      1) a lack of integrity and of 'flexible solidity' in hand structure and
      2) a lack of exactitude and accuracy in the contraction of muscles
      and in the control of the limbs producing the sound.

To have a quick key descent without roughness, you must avoid *jamming*—energy being lost through misaligned joints. If you try too hard to make a big sound, you are likely to lose your optimal alignment and get 'jammed up.' When you think, "now it's got to be loud (or brilliant)," you tend to get convulsive. This reduces accuracy in your attack just when you need it the most.

Lack of exactitude in the muscular activity behind an attack forces you, after playing a note or chord, to 'hold on' with certain muscles in order to stabilize a misaligned skeletal structure. Thus the complicated post-attack sequence of movements (so crucial to the completion of one note's sounding and its continuation into the next) is interrupted or at least inhibited. You end up feeling 'jammed', and the music does too! It is crucial that muscular activity, even at its most effortful, does not disturb your natural skeletal alignment. Only then can natural musical movement proceed unimpeded.

You may well improve your tone by feeling as if you *are* slowing the key down. But what you are actually doing is adjusting the operational speed of your complex system of reflexes and reactions to effective levels. Remember, it's a subjective perception: for instance, I was trying to get a student to repair her harsh tone, going through a detailed explanation of hand structure, legato, arm movement, my whole spiel. Finally she got it; her tone improved. She turned to me and said, "Oh, it's simple, I just tried to slow down the key"!

I had purposefully avoided that mode of description as being overly subjective — I did not want to address only perception but really deal with what was actually going on. And yet, the student may not *care* about what is actually going on, but only about a good result! Not all of us are cursed (or blessed depending on how you look at it!) with an analytical mind. What works for you? Going through a whole analytical process or simply slowing the key down?

If you calm down, you increase your chances of organizing yourself properly and avoid a type of hitting where your contact with the key is inexact. One of Moshe Feldenkrais' favorite sayings was "go slow in order to go fast." Here you can see exactly what he means. Calm down, become more aware, get centered: you will *feel* like you're moving more slowly but you can make that key go as fast as you like and still sound great![1]

---

[1] See chapter 19, *Replacing Arm Swoop with Cobra Strike.*

7 FORM FOLLOWS FUNCTION

Aim for variety of tone, not only beauty

For a complete piano technique, is it really only beauty of tone we want? What about all those motoric Prokofiev movements that require a mechanistic, biting, almost harsh sound? What about scherzando, staccatissimo passages in Beethoven? What about those explosive fortissimo interlocking octave passages in Liszt or Tchaikowsky? Is not 'correct tone' that which reflects the *emotional* tone of the music? Thus the more variety and larger scope of tonal color we have in our technical repertoire, the more effective our orchestration and emotional coloring. For this we need the widest possible variety of touches, the greatest possible facility and strength.

Even sounds that under normal circumstances would be consigned to the garbage heap can be produced in a physiologically sophisticated manner. Even 'ugly' can be done beautifully!

Any tone, movement or position can be correct, given the appropriate context

When the context for your technical approach is musical rather than mechanical, a whole new set of physiological demands, a completely new category of mechanical problems arises! In the search for a wider variety of sounds we need to create new forms of technique and even shape our hands into new, unaccustomed forms—forms that can create the sounds we seek.

Correct positions, movements become the byproduct of appropriate musical activity

A pianist's *function* can be defined as follows: to draw from the instrument a sound appropriate to the music's character in the most orchestrally rich and emotionally significant way. Your physical *form*, how you organize yourself technically, will be the result of your orientation towards this goal. Thus the form into which you shape your hand and arm, your 'position', stems from the musical function rather than being a goal in itself. Your wrist may be low one minute, high the next, relatively stiff or loose, depending on the type of sound you want to produce. The correct movement becomes that which articulates the desired musical shape. Technique's main concern should be maximizing the orchestral, coloristic possibilities of the instrument.

Minimizing the risk of injury should not be the goal of technique, but it certainly can be a welcome byproduct, because as it turns out, the most effective way to maximize orchestral color is also usually the healthiest! So instead of trying to avoid excess tension, just make the music speak! Instead of avoiding twisting and stretching, why not learn how to twist and stretch cleverly, to utilize tension intelligently? Your repertoire of effective movements should naturally expand to accommodate your expanding repertoire of musical goals and gestures, your increasing musical capability.

Use extremes effectively—healthy finger curling

Expanding your repertoire of movements will mean learning to *use* the extreme ranges of a physical movement rather than avoiding them. This can develop rather that hurt you if done intelligently. Only by reaching the extremes of your range effortlessly, elegantly, and free of excess tension can you utilize all your movement capabilities.

For example, there is a prevalent theory that curling the fingers inhibits movement whereas merely curving them makes your movement much easier. The idea is that curving involves only short flexors whereas curling employs those nasty long ones! This is an accurate theory as far as it goes, and there is a whole crucial aspect of technique based on exactly this concept. In part VIII, *Natural Finger Shape,* we will explore how maintaining the fingers' naturally curved shape opens up a whole new dimension of subtlety, exactitude, ease and power in finger movement.

Remember, however, that our aim is to have as wide a variety of tone colors and thus of physical movements as possible. It is true that curling the fingers distorts them from their natural shape, but curling the fingers is a primary component of that most basic and useful of hand functions, grasping. Your long flexors are there for a good reason! Just because curving the finger is less stressful than curling doesn't mean you must never curl. Choose the movement that achieves your musical goal, regardless of the amount of effort involved (as long as that effort is educated). Why not find a way to *make* the greater effort, in an elegant, sensible way, in a way that does not hurt you? You cannot and should not always avoid using your long flexors. Imagine not being allowed to curl your fingers! Imagine not being allowed to hold on to anything! You need long flexors for strength, color, taking the garbage out, all sorts of things! There *is* a way to use them healthily.

Dual muscular pull: the effective balance of opposing forces

We must do away with this fear that tension will interfere with, or limit, motion. Without tension there is no life at all, and after all, any motion needs limits. Consider the common misconception that dual muscular pull is bad because it creates tension. The fact is, flexors and extensors always work together. Without the regulatory effect of one, the other could not operate in a controlled fashion. The extensor acts as a brake ensuring that the flexor's motion doesn't go too far, and vice versa. Thus dual muscular pull, by the very nature of physiological function, must *always* be present in movement!

However, it is detrimental if done in an overly effortful or unbalanced way. This harmful dual pull is a type of anti-movement akin to the habitual contractions discussed earlier. Indeed, reducing dual muscular pull to the minimum can increase movement effectiveness to the maximum. Discrimination allows us to recognize perceptively whether dual muscular pull is functioning counterproductively or as it should, and to fine-tune it to optimal levels.

When dual muscular pull functions normally, you will not experience it as such! Effective movement is for the most part perceived as effortless, easy, because the balance of opposing forces is precisely optimal. There is no superfluous contraction or wasted effort—it just feels easy.

Hand-arm fixation—a positive use of stiffness

Yet sometimes we *must* use a perceived effortful fixation, caused by two opposing muscle groups working purposefully one against the other, to achieve our musical ends. Fixation is a crucial tool in producing many types of **forte** legato, large blocks of orchestral sound or the type of percussive ostinati we associate with Prokofiev. For these it is often necessary to stiffen your hand, fingers and sometimes your wrist and arm as well to the point of a cement-like rigidity! This gives you precise control of the duration of your staccatos, most of which in Prokofiev should be slightly on the long side to give them motoric meat, a beefy sound. Here again a *form* (the stiffened hand) not generally associated with piano playing is brought in to fulfil the required musical *function*.

Often one must really dig in to the key and hold on heartily to produce a rich, singing *cantabile*. This kind of 'flexible hand fixation' feels like clinging, hanging on for dear life, but your sound will not be harsh if your arm movement counterbalances the effect of your stiffened hand. The hand stiffens even as the arm 'plasticizes' itself. Here it is a balance of opposing qualities of force that creates a symbiosis.

8 ARM WEIGHT

The idea of using arm weight to produce beautiful tone is one of the most widely held tenets of piano technique. There is much truth in the concept of arm weight, but it is rife with pianistic dangers as well.

'Arm weight' theory says that allowing the arm's mass to be transmitted unhindered through the finger into the key produces good piano tone, whereas moving the key by muscular contraction or tension results in a forced or harsh tone. On the other hand, the older 'finger action' theory sees the muscular activity of the fingers as generating piano sound—the arm provides only the spatial positioning needed for the fingers to be placed accurately on their notes.

We need a more global understanding of human movement

The debate between the arm weight and finger articulation schools is still going on because neither side will ever be proved correct. They're both right and both wrong—both points of view indicate an incomplete understanding of human movement.

The nature of freedom

Is dropping the weight of your arm into the key to produce the most beautiful sound really free? Well, maybe—just like jumping out of a plane without a parachute is free! Perhaps a weight in free fall is most free but it is also most dead! 'Most free' is not necessarily best. Our goal is not uncontrolled freedom but a *capable* freedom—to create pianistic, dramatic color with maximal variety.

Muscles directing the motion of arm mass

Arm weight does play a crucial role in tone production, but its quality is anything but dead. It is an active, intelligent mass, flexible in its actions, not the weight of an inert, inactive substance such as wood or lead. The key point: although the weight of your muscles indeed can impart momentum and power to the arm, those very same muscles also *direct* their own action. The very substance that constitutes that weight also activates it. The mass of your arm moves, but its own muscles move it!

If you are too tight, your muscles cannot move freely. Thus by cultivating a feeling of arm weight, you may indeed be helping yourself. You may think you are letting weight generate tone but actually you are just relaxing enough so your muscles can work well! Up to a certain point, the more you feel your arm's weight, the less you are inhibiting its free action.

In David Dubal's film, *The Golden Age of Pianism*, there is a clip of Claudio Arrau playing Mendelssohn's Rondo Capriccioso. This is a wonderful example of a pianist using the perceptive mindset of the arm weight school to produce great results. You can see him tangibly letting his arms drop in. His fingers are so loose they seem like strands of spaghetti! Yet they *move*. They look so relaxed it seems a miracle that he can play at all, let alone hit all the right notes. Yet the playing is wonderfully alive, light yet full-toned, exuberant. Arrau's relaxation allows a naturally vivacious enervation of the finger muscles. But do you know how many hours a day Arrau played in his youth to arrive at that wonderfully relaxed, capable technical aliveness? He practiced so incessantly that one of his neighbors ended up having a nervous breakdown![1] His fingers *moved* even while he cultivated arm weight, because the reflexes had been built in.

Balance of activity, relaxation

Arrau demonstrated an optimal cultivation of the arm weight philosophy. But taken too far, it can lead to negative consequences. Your arm possesses a certain mass. The most efficient way to employ this mass in the generation of piano tone is to maintain optimum balance between relaxation and activity. For the results of muscular effort to move freely through the bones and flesh of the arm into the piano, it is true that they must not be inhibited by an overly tense muscle tonus. But it is equally true that too much relaxation renders your playing ineffectual—your muscles simply do not move enough to do their job!

---

[1] Joseph Horowitz, *Conversations with Arrau* (New York: Knopf, 1982).

Arm weight never the sole ingredient in a movement

A common negative result of using arm weight technique to produce your tone: you relax a little too much, and reduced activity in your hand weakens its structure. You no longer have perfect contact with the key. Your arm is now producing beautiful tone, but your hand can no longer effectively manage the relationship of one tone to the next! It is as if this arm relaxation becomes contagious and renders the fingers overly inactive as well. Your fingers are no longer in command, hence an insidious roughness, a lack of control in your legato sound.

Over-relaxation leads to excess tension

Furthermore, the loss of structure and function must now be compensated by muscular contractions elsewhere, but these contractions stabilize rather than activate—they inhibit rather than facilitate movement. Consider the extreme case: total relaxation, which equals total inactivity. When both sets of muscles around a joint are overly inactive, the joint collapses—it does not maintain it optimal orientation to the rest of the body. This relaxation does *not* equal a state of rest but of deadness! There is no functionality. Now other parts must carry the load for this overly loose area. Here counterproductive tension in one place results not from over-contraction but from over-relaxation elsewhere!

Appropriate activity leads to healthy tone

In 'tone production' there is a symbiotic relationship between the muscles' activity and their physical mass. This is the new light in which we need to examine the whole question of arm weight.

Lie on your back; 'play the piano' on the underside of a table. Try to produce various types of 'tone': forte, piano, fat, thin, staccato, legato. You will see that you can produce all the gamut of noises that you can when playing the top of that same table.

Where is your arm weight now? It is plain to see that activity is doing the job, not weight. This shows how your muscles activate their own mass when acting against, instead of with, gravity. Observe yourself carefully when you return to the keyboard and you'll have to admit: this same type of activity goes on when you act *with* gravity. But also notice that your arm moves freely in both cases—its mass *is* involved and certainly not excluded from the movement process.

Can you see clearly that it is not weight but activity, sensibly guiding your arm mass, creating forces that manifest through your skeletal structures, that creates piano tone? Can you feel how the inner activity of your upper arm translates down through the freely transmitting forearm to give you true power? You may well *experience* the mass of your arm as weight, because you are responding with sensitivity to your own actions rather than being blocked up in over-contraction. But your main sensation may just as well be one of locked contact with the board (for massive chords and sonorities), a flowing weight*less*ness based on 'T'ai Chi walking' legato (see applications #10.1, 10.2, 10.3 on pages 55, 57, and 60), or a flying activity for vigorous staccato strokes.

The problem of subjective perception

Just as in 'slowing the key down', here again we confront the problem of subjective perception. Although you may *feel* your weight producing your tone, I can assure you that with no muscular activity on your part, your piano will not even peep!

Consider a phrase of let's say five notes. Logically speaking, if arm weight generates tone, then there must be a movement of your arm into the key on each note. With no arm movement there would be no possibility for its weight to express itself. However these movements will most likely create bumps in your tone that destroy any sense of phrase.

Either that or some imaginary 'momentum' in your forearm continues to have an effect on your tone although your forearm isn't actually dropping into each subsequent note of the phrase. If so then an extremely stable and functional hand structure is the only thing preventing those bumps in the line, and we are thus back at hand activity playing the major role in 'tone production'. You may well feel some sort of 'momentum', but your hand must do a great deal of work to control the effects of that momentum.

Maintain global view

The finger-action camp might not have gone so far wrong if they had managed to maintain a global outlook. But somehow that idea evolved mono-thematically, to the exclusion of all other functional elements. Finger action was cultivated; all the supportive functions were ignored. This of course was disastrous. Why it happened this way may again be traced back to the problem of subjective perception.

For example, if I am well organized physically, my wrist might well remain motionless enough that I could balance an eraser on it while playing. Instead of a lot of external movement, my arm has an internal freedom that allows everything to work well. Imagine now that some pedagogue observes a great master playing with this unmoving wrist but sees it only in its external aspect, understanding nothing of the sophisticated internal organization involved. He puts erasers on his students' wrists, and of course they soon go into spasm. Where form should follow function, here he cultivates form at the *expense* of function.

His students cannot succeed in this because they didn't learn how! They did not follow the long, complex two-step process that learning to play this way entails. First the proper sequence of participatory arm movements must be learned externally. Only then can you begin the long process of internalization, reducing the amount of visible, external movement but retaining the internal muscular activity that gives you the musical result.

Participation of all muscles may not be perceived as such

Thus if you try to imitate the external appearance of an unmoving arm without learning the internal organization necessary to effective finger action, your arm will become overly tense and your finger movements will have no chance of being efficient. Your fingers are the prime agents of movement that creates tone, but all other parts of yourself must be involved as well to an appropriate degree. This may seem strange to you until you realize that we need not perceive that involvement of our body as movement or effort. We may not feel muscle contraction elsewhere in our body when our fingers move, unless it is an inappropriate, overly effortful contraction.

For instance, have you ever noticed the various muscles rippling under the skin of your forearm as you move your finger, all the more so the more you relax your arm? These are the visible signs of the internal organization I'm talking about. All these muscles are engaged in either generating or supporting the movement, though you may only feel you're moving your finger.

Another example: when you entertain the idea of involving your back in playing, it is incorrect to feel the involvement of your back as movement or effort. The involvement is rather one of non-effort, a strangely alive sensation as if there is indeed activity but no movement. The more your spine floats erect in gravity with a minimum of help from muscular contraction to hold it there, the freer all its surrounding musculature is for that supportive 'non-activity'. Take care: leaning against a chair back to relieve those muscles of their work will *not* achieve the same results. Now you have *deprived* your spine of its fundamental relationship to gravity and thus of its functionality. Here the surrounding musculature tends to over-relax, to become somewhat inert, lifeless.

Instead, while sitting, try to feel just *how* your skeleton's weight rests on your thigh muscles: how do they bear that weight? Do they tense or stay relaxed, allowing you to sink into the bench? Notice that the moment any inappropriate tension develops elsewhere in your system you can no longer monitor this. You have lost that quality of *effective* stillness, the relaxed, *alive* stability that allows the passive ancillary actions of other body parts to participate in the active movement of one part.

The ultra-relaxed, ultra-alive movement of Feldenkrais Method

This alive, stable relaxedness can be cultivated through lessons in Feldenkrais Method, which is taught in two formats, group Awareness Through Movement classes (ATM), and private one-to-one Functional Integration sessions (FI). In a really good FI and sometimes even in an ATM session you may end up feeling like a sack full of gelatin in which your skeleton is floating. That exceptional degree of relaxation facilitates the learning of a new, more sophisticated type of movement based on a heightened sense of one's own skeletal structure. You can feel each link in a chain of bones 'coupling in' to a movement one by one, just as a whole row of dominoes falls almost but not quite simultaneously. Because the bones are doing almost all the work, you get more movement with less effort. It's a wonderful feeling, but I have had students complain after such an FI that they couldn't play—they were too relaxed!

They missed the point. If they had taken the trouble to *stay with* that feeling, and to discover that it is possible to perform the actions of playing without losing that exceptional degree of sensitivity, they might well have figured out how to use that newfound physical organization at the keyboard. When playing, there's a sense of the bones of the hand swimming in a sort of 'muscle soup'. The bones themselves are able to find their natural alignment because there are none of the normal muscular efforts preventing them from doing so. Then, the amount of extra effort required to activate these bones is surprisingly little—so little in fact that it can be done without losing the feeling of 'soup' but maintaining a contact that is exceptionally profound because it lacks the normal feeling of forced-ness.

The contact is bone to bone, but the heightened relaxation loosens the muscles around the joint so much that there is kinesthetic feeling within the joint itself even as it maintains stability. The bones feel solidly connected without being fused— this is a connection that enhances rather than inhibits movement.

Relaxation to facilitate effective activity

Because of your exceptionally relaxed state, you do feel your arm's weight to an unusual degree. But the *functionality*, the *intentionality* of your muscular activity will be the primary focus of your awareness—your arm weight, although felt, is only a background factor. You do feel as if you are using the mass of your arms because you have relaxed these muscles to a certain extent. Remember, however, the actual function of this relaxation is not to generate tone with arm weight but to facilitate the imperceptible yet crucial participation of all the appropriate muscles and bones in movement. Activity, not weight, produces piano tone—activity not of the finger alone but of the whole body. Different *qualities* of interdependent muscular activity can interact simultaneously to create various compound movements. The movements can be relaxed but not dead in quality. Be intentionally active to be effectively free.

The finger-action camp held an overly limited view on the nature of tone generation that led to all sorts of pianistic and health problems. But let's face it, the arm-weight camp hardly approached any closer to a plausible explanation for the multitude of complex processes involved in coupling one's hand to the keyboard.

9 MATTHAY, MOSHE AND MOVEMENT

Along with Ludwig Deppe (1828-1890) and Rudolph Maria Breithaupt (1873-1945), Tobias Matthay (1858-1945) was one of the original proponents of the use of arm weight and thus occupies a premier position in the history of the development of piano technique. Matthay was a revolutionary in his time, only to be superceded by revolutionaries of a later era. One of these, Moshe Feldenkrais, an engineer, physicist, judo champion and anatomist, discovered that many of our perceived 'givens', might not only be changeable but even totally inaccurate. That is, accepted assumptions about the nature of our physical state can lead to misconceptions and faulty understanding of pianistic technique and function. Examining these notions in the light of new knowledge can lead to unexpected improvement.

Upright stance an imperfect evolutionary adaptation?

For example, before I studied Feldenkrais Method I thought the structure of the human body was an imperfect advancement on that of the apes. I couldn't find a way to feel comfortable standing fully upright, and I perceived this to be a flaw in the construction of my skeleton, my bone structure—something unchangeable. I reasoned that we humans, in our evolution from the forward slant of the apes to a fully upright stance, did not quite make it.

Feldenkrais to melt 'immoveable' structures

By the end of my Feldenkrais training, in which we investigated and relearned most of the basic human functional movements, important among which are torso flexion and extension, I had discovered how to stand fully upright. Lo and behold, those seemingly immoveable skeletal strictures were actually habitual, constant *muscular contractions*, so immutable in their activity that they

47

really felt like bone structures to me.

Improvements in my breathing, with increased movement of all the individual parts of my rib cage, and freeing up and 'liquidifying' the movement of my pelvis (the body's center of gravity and main foundation for generation of powerful movements) were two key contributors to my newfound ability to 'walk tall'. These improvements were not arrived at so easily: it was a long-term, complex and powerful process of change that held many implications for my future growth, both physical and emotional.

Rotation necessary to lay hand palm down?

Tobias Matthay's view of rotation is another example of inaccurate perceptions leading to faulty conclusions, an example more directly related to piano. Matthay postulated that we cannot even play one note without first rotating our hand from its 'natural' vertical position with our palm turned inward, to the horizontal with our palm lying flat. For Matthay this rotation to the horizontal was a departure from the neutral 'at rest' state. It required a certain minimal effort, without which his thumb would tend to rise back up and to the outside. Thus he asserted that "visible or invisible arm rotation", compensating that tendency, must always be present in our playing.[1]

A new perception of normal

However, if your arms hang by your side with your palms turned inward and your thumbs pointing forward, as most of ours normally do, they are not at rest! It is unnecessary habitual muscle contractions in the shoulder area that keep them there. Perhaps the inculcation of the 'military stance', chest out, shoulders back', so prevalent in our Western culture, has something to do with this unnatural but ingrained habit.

At one point in my Feldenkrais training we did a series of lessons designed to free up movement in the shoulders. Before these lessons most of us stood with palms facing inwards. But by the end almost all of us were standing with our thumbs aligned along our pant seams, palms pointing to the rear. The amazing thing is, we achieved this radical alteration with no physical effort. In fact, it was

---

[1] Tobias Matthay, *The Visible and Invisible in Pianoforte Technique* (London: H. Milford, Oxford University Press, 1932).

through a *cessation* of involuntary physical effort that we were able to do it!

The effort we expended was instead mental, as we directed our attention to particular sensations associated with specific single movements. As various habitual contractions first came into our awareness and then melted away, our breathing became deeper, freer. Our chests filled out naturally. Because we did not force this but simply allowed it to happen, ironically the result vis-à-vis arm position was the opposite of what the stiff, held-upright army style posture gives.

There is much truth in what Matthay saw. Rotation is a key element of piano technique, but not in the sense of the compensatory action Matthay envisioned. Rotation is simply the most efficient way to achieve certain technical goals.[2] Unfortunately, by the time Tobias Matthay had completed his work, Moshe Feldenkrais was still young, his method still far from being formulated. Matthay did not have the opportunity for his shoulders to become normal instead of merely 'average'. And so one of the central pillars of his system is based on a misperception.

It is my hope that through investigation of these and other issues in an informed and perceptive way, your curiosity too might be rewarded with just as startling improvements as those described here. The moral once again, as Feldenkrais was so fond of saying: if you know what you're doing you can do what you want.[3,4]

---

[2] See part VIII, *Rotation*.
[3] More principles of movement and learning as related to piano can be found in appendix II.
[4] For more on why our upright stance is indeed optimal and not an imperfection in our evolution, see part VIII, *Rotation*.

III

HAND STRENGTH AND FUNCTION A

PERFECTING LEGATO

10 Physical Legato Is the Foundation of Piano Technique

This new view of movement as it relates to piano playing is rich in its substance and also in the myriad details of its application. But piano playing is a pragmatic undertaking—how can we possibly do justice to Beethoven or Chopin if our minds are preoccupied with all this new information?

Well of course, we can't. All this must be integrated. We still are nowhere near the sophisticated simplicity of an evolved technique, the fusion of these many disparate elements into a unified gestalt. How can we at least begin to apply this new theoretical framework to the practical demands of piano playing?

The logical starting point is legato, the physical joining of one note to another. As I have said, legato is a keystone of any musician's technique, but for pianists it is of particular importance: it is the pianist's rock in time of trouble, the firm foundation, a point of physical reference and stability. In clarifying legato we create a central foundation from which we can develop other aspects of technique.

A template for control

Through a perfect physical legato the illusion of singing can most dependably be created at the piano. Some pianists assert that it is possible to play a perfectly even, absolutely controlled melody without physically joining the notes. I grant this,[1] but it is a lot more difficult, and the possibility for error is magnified a hundredfold. Through physical legato we can most surely avoid unintended accents and irregularities, even one of which is enough to destroy the whole effect of a shaped melody.

---

[1] See reference to body-building pianist, *Even a pencil can play legato* in chapter 32, *The Underlying Musical Purpose of Arm Movement.*

Although we can achieve beautiful melodic evenness without physically joining notes,[2] physical legato provides us with the template for evenness, a physical feeling of evenness that we can relate to the aural impression we seek. Legato is the most dependable physical basis we have for musical control. The acquisition of a perfect physical legato is almost as difficult as controlling a melody without legato touch—yet once you have it you are on infinitely surer pianistic ground.

The almost universal absence of real mastery of legato is a serious unacknowledged fact in the piano world. The problem is, we think we already have it, and so do not trouble ourselves to investigate further. But in fact, the leap from the legato most of us employ to an ideal legato is so great that many pianists attempting it will probably feel as if they are reinventing their hand.

T'ai Chi walking and legato

Crucial to the development of a controlled legato is the 'functional strength' we have already discussed at length (see chapters 4, 6, 7). To help us make the jump from the theoretical to the practical, I'd like to refer to the ancient Chinese martial art, T'ai Chi Chuan. Many articles recently have linked T'ai Chi to piano, talking about the soft, flowing quality of movement, the circular motions that are so much more graceful and effective than linear, angular moves. This is all very true, but neglects to address the foundation upon which all this refinement rests. There is one essential element fundamental to both T'ai Chi and legato at the piano that wears quite a different face from that of softness and flowing movement.

In T'ai Chi you first learn to walk. You acquire your physical base. Flowing circles and softness are all fine and lovely, but for walking, just 'soft' just doesn't work! There's no structure! Let's look at how the legs in T'ai Chi walking are similar to fingers on the keys, and for best results, don't just read this exercise: try it!

---

[2] See paragraphs on inflected legato in chapter 23, *The Octave Arm-Sweep.*

Application 10.1
LEGATO I: T'AI CHI WALKING

Step 1: Stand with your feet shoulder width apart. Bend your knees, slightly lowering your *d'an tien* (a point three centimeters below the belly button, for the Chinese the physical-emotional-spiritual center of the body).

Step 2: *Slowly* shift your weight onto one leg. This leg is now the *yang* leg, the one where all your power is concentrated. This frees your *yin* leg for light, nimble movement.

Step 3: When it comes time to actually walk, you'll first tend to fall onto your *yin* foot, shifting your weight along with your foot. No! There must be a differentiation between *yin* and *yang!* You must place that *yin* foot at a 45-degree angle a comfortable, moderate distance in front of you *without* transferring any weight onto it. Try reducing the distance at first, giving yourself a better chance to let your foot snake out, touch the ground, feel it, sense it, as a Buddhist monk does when walking on rice paper without crackling it. Your sensing leg feels almost weightless, completely capable of light, feather-like movement, while your center of gravity is still solidly grounded in the *yang* leg. (At first you may find this hard on your knees. Don't worry, it's normal!)

Step 4: Here your *yang* leg is solid but not totally rigid. It feels like the spring assembly on a car: not a spiral-type spring but a leaf spring that is trying to spring back as pressure is exerted on it. Bend your *yang* knee even a little more, then straighten it slightly so that your erect torso bobs lightly up and down like the body of a car on its springs. Have your *yin* leg maintain its spatial relation to your body, making your *yin* foot leave the ground and return, slapping the surface lightly, sensing it. This helps you become sure of your grounding in two ways. You are firmly rooted in your *yang* leg and can feel your stability, while your *yin* leg, by sensing, has a chance to prepare itself to receive your body weight.

Step 5: When you feel sure in this differentiation of function between one leg and the other, begin to shift your weight slowly, gradually. Feel every iota of the movement, each degree. Notice that somewhere around the midpoint in this transition you will feel like you have two *yang* legs. At this point your front leg has begun to bear some weight but your back leg has not yet really begun to ease off. When your weight finally does come to rest fully on your front leg, its knee now well bent, it becomes your new *yang* leg. Now your *back* leg becomes feather-light. This is why feeling each increment of the movement is so important: your two legs are exchanging their *yin* and *yang* functions. The difference in feeling between *yin* and *yang* is huge. The slower and more gently you move, the more you can begin to sense the profoundness of this difference.

front stance   back stance

Illustration 10.1: T'ai chi walking

Step 6: Only now can you begin to take your next step. That is, remove your back leg from the ground and draw your foot to a point hovering beside your standing ankle. Then let it snake out diagonally and use *it* now, your new *yin* leg, to sense the ground further in front of you. The clear separation of function of your legs is always maintained: one is the foundation sprig, the other a mobile sensing antenna. Only when this separation is felt and understood clearly can the moment of *transition* be managed skillfully, effectively, elegantly.

Step 7: Perhaps by now you feel you have attained a certain degree of mastery over this strange but educative mode of locomotion. Now try all of this but walking backwards instead of forwards. This will certainly show you how (im?)perfectly you've learned it! Here's your chance to smooth out any bugs that still may remain in the system.

Application 10.2
LEGATO II: 'FINGERSTANDS': THE PIANISTIC EQUIVALENT OF HANDSTANDS

Why so much detailed concern over the mechanics of T'ai Chi walking? We want the body to learn it, sense it as thoroughly as possible, because the next step will be to transfer that sense of structural security and functionality to our piano playing mechanism. First, let's give your hands and arms a sense of 'standing'.

> Step 1: Press your fingertips to a wall, keeping your palms and wrists as far removed from the wall as possible. Your fingers should be comfortably spaced, your thumb and fifth finger somewhat less than an octave but more than a fifth apart. Now lean into the wall; actually try to move the wall but with your fingertips not your palms. Make sure your fingers keep standing by first ensuring that none of their joints are collapsed. Thus each knuckle should create a little hummock along your metacarpal ridge,[3] where your fingers join your hand.

Illustration 10.2: Fingerstands against a wall

Step 2: Now have your whole body adopt a stance as if you really are going to push that wall over. Maybe one leg is back a little; your

---

[103] For anatomical terms see end of chapter 2.

wrists are not too high, not too low. Your elbows are not too out, not too in. Your arms are almost straight but your elbows are not locked. Locking them would appear to increase stability but at the cost of a vastly reduced functionality. Everything is just where it needs to be so that all the power of your body goes right into the wall in a functional way. Make sure you do not collapse your sternum (your breastbone). Doing so would increase your effortfulness dramatically. When you have organized all this very well, then *really* push—with all your might! Notice that correct alignment of your bones is far more effective than muscular effort in transmitting your body's force through to the wall.

Step 3: What is happening with the joints of your fingers? Are they collapsing? They should not! This exercise quickly helps you pinpoint weak spots in your skeletal structural alignment, especially in your fingers and even more especially your thumb. *It must not collapse!* Try pushing the wall with your thumbs alone, like a ninja warrior taking someone's eyes out. One or the other of the thumb joints tends to collapse.

Sometimes you will stop one joint from collapsing only to have the other one cave in. But both joints must stand up stably. Notice that a certain adjustment in your shoulder can help a great deal in finding an alignment where your distal joint stands well.

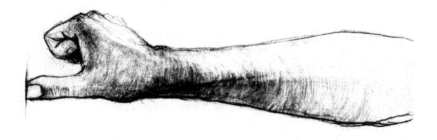

Illustration 10.3: Well-aligned standing thumb

When you can do this (and for many it's not such a simple thing), then one by one add the other fingers to the system. In the end you should be able to push that wall to your heart's content, with no adverse effects on your fingers' natural, slightly curved position.

Step 4: Go back to the piano but don't sit down on the bench yet—remain standing. Now with your hands, stand on some block chords, say C-E-F-G-A in your right hand, C-D-E-F-A in your left. Find the same feeling of structural solidity and power you had at the wall. Your wrists will be somewhat high, but their height does not affect your finger joints' standing well and strong. When you have found this while standing at the piano, then see what adjustments you need to maintain that feeling of wonderful strength and security of touch when you sit down.

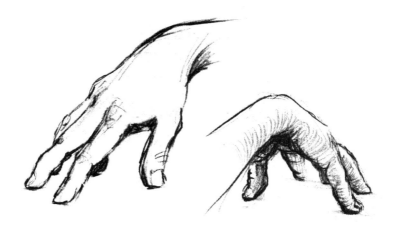

Illustration 10.4: Standing hand with a sitting body

Application 10.3
LEGATO III: 'WALKING' ON THE KEYBOARD

Discrimination of functions

Try to maintain this sense of power and stability as we now introduce a new element, a discrimination of functions. While one finger maintains the stability it acquired in fingerstands, its neighbor will begin to move to take a step, snaking out to feel the key antenna-like, as your legs did in T'ai Chi walking.

> Step 1: Play one note. The finger that plays it becomes your *yang,* your foundation, your support. Your next finger, because it is *yin,* can feel its note, gauge the key exactly, even feel the very weight of the hammer as you might measure the weight of a book by holding it at arm's length and jogging it up and down gently.

> Step 2: Only when your *yin* finger has adequately felt its key does it play the next note while your *yang* finger *does not release the first note.* The moment when two keys are depressed is crucial. Here the two fingers exchange their *yin* and *yang* functions just as your legs did, while both maintain a perfect stance—total contact with the keybed. This means that for a moment you feel as if you have two *yang* fingers—you are already leaning healthily into your *yin* finger but have not yet begun to release your weight from the initial *yang* finger. This sense of walking, of shifting your weight so to speak, from the bottom of one key to the bottom of the next, allows you to connect your two fingers on the keybed.

> A very slight adjustment of your wrist facilitates this. Don't actively move your wrist so much, but simply let it follow your hand through its slight shift in position from one note to the next.

This procedure is called overholding, and there is a crucial musical as well as physical reason fo doing it. As I mentioned earlier, singers can join a series of melodic tones seamlessly.

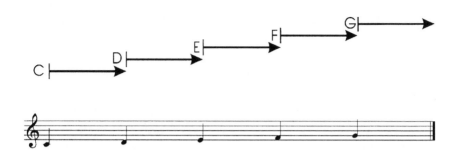

Illustration 10.5: Graph of vocalist's melodic line

The piano, however is a percussive instrument. Sound is produced by felt-covered hammers hitting strings. Thus if we merely try to reproduce this seamless joining, the sound of each hammer's impact will break the smooth line. When you overhold notes, there is a moment during each melodic change when two notes are sounding simultaneously, even if they are dissonant next-door neighbors. This blends the notes in our ear and masks the percussive effect. Blending the notes more than they 'should' be counteracts the percussive attack, and somehow our brain computes all that to produce the impression of a smooth line.

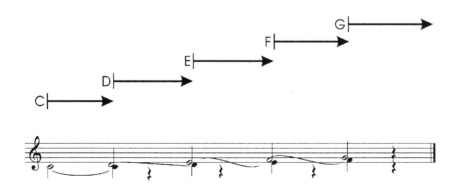

Illustration 10.6: Graph of pianist's melodic line

When you first try this, the more you overhold (the further you extend each line in the graph to the right), the easier it is to get the hang of it, and the clearer the aural result. Be sure not to make an individual wrist movement on each note — this would increase dramatically the risk of a 'bump', a shock that would again break the melodic line. The chain of small wrist adjustments should in the end resemble a smooth, subtle gliding arm movement through a whole group of notes.

Just as in securely shifting your weight from one leg to the other, here as well there is at no moment any loss of structure or support, therefore in no way is your *ability* ever impaired. One fingertip connects to the other through the keybed, and your metacarpal-phalangeal finger joints, your knuckles, are also joined, creating a tetrahedral structure whose four corners are the two fingertips and two knuckles.

This is crucial, that legato is felt not just at the fingertips but across the metacarpal-phalangeal joints.

Illustration 10.7: Legato at the midpoint: the tetrahedral structure of two yang *fingers*

Illustration 10.8: Sensation of the tetrahedron maintained in curved-finger legato

When we walk on the street, we do not move from one foot to the other with a hop but with a sure stride. It is surprising how far we can stray from this sureness of step in our legato touch on the keyboard!

Illustration 10.9: The inner feeling of the curved finger tetrahedron

Illustration 10.8 visually heightens contrast between the structurally secure tetrahedron and the other fingers that remain at rest. Although your hand might never assume such a 'deformed' shape, the inner feeling of functional differentiation might indeed approach what is represented visually here.

11 A Capable Hand Can Free
Your Arm

Developing true ability below your wrist through the perfecting of your legato touch has some interesting ramifications, not the least important of which is the liberating effect on everything above it.

Application 11.1
Legato IV: Overholding I

Overholding, arm freedom and finger insubordination

> Step 1: Play a small legato passage as in the previous exercise, still omitting your thumb. But now after each finger has depressed its note, do not let the previous finger release its key. Instead, when you have played four notes you will now be holding them all down — you have now recreated the totally secure structure you first established in 'fingerstands'.

Example 11.1: Maximum overholding in a four-note scale

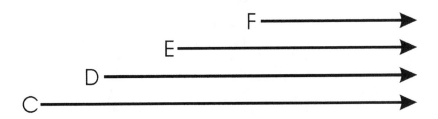

Illustration 11.1: Graph of note durations in maximal overholding

This is the best preliminary exercise to get the feeling of overholding into your hand.

This process of building up that structure from an initial single finger attack is called overholding even when done with as few as two notes. When all your fingers and their four hillock metacarpal-phalangeals hold on to their keys securely, your arm can free up behind your hand and your hand itself can feel a new strength.

It really feels like standing on the keyboard, but not standing like a statue! In 'fingerstands' against a wall, your whole hand-arm-torso structure was secure, almost rigid, for maximum transmission of power. Now we have modified that. Just as in normal standing you can move your body around on the stable base of your legs, so now should your arm be free to move, supported by the standing base of your fingers and hand on the keyboard.

Step 2: Try standing on only two fingers and moving your arm without disturbing the security of your finger/hand structure. You should be able to loosen your arm or have it move slightly in any direction without disturbing your hand's stable standing on the board.

Step 3: You can cultivate this capability by playing a mini-scale of four notes ascending and descending overholding all notes and moving your arm through the whole group—one small, smooth lateral movement instead of an individual relaxing movement on each note. Here we differentiate arm and finger function. Fingers play notes while the arm shapes the phrase. If you succeed in this you are no longer typing out notes but creating a musical shape. This is a crucial difference, an excellent way to transform note by note playing into something sinuous and lovely.[1]

Step 4: As you play this overheld mini-scale, make sure that you only raise the finger that is about to play. All the others securely hold their key in its keybed. Many times when I first give this exercise, fingers are popping up all over the place—one finger does not hold its note down as long as it should, but lets go prematurely, unbeknownst to the student! That's amazing—to be so out of touch with one's own mechanism. You think you can command your finger to hold its note, but it does not follow orders! This is insubordination, but you don't even notice!

Try again, and this time, really try to zero in on that moment when one of your fingers surreptitiously begins to release its key out of turn. Can you catch yourself in this? Here's an opportunity to discover how much your fingers lack independence. Only when you really make all your fingers do their job will you find that new feeling of strength in your hand and the corresponding looseness in your arm. Your arm naturally becomes quite flexible only when it 'walks' on the very firm base provided by a truly functional hand.

Overholding allows you to experience the interdependence of your fingers—they stand together. Ironically, this interdependence is absolutely necessary for the eventual development of their independence. I believe that Pischna originally developed his exercises with just this goal in mind. Doing Pischna while attending to both absolute finger control/stability and arm fluidity sheds potent light on the finger independence/interdependence relationship.

Overhold or articulate, without strangling the light breath movement of your arm

Take care: there is a problem in learning legato through overholding. Because your fingers are barely moving, your arm has an even greater tendency, to freeze into immobility instead of maintaining a neutral move-ability even though it now finds itself on firm ground. When you try and remedy that with increased finger articulation your arm now begins to breathe, to move a bit but you lose the legato! The real art comes in being able to increase the amount of finger articulation even to

---

[1] For much more on this topic see section VI, *Above the Hand: the Role of the Wrist and Arm.*

an energetic, maximally reaching for the sky movement, while continuing to maintain the perfect joining of key bottom to key bottom, through maintenance of hand structure integrity and fluid arm movement.

Remember: legato means that between every two notes there is a moment when both keys are held down all the way to the keybed, and in that instant your arm does not block but continues to flow. Check visually—you should be able to see this clearly, and when you do, notice what a difference you *hear*. This can be felt even in a slow trill between two notes. You must find the feeling of absolute evenness, physically as well as tonally. Develop your ability to hear the roughness of the sound when you're not doing this perfectly. Improve your sound by becoming stronger in the finger but looser in the arm. Your arm can remain free on each note only when the bridge from one metacarpal-phalangeal to another is secure.

Overhold even in performance

Note that you can overhold sometimes as many as four fingers even in performance, as long as you overhold smoothly not stiffly. In a large hall it is often possible to enrich your tone this way—the big acoustic masks the blurring of tones we would normally avoid. Your fingers manage the perfect legato while your arm never presses down; instead it makes the phrase.

Differentiation of arm and finger

If your arm is pressing to create legato, it means only that your fingers did not do their job. When your fingers achieve a stable transfer of weight from one to the next, you'll notice your arm is completely freed up. The connection is present but not stiff. When it is functional, your structure can be strong without becoming rigid.

No more 'pianistic polio'!

You've seen poor souls who have been left half-crippled by polio or some childhood disease, limping down the street. Did you ever stop to think that there could exist a pianistic version of this? When you learn to stand up well on the keyboard you acquire a much greater capacity to control what you're doing. No more 'pianistic polio'!

"If I hang on to make a true legato, I'm stretched, tight."

…complains one student. But if you don't hang on, you have no control! There must be a way to hang on without stretching tight. Ask yourself, "With *what* am I hanging on tight?" If everything below your wrist is doing its job, you should have no problem with this—there should be no tightness above. You feel stretched tight in some parts because not all your other parts are participating as they should. Your arm *can* move to shape the phrase *and* simultaneously free up all those muscles that would 'normally' stretch tight, if appropriate activity in the hand frees them. Contact with the key has become a wonderful, elegant thing, allowing you to control musical inflection because you can now *sense* in the most practical meaning of the word.

IV

HAND STRENGTH AND FUNCTION B

THE SPECIAL ROLE OF THE THUMB AND ITS RELATIONSHIP TO THE FOREFINGER

12 THE THUMB AND GRASPING

We are looking at the importance of hand structure and function in legato, but you may have noticed that the arm somehow keeps creeping into the discussion. This is unavoidable: its crucial supporting role is the third major component of legato. For the moment we will continue our elucidation of finger and hand function, but in part VI, *Above the Hand: The Role of the Wrist and Arm in Legato*, we will consider the arm's role in greater depth. Some of you may want to turn there now and immediately follow our examination of legato to its conclusion.

In the legato exercises of the preceding chapter I avoided the thumb because of its problematic nature: it is generally more difficult to maintain legato between thumb and finger than between two fingers. Now try overholding five notes instead of four (play 5-4-3-2-1)—you'll quickly see that we have a special difficulty here. When you arrive at your thumb's note, your other fingers have a stronger tendency than ever to collapse. There are good reasons for this that merit more detailed scrutiny.

Special structure of the thumb

How does your thumb relate to the rest of your hand? Your thumb is a unique digit in that it has only two phalanges, not three as the other fingers do. However it has more possibility for movement than the fingers, not less, because of a crucial structural difference. Whereas the metacarpal bone of each finger is fixed quite firmly in the hand itself, the metacarpal of the thumb is free to move. In fact it functions as a third phalange but one with much more freedom of movement than those of the fingers, because it attaches directly to the wrist.

Your thumb has four types of free movement, one more than your other fingers. Try each of these as I name them now. The three types of movement common to all your digits are

> 1) *flexion* (curling) and *extension* (straightening)
>
> 2) *straight up and down* (the extended digit moves on the vertical plane without flexing)
>
> 3) *abduction* (spreading the fingers apart from one another), and *adduction* (clamping them together).

This third is the only way monkeys can grasp, the rudimentary way they use their thumb to hold on to things. Their thumb cannot do the fourth movement, which is unique to humankind:

> 4) *opposition and reverse opposition*, by which the thumb can be brought across, or opposed to, the palm and to the tips of the slightly flexed fingers then taken away again. This motion forms a basis far more effective than adduction for the handling of tools, weapons, and instruments: the fundamental movement of the human hand, grasping and releasing.

Application 12.1
GRASPING I

Grasp to experience the innate strength of your hand

> Step 1: This most basic function of the hand can provide us with a graphic experience of the strength it needs to develop. Grab someone's forearm with your fingers over and thumb underneath. Squeeze and pull it towards you. Have your accomplice resist, keeping his or her forearm parallel between your two bodies. You are now holding on to something, grasping. This is your hand's most basic action and one that only the human hand is designed to do. And you may notice that if needs be, you can do it with great strength, as most of us can. This natural strength of your hand could work wonders if you could allow it to express

itself in your playing. The strength of the grasping function *can* be directly incorporated into your playing if you are savvy enough to make the connection.

Role of the thumb

Notice the importance of the thumb's role in grasping. Because it is opposable to the rest of your hand, it constitutes no less than 50 percent of the function we're dealing with. Try grasping more with your thumb and less with your fingers, then decrease your thumb's exertion and have your four fingers make more of the effort. Can you see how your thumb provides one entire half of the support for your hand on the keyboard; the rest being the job of your other four fingers combined? This is even reflected anatomically. The thumb's main muscle forms the largest part of the heel of the hand, almost equal in bulk to the muscles of all the other fingers put together. Once again, anatomical form reflects function.

In grasping, the thumb is under, the fingers over—their work is divided half and half. On the keyboard, although the thumb appears no longer to be opposed to the fingers, one of its motions actually remains that of opposition—the division of labor is the same.

Make this radically new sensation familiar

Step 2: Trying to maintain this feeling of capable grasping, let's review overholding (Application 11.1, page 64), but now including your thumb. Play a five-note scale overholding maximally.

Example 12.1: Overholding five notes

Can you remember the sense of grasping your colleague's arm
with great strength, and transfer that sensation to this exercise?
Can you make the connection between grasping and legato? Notice
that the more you 'grasp' while overholding, the more your hand
structure stands up, strengthening and evolving itself.

Fool around with it. Go slowly, take time to get used to it, explore. There are many variations and ramifications to what we
are doing here. For instance, just because you are holding the
notes firmly does not mean you *must* play them loudly. Try vary-
ing your dynamics: play the phrase ***ppp***, or make a diminuendo or
some other shape while maintaining your firm touch. Try playing
the notes softly, then while continuing to hold all the keys down,
increase your pressure to the maximum. Can you feel the powerful effort of grasping all the way up your arm to your shoulder?

Step 3: Now let's take a simple example from the literature to see
how this applies in practice. In the Beethoven Sonata in F minor,
Op. 2 #1, at measure 33, there is a scale in eighth notes.

Example 12.2: Beethoven: Sonata in F minor, Op. 2 #1, *1st mvt., mm. 33-35*

As you play the high note, hold on to your thumb note firmly,
ensuring that your thumb-second finger assembly does not collapse. In each subsequent note of the falling scale, keep the structure of your hand secure, even helping in the first few tries by
continuing to overhold your thumb note and the proceeding ones.
The crucial moment comes when you arrive at your second finger's D flat and your thumb is about to play again. Take care!
Here is where you are bound to fall. You may find it difficult to

notice at first, but I can assure you there is an almost 100 percent chance that your structure is weakening here. Virtually all my students suffer from it *and do not realize it.* Can you catch yourself in the moment when unawares to you the space between thumb and second is diminishing somehow? Can you repair this? You may want to skip ahead at this point to try application #43.3, steps 4 and 5 (the thumb swing exercise at page 265-66) to elucidate this problem in an effective way.

Step 4: If you can now manage to maintain real support between your second finger and thumb as you play C, you have solved one big problem only to arrive at another major hurdle. Passing your fourth finger over your thumb, you will again notice a strong, almost irresistible tendency for your thumb-forefinger structure to weaken (see illustration 43.5, *Pass fourth over thumb*, page 267). Play your fourth finger's note while overholding your thumb note. Did the structure collapse in any way? Stand it up again! Even use your other hand to lift your right hand knuckle up from underneath and restore it to its rightful place as the keystone of the arch. Practice this until you can totally maintain the arch even while playing. It must not collape even for an instant.

Do you remember Feldenkrais' catch phrase, "If you know what you're doing, you can do what you want"? Through understanding grasping, you can come to know what your thumb and fingers can *do*. The more it becomes alive to its own function, the more your hand will be able to serve you well—to do what you want.

13 Thumb Pushups: The Hand as Suspension Spring

The transition from thumb function in grasping to its role in playing piano is not so simple. How can your thumb express its natural strength when it cannot grasp but must stand alone on the keyboard, relatively independent from the rest of the hand? The series of exercises I call thumb pushups explores the development of thumb strength and function where we need it—in playing.

Application 13.1
Thumb I: Thumb Pushups

Arm pressure imitates body weight

Do you remember how your thumb tended to collapse in application 10.2, pushing against the wall? Let's return to this problem and try in a more detailed way to resolve it once and for all.

> Step 1: Put your thumb on a key, then 'standing' on it, stretch your four fingers, lifting them as high as you can. Point them to the ceiling, all the while letting a considerable, even close to unbearable amount of weight press down through the thumb into the key. Here the continuous pressure of your arm exerted on your thumb and hand imitates the weight of your body on your hands and arms in real pushups.

Remember, if you have any concerns at all about tendonitis, **go gently here. Proceed with caution!** *Perhaps start by imitating your weight when you were just a baby, then proceeding to when you were five, ten, fifteen years old.*

Illustration 13.1: Thumb Pushups I—reach to the sky

Step 2: Continuing to exert pressure with your arm, make your wrist as high as possible, as if you were using your thumb as a screwdriver. Now take a look—has either of your thumb joints collapsed? We all have differently arranged thumbs—for some of you the distal joint might be the main problem, for others the proximal. Still others of you will fix one joint ('un-collapse' it) only to have the other collapse—it goes back and forth.

Find a neutral position where neither joint collapses. Exerting a high amount of pressure will show you most clearly where the structural weaknesses in your alignments exist. If you cannot render your thumb uncollapsible while maintaining pressure on it, now try reducing the amount of pressure on your thumb until it becomes easier to form your joints into some sort of sensible alignment. Use the information you got from the high-pressure push to adjust your alignment at a lighter, more manageable level of effort.

You may feel a bit like Bambi as you wobble about on your thumb, trying to find a stable way of standing. Don't get discouraged but stay with the new experience rather than falling back into your old organization, your tried and true (but perhaps not so useful) technical solutions.

Step 3: Once you've found that neutral, un-collapsed position, confirm that it's *the* one by once again gradually increasing pressure on your screwdriver/thumb while now maintaining its supported, uncollapsed structure. If either joint again collapses, it shows that you still have some adjusting to do. Finding the skeletal arrangement that will bear even excessive amounts of weight without collapsing is the beginning of true strength and function for your thumb and indeed for your whole hand.

Thumb-forefinger isometrics

Step 4: Now from its 'reach for the sky' position, begin ever so slowly to bring your second finger down to play the adjacent note. Keep lots of pressure on your hand, as if there was some huge weight exerting itself on it, and your thumb must work hard to keep that weight from crushing your hand down. In addition, act as if there is some huge force keeping your thumb and forefinger apart, preventing your fingertip from descending, and you must work against this force to bring your forefinger into play. I believe this deliberately setting the efforts of two opposing muscle groups against each other is called isometrics. Notice how this gives you unbelievable exactitude and control over the sound of this note.

Illustration 13.2: Thumb Pushups II—gradually descend

Step 5: When you release your second finger's note, still holding
your thumb note and maintaining pressure, let your second finger
rise slowly again to its fully open position. Still later you can try
letting your forefinger *spring* up again to full extension. You should
feel that the structure joining thumb to forefinger is like the suspension springs of an automobile, stable yet active. It resembles
the pelvic connection between the legs in T'ai Chi walking—here
the hand is equivalent to the pelvis.

In thumb pushups the space between thumb and forefinger opens and closes
just as the elbow does in real pushups. The hypothetical maximum range in
real pushups is almost 180 degrees. How close can you get to this in thumb
pushups? Presumably you can close your thumb-forefinger joint to 0 degrees,
but only those of us who are double-jointed can open it all the way to 180
degrees. Nevertheless, the closer you can approach a full opening of the joint,
the better for you!

When considering structural functionality and security in the fingers and hand,
one of the best places to start is in scales. Often we neglect to play a true legato

even between thumb and forefinger. We often do not physically connect two notes because we are not sensitive to the possibilities for structural security in the whole arch system that connects the two digits in question through the hand. We want to play in a relaxed manner, but inadvertently sabotage our hand's inherent structural functionality in the process. How often have you caught the knuckle of your second finger collapsing as you play the thumb note that follows? The aim of thumb pushups is to increase our sensitivity to this problem, to educate our nervous system so it can notice the problem when it occurs and effectively repair it.

> Step 6: When you have mastered this first version of thumb-forefinger isometrics, try the variation of letting your second finger descend alternately to the left and right of your thumb, continuing in the spirit of isometric exercise.

Pass fourth finger over while thumb continues to push up

An even clearer illustration of this collapsing problem can be found in passing your third or fourth finger over the thumb. Let's start with the more difficult variant:

> Step 7: Play a thumb note and then cross your fourth finger over to play the next note of a scale, all the time continuing to press down on your thumb. Make your thumb as strong as possible, as if you were doing thumb pushups. Now, while still holding your thumb note, raise your fourth finger and play it again. Do you see how insidious the tendency is for your hand structure to collapse? Do you see how unused you are to providing a stable platform from which the fourth finger can play? This platform can be stable only to the degree that your thumb does its job. For the moment it is the flexible but dependable pillar on which that platform rests. Your hand depends on it for stability.

14 Clarification of the Thumb-Forefinger Relationship

When I was younger I used to draw a lobster claw in my scores at points where I felt structural integrity between the thumb and forefinger was needed. I was still laboring under the illusion that this integrity could be achieved by fixing the structure (as in 'fixative', not as in 'repair'): making it solid.

Develop strength while maintaining sensitivity

But the integrity must be *functional.* Consider three hypothetical levels of strength: the first, weakness, the second, the maximum you can attain at present. This second is better but not optimal if it hinders free movement in any way. The third, most desirable level of strength is much stronger than level two, but with this greater strength you do not attain more force so much as a new quality—unimpeded freedom of movement. There is a new level of *organization.*

The mistake one generation of pedagogues made was to neglect the development of strength in their attempt to restore free movement to the playing mechanism. I remember my teacher cautioning me not to lift any heavy object, as it would disturb my growing ability to discriminate the fine differences in sensation that we were then cultivating. For many, avoiding stressful effort in the hand is necessary at a certain stage. But once you have acquired the discriminatory ability, then you must develop strength as well, or else you're lost! Ideally, the two capacities develop side-by-side, one never outstripping the other by too much.

Mysterious inactivity of the second finger in a typical Chopin figuration

The coda of Chopin's G minor Ballade is a supreme test of pianistic virtuosity. The most obvious difficulty is coordinating the left hand leaps with the

right hand's melody in broken chords. But the solution of an underlying problem offers us the key to mastering these three knuckle-busting pages. We will
study the figuration found in measures such as 222-224, where the melody
lies in the thumb while above it the second and fifth fingers play open sixth
chords, harmonizing the melody notes off the beat.

Example 14.1: Chopin: Ballade in G minor, Op. 23, *mm. 222-224*

An even clearer instance of this same right hand figuration can be found in
the F major Ballade at measure 48,

Example 14.2: Chopin: Ballade in F major, Op. 38, *mm. 47-48*

and Chopin goes so far as to devote a whole etude, Op. 10 #10 in A flat
major, to this pattern.

Example 14.3: Chopin: Etude in A flat major, *mm. 1-2*

I had one student for whom this passage was particularly problematical. Throughout his performance, the notes of his right hand second finger remained for the most part inaudible although it did seem to make some attempt to depress its notes. It was strange to me, as this boy plays many other works with consummate virtuosity—great sound, fingers that move, and a heartfelt passion that leaves you gasping. Why the problem here?

Application 14.1
THUMB II: THUMB AND FOREFINGER

Rigid strength inadequate

In the process of strengthening the structure between his thumb and forefinger he rigidified it, bound it up. He reached only the second level of strength. He needed to go further, to gain an even greater strength, one that is not binding and rigidifying but *functional.* How to develop that quality of strength? Do this exercise yourself as you follow my description of how we approached the problem.

Anchor hand on its heel, freely swing second in

> Step 1: I had him place the heel of his hand, and especially the large muscle of his thumb, on the closed fallboard of the piano. With his hand and arm thus stabilized I had him swing his fore-

finger vigorously into the fallboard, giving us a resounding
wooden 'thwack' with each strike of his fingertip.

Illustration 14.1: Heel fixed, forefinger swings in—'Thwap!'

We ensured that his hand and arm stayed free, perhaps swinging
slightly or at least moving in sympathy with the finger—there was
no rigidity in the arm inhibiting the energetic movement of his
finger. His thumb muscle, firmly resting on the fallboard, provided all the structural stability he needed.

Strong thumb muscle does not rigidify second finger

Step 2: Then I had his thumb stand up on the keyboard while he
repeated this same action of his second finger. It was impossible!
No more the resounding *thwack* from his fingertip. All that remained was in ineffectual *bip*. When the fallboard provided support, his forefinger could move very effectively. But when his
thumb, instead of passively resting on the fallboard, was called to
activate, when that big, substantial, capable muscle itself was required to provide the support, it could not, and the forefinger
was left helpless. Or else in providing support, the thumb muscles
rigidified, obstructing the second finger's free movement.

Illustration 14.2: Thumb stands, forefinger swings in—'Bip!'

What happens when you try this variation? This exercise educates with graphic clarity: it shows what is possible, what has not yet been achieved, and how to achieve it. Can you call upon your thumb to work in such a way that it facilitates and supports, empowers the active, energetic free movement of your other fingers rather than inhibiting by default or paralysis?

> Step 3: Try now to play these measures (or others with similar figuration), omitting all the fifth finger's notes. Clarify the problem by isolating it. As you pass between your second finger and thumb, each digit in turn should serve as a support for the other, providing a foundation from which you can make a vigorous and accurate stroke into the key. For a detailed description of this, turn to part V, *Maximal Articulation of the Fingers.*

Example 14.4: Chopin: Ballade in G minor, *mm. 222-224, omitting all fifth fingers*

Thumb can support even when not standing: there's more than one way to skin a cat!

When you stand up on your thumb, does it provide the functional stability you need? Could it provide the same functional stability while not standing? Kemal Gekich describes another strategy for use of your thumb that looks totally different but achieves similar ends:

> I am suspicious about the role of thumb. I started to think about the possibility that the thumb actually should not do any big and independent work. On the contrary, there are indications that the hand works best when the role of thumb is reduced to an absolute minimum, clinging to the palm of the hand, more precisely to the forefinger, and opening only when this is absolutely unavoidable.
>
> Step 4: Try it for yourself, play one of the easier scales, let's say, D-flat major, or B-major or E-major with your right hand, trying to keep your thumb and forefinger as much in permanent contact as is work-able *so they operate as one single unit* [italics mine]. Observe how your hand behaves in order to compensate. This opens many new vistas. Try trills also, with your thumb and forefinger in contact. You will see that the way you execute these will be significantly altered, and this alteration contains the seed of an idea of effective movement that agrees very well with the general nature of moving at the keyboard.[1]

At first glance this idea seems in total opposition to my 'standing on the thumb' exercises, which are designed to increase stability of structure by firming up the arch of the hand, of which the thumb is always one of the crucial pillars. But remember, I give these exercises in the context of *function*, not structure. Stable structure is only a result of good function! When you clamp your thumb to the side of your hand, you activate its function just as much as if you stand on it—possibly even more so, which is perhaps why Gekich got the idea! And of course a functional thumb freed from its connection to the key will be a lot more use to us in most piano playing. Here we achieve the requisite active participation of the thumb without it needing to be clamped to the board or even brushing the keys[2] to ensure its independence. The thumb is active not limp, not a dead weight but pulling its weight in terms of functionality.

---

[1] Kemal Gekich, unpublished email, October 2000.
[2] See next chapter.

When we try this, the first tendency is for everything to freeze into immobility. But if you again follow the idea of loosening everything around the point of effortful focus (in this case the clamping of the thumb to the forefinger), your fingers are once more afforded the opportunity to work in a new way.

Application 14.2
THUMB III: OPPOSITE DIRECTION THUMB STROKE

Have you noticed that there is more than one way to stand on your thumb? Normally your thumb strokes in a circle down and in, the movement of opposition, and if the stroke is continued the thumb ends up somewhere underneath the hand. It is possible to use this stroke to stand up on your thumb. But if you cross one of your fingers over your thumb, you'll see your thumb tending to move in a completely different manner.

Thumb often plays by opening not closing

> With your third or fourth finger crossed over your thumb, stand on your finger's note and play your thumb note. Notice your thumb *begins* its stroke from somewhere underneath your palm. Your thumb does not circle inward at all but rather extends, opening *out and down* from your hand. It actually seems to play backwards, a movement of *reverse* opposition! If it does this but the keyboard gets in the way, then your hand will end up standing on your thumb as a result of an opposite direction thumb stroke. Notice how this move comes in handy in strengthening the whole thumb-forefinger assembly.

This movement is not abduction, which only takes your thumb laterally away from your hand. Whereas normally we are used to opposing our thumb, drawing it in somewhere underneath our hand, it is surprising how often in piano playing you are 'reverse opposing' it. Can you find instances where you have been doing this but hadn't noticed? Can you find places in the repertoire where you are not doing this but might be better off if you did?

Can you develop a hybrid movement that lies somewhere between adduction/abduction and opposition/reverse opposition? Where have you already been doing this one unawares?

15 QUALITY OF MOVEMENT IN THUMB PUSHUPS

Perceive every part of every step

Moshe Feldenkrais loved to say, "My principle is that there are no principles", usually just before he explained one of his principles to you. The one we'll look at in this chapter goes as follows: the more segments or discrete parts of a movement you can perceive when you slow it down, the more highly evolved the movement is. The fewer steps along the way you can perceive, the more primitive a movement you are likely to be doing. If you normally move quickly from point A to point B but cannot in practice reduce the speed of the movement in order to sense all the intermediate points, then it's likely the move is not being done in the most sophisticated or effective way.

Uncovering the real source of a problem in the Italian Concerto

This came up in a lesson on the third movement of Bach's Italian Concerto, which my student played well but with a sound that was somehow not so extraordinary. Her sound was good but nothing special, and I wanted to discover why. In fact, she did not move her fingers—not really! Thus her sound lacked color, differentiation.

Example 15.1: Bach: Italian Concerto, *3rd mvt. mm. 1-4*

But when we started to investigate *why* she wasn't moving them, we opened a Pandora's box!

Application 15.1
Thumb IV: Smooth Movement

Sudden movements lack dimensionality

It didn't take long: the opening octave leap, syncopation and rising scale were all the material we needed.

I asked her to brighten up the scale a little. She couldn't. "No, that's not it," I said. "Move your fingers even more". She didn't. Well, why not? First problem: the transition from thumb to second finger. "Hmmm—not working all that well." Now try doing this as you read along...

> Step 1: "Hold the keys of fingers 2, 3, 4 and 5 down and play your thumb. Don't let your metacarpal ridge collapse!" (It collapses).

> Step 2: "OK, now hold them again but instead of playing your thumb, raise it." She raised her thumb so suddenly, with such a jerk, that she only had the up position and down position of her thumb, nothing in between—like an on-off switch. Aha! We found a clue to the real problem! How does *your* thumb behave here?

Find the thumb movement's three-dimensional path

> Step 3: When I finally got her to slow down, she discovered the path through which her thumb was moving for the first time! She had really never experienced each micro-millimeter of the arc through which her thumb travels to get from a raised position down into the key. This was a whole new world for her— and so simple to discover. The band of four fingers holding their notes down made a solid bridge, and it was this support that allowed for the excruciatingly slow thumb movement from its lowest to highest position and back again. Do this in a more and

more relaxed way to feel the path of movement with ever-increasing richness.

Thumb stays resting on key: contrary strategy gives further clarification of function

I told this student to practice with a large thumb stroke so she could feel the full path of her thumb movement. But what does your thumb do when it's not playing? We can learn much about total hand organization by observing what some parts of it do when not in use. If, as your fingers play, your thumb also wants to activate, to pop up in the air, wave itself around and go flying off in all directions, this is just another sign of a disorganized hand. Your thumb has no real independence if it engages in sympathetic movements provoked by the other fingers. Earlier we read Kemal Gekich's solution to this problem. Here is another, contrasting strategy that achieves similar ends.

> Step 4: Try as your fingers play, to leave your thumb on key—it should remain constantly brushing the key top, leaving absolutely no air space between itself and the key. You must be extremely rigorous with yourself in this. Your thumb does not play but does not wave itself around in the air either. This instantly shows you how many bad habits your hand may possess. By forcing your thumb just to *touch* its note, to constantly brush the white keys without flying around in the air, you force your hand into a totally new organization—an organization of power and control. You have established your thumb's independence from your fingers. And most important, the force you used was *mental* not physical!

Of course you're not going to play piano your whole life with your thumb grazing the white keys, but this is a great exercise to clarify function. Which of these various exercises from the last four chapters provides you with the most graphic understanding of your thumb's role—an understanding that empowers you? Perhaps this next chapter can sum it all up.

16 Forefinger Arc Swings for Thumb Function

Many of these preliminary exercises focus on developing strength—they don't seem to be so much in the spirit of Feldenkrais Method, which develops function mainly through the cultivation of a sensitive, relaxed quality of movement. There's a good reason for this. Walking is an integral part of our daily life. Our pelvis' ability to stand is already developed; it only needs refinement. But many pianists have never experienced the 'pelvic' nature of the thumb-forefinger assembly—many of you will by now have 'stood up' really well on the keyboard for the first time. This next application approaches the problem from a more classically 'Feldenkrais' point of view, and also introduces arm rotation, to be discussed more fully in a later section.

Application 16.1
Thumb V: The Forefinger as a Windshield Wiper

This application can be done either sitting or lying comfortably on your back on a firm surface such as the floor.

> Step 1: Lay your right hand on a flat surface, your fingers spread as wide as they can comfortably. Now put your forefinger on that surface as far to the left of your thumb as possible. How did you do it? Probably you rotated your forearm and your elbow rose up in the air. Your forefinger probably travelled through an arc resembling that of a windshield wiper.

Did your thumb stand up? Is it standing now or are you lying on the whole inside surface of your hand between thumb and forefinger? Let's investigate some variants.

Step 2: Do the 'windshield wiper' movement of your second finger, placing it alternately as far to the left and to the right, and on purpose do not stand up on your thumb. Instead let it function like a log roller—*roll* on all three of its phalanges as your forefinger arcs from side to side. Here it remains totally passive, and your arm does all the work. This gives your thumb a nice massage, but doesn't contribute much to our concern with its standing function. What it *does* do is allow you to *feel* each joint of your thmb in all their magnificent moveable splendor.

Step 3: Repeat the movement, now bringing your fingertip to the highest possible point in space at the midpoint of the arc. Your thumb tip still touches the surface but now your thumb stands up at the midpoint of the arc (as it did in thumb pushups), returning to a passive state at each extreme.

How much of the energy for this movement now comes from your thumb itself; how much still comes from your arm? Try it both ways, first with your thumb actively pressing your forefinger up into the air, or conversely with your arm providing the impetus to launch your forefinger into space. Note in this second variant that your arm only *seems* to be doing the whole job—your thumb still activates though it is not so obvious.

Step 4: Repeat the movement, now standing on your thumb the whole time. Don't let it sink down into passivity at the extremes of the arc.

Notice that if your thumb stands at a certain moderate angle, great speed is possible once you have gotten used to the organization of the movement. Try standing at different angles, noticing which ones help or hinder ease of movement. Notice as well how the movement of your elbow naturally minimizes to increase efficiency.

Try striking with your pinkie instead of your forefinger on the right side. Not only is the ease of the movement increased but your striking range as well.

Now do the movement very quickly a few times, then let it go.

Step 5: All the above with your left hand.

In this application we arrived at true thumb functionality without extreme pressing or exerting any excessive stress on it. All we did was cultivate a movement where your thumb *had* to do its job! How did it fare in this? How long did it take for your thumb to tire? Was it not used to this kind of activity? In actual playing, how much should we use pressing to maintain that integrity of thumb function—could not *movement* rather than pressing keep our thumb in functional shape? And to what degree should our arm take over the work?

These questions will be addressed in subsequent chapters, but the following steps may already shed some light on the matter. If this were a 'real' *Awareness Through Movement* lesson it might continue something like this:

Step 6: Return to step 2 and try again, now casting your attention on other parts of your body. Where else does this movement resonate? In sitting, it is important that your knees and feet are comfortably (about shoulder width) apart, your torso comfortably erect. As you do the 'windshield wiper' movement can you feel what is happening in your right shoulder blade? Does it slide on your ribs? How much so, and in what direction? How about your left arm? If your left hand is lying on the same surface, shoulder width apart from your right hand, does your left elbow fall slightly to the inside as your right elbow lifts? Does your rib cage move to the right? Can you detect any motion even in your right knee? Does it perhaps move infinitesimally forward as you swing your right forefinger to the left? If so, what is happening in your pelvis to allow this? Does your left knee move back as the right moves forward?

In lying, what can you discover about these 'movement resonances' elsewhere in your body?

For each of these details, when you notice if there is some movement in some other part of your body, does that movement tend to increase once your attention is focused on it? Can you let that happen without forcing it to happen? By relaxing and softening rather than trying harder we can cultivate that quality of total body cooperation without exertion. As if the bones of your whole skeleton constitute a series of dominoes and when one moves it starts a chain reaction through all the others.

Steps 7, 8: Return to steps 3 and 4, now following the same investigative exploration as in step 6.

Step 9: Perhaps by now you have discovered a way to do this simple little 'windshield wiper' movement of the second finger so that your whole body participates, your torso swaying slightly and your pelvis swivelling, not because you made an effort in that direction but because you *allowed* your body simply to resonate to the initial impulse of the movement. But of course we cannot do this kind of thing while playing piano—it's unthinkable! Aren't we trying to minimize external movement not enhance it? What does this have to do with the 'meditative stillness' mentioned earlier to which we may well aspire?

Step 10: Try the movement now with both hands at once. How does your torso and pelvis participate now? There is no more swaying because the two arms cancel out each other's influence. But you still may be able to detect a slight forward and back rocking motion in your pelvis and torso.

Step 11: Try playing any normal passage, anything you like, *continuing to monitor your pelvis and torso.* The point is not that they move or not move, but rather that you *feel* whether there is any resonance of movement going on there or not. It is simply the process of *staying in touch with it* that cultivates effective whole body participation. But even this is not the final step.

Step 12: Leave only 5 percent of your consciousness on this monitoring process, or perhaps even none at all, devoting all the rest of your attention to the music. But let that process of body awareness continue in your automatic reflexes. If you have trained it well, it should continue to operate on its own. *Now* we are approaching something akin to how you should be functioning in performance.

V
HAND STRENGTH AND FUNCTION C

OCTAVES TO SYNTHESIZE HAND AND ARM FUNCTION

17 FROM THE THUMB ACROSS TO THE FIFTH FINGER: HAND STRUCTURE AND FUNCTION IN OCTAVE PLAYING

At this point we have set down some basic principles about optimal hand function, and are now beginning to see how these apply in practice. After the thumb-forefinger assembly the next stop on our functional tour of the piano playing apparatus is the fifth finger, or more exactly, the bridge between thumb and fifth. This bridge is an integral part of virtually all piano playing, but we can most clearly examine it in octaves. Once again in octaves the role of the arm is difficult to ignore, and so this chapter also serves as a transition to part VII, *Above the Hand: The Role of the Wrist and Arm in Legato*.

If the stretch to an octave imposes too great an extension on your hand, all the following exercises can be done using a smaller interval, even as small as a fifth.

Application 17.1
OCTAVES I: REVIEW OF STRENGTH AND STRUCTURE

This lesson I gave a student whose octaves worked well in a *piano* dynamic, but whose arm would seize up in *forte*. Her hand wasn't *supporting* the forces coming down through her arm. This logical sequence is designed to build up your hand structure and function step by step.

> Step 1: First review the role of your thumb. Play a note with your thumb, hold it and exert as much weight as possible on it. You will notice that the space between your thumb and second finger will tend to collapse.

Open that space

> Work against this tendency: Keep pressing down but use your thumb
> muscles to *open* that space. Try to touch the ceiling with your fingers.

Open and close thumb to move hand right and left

> Step 2: Maintaining that space between thumb and forefinger open,
> move your hand laterally right and left. Again, activate your thumb
> muscles as much as possible. Now you are using them to locomote
> this movement—it is your thumb actually opening and closing that
> moves your hand. The more pressure you maintain on your hand
> structure, the more exercise you are giving those thumb muscles, the
> more you are improving their functionality as well as the functionality
> of that whole structure.

Pushups

> Step 3: Having mastered the feeling of the thumb carrying the hand,
> continue to move your hand laterally and now have a finger play a
> note to the right and then left of your thumb. Still try to touch the
> ceiling with your fingers between each note, all the time maintaining
> that pressure, exerting maximum weight on the thumb. Now this
> resembles the thumb pushups described earlier.

Application 17.2
OCTAVES II: FIFTH FINGER PULL-UPS

Thumb-forefinger exercises strengthen the inner side of the hand, but what
about the outside? For the fifth finger and outer ridge of the hand, try this:

> Step 1: Curl your middle three fingers so their tips touch your
> palm or even better the pads underneath your knuckles. Place
> your fisted hand on the keyboard with your fifth on let's say C#
> for your right hand or D# for your left hand (F# right or A# left
> are also possible). Clamp the heel of your thumb to the white

keys so it cannot move. This provides a point of fixation for your arm.

Step 2: Pressing the pad of your fifth as firmly as possible into the black key, draw your finger back towards you. Your finger pad slides towards you on the key surface even as it remains clamped to the key. Do not curl your fifth finger but leave it straight, even hyper-extended. Do you notice what happens to the top knuckle (your fifth finger's metacarpal-phalangeal joint)? It and the whole outside of your hand should stand up. Even your elbow will rise a bit. This exercise activates and strengthens the whole outer ridge of your hand, from whence much of the fifth finger's strength originates.

Illustration 17.1:

a)Heel fixed, fingers curled   b) Fifth pulled back

Application 17.3
OCTAVES III: THE ARCH FROM THUMB ACROSS
TO FIFTH

Maintain at least some small degree of arch in octave hand extension

Now let's approach those octaves. If your hand is very small you might want to try this with the interval of a seventh or sixth at first instead of the full octave.

Step 1: Play an octave with the center part of your hand drooped onto the keyboard. The ridge of your palm that runs along under your knuckles almost mashes down its notes. *Feel* those middle keys with your palm; get a sensorily rich impression of where you are on the keys. Rub those keys with your palm; let them give you a massage.

Step 2: Now try to draw the tips of your thumb and fifth closer together. Of course they cannot approach one another because they are holding onto their keys. Instead, your efforts result in the central part of your hand rising, creating an arch form. Your palm now leaves the keys. For loud, juicy octaves it is not necessary to bang but rather simply to *maintain the integrity of that bridge*, so that the grasping function between thumb and fifth is repeatedly activated.

Center of gravity is over thumb not fifth

Step 3: Because we are taught to voice the fifth finger note in right hand octaves, we tend to commit a common error at this point: we focus the arm's center of gravity over that finger so that the outer edge of the forearm and the fifth finger form a continuous line while the thumb protrudes to the inside somewhere. This is a *big* mistake! According to natural structural design, the whole locus of hand strength and security is centered on the thumb. Thus the arm and *thumb* should line up—the inner edge of the forearm and the thumb should form a continuous line. Notice that your hand is turned out as a result.

The bipartite hand: ballet dancer-like turnout

Do you recall our discussion about the division of labor between the thumb and the group of four fingers? Because form reflects function, it follows logically that the structure of your hand also would be bipartite: the four fingers together folding in to meet the lone thumb. Thus in playing we will often turn our hands out so far that the thumb tip is just as close to the keys as the fingertips. I remember one Feldenkrais practitioner telling me that my hands had more 'turnout'—like a ballet dancer's feet—than he'd ever seen. He saw it as a professional deformation; I see it rather as an optimal adaptation—once again, form following function.

Voicing the top even when physical structure is centered over the lower voice

"If I can't lean my hand directly on my fifth finger, how then to bring out my top voice?" asks the despondent student. Quite simple. Remember the original exercises of this lesson? Let's try one more variant in our thumb pushups review.

> Step 4: Balance your hand on your thumb again, and now rotate your forearm so that your elbow and fifth finger rise. However, this time leave your fifth still pointing down towards the key—only let its metacarpal-phalangeal rise. As your hand descends, play the fifth finger and note the resulting juicy, singing, alive tone. *This* is the way to bring out the top voice! When you maintain a hand alignment that *consolidates* its strength, you can use it as a base to produce whatever voicing you want.

Application 17.4
LEGATO V: OVERHOLDING II, GRASPING II

Overholding in Hanon

One more exercise to clarify and consolidate what we've learned. This time, believe it or not, we go back to good old, tried and true Hanon exercises. For instance let's now take Hanon #1, but use it to create an evolved version of our five-note overholding exercise.

> Step 1: Play your first thumb note C with a good, healthy *forte* or more. Overholding your thumb, play the next three notes *pp*, and

hold all those notes down as well. The top note, your fifth finger's A, **forte** or more again, the three middle notes again **pp**. Always hold down all keys possible, especially your thumb and fifth finger! Notice that this creates once again the bridge structure we have been investigating, and that the structure based on the outer fingers is so stable that the middle three fingers simply can drop in like feathers, with no effort.

Example 17.1: Hanon exercise

However, do not neglect the bridge in the reverse situation: during the **forte** attack of the two outer fingers, especially the thumb, it is the middle three fingers that must provide the security of a totally sound bridge, even though they have just finished playing a non-pressing, feather-light legato. Be on your guard!

When this variation on Hanon is done properly, it literally sounds as if you have transformed your piano into two instruments—loud, sonorous, singing brass fanfares and a whispering zither-like accompaniment. Success in this exercise is not measured only by the incredibly graphic differentiation and discrimination in the feeling of your hand but first and foremost in your sound!

The same structural relationships empower passagework

In this modified Hanon the tendency to collapse (especially between your thumb and forefinger) will be highlighted because of the dynamic differentiation you are attempting. Thus you have an even richer opportunity to overcome this insidious habit. Remember, don't correct it by rigidifying structure but by finding a natural stability based on optimal bone alignment.

Step 2: Turn your attention once again to single note passagework. Has your work on the hand's arch structure in octaves, and extreme dynamic differentiation in Hanon enlightened you, increased your ability to detect when your hand structure weakens going across the thumb? The sensory learning inherent in these exercises should help you to *prevent that momentary failing of structure* that is an epidemic yet mostly unacknowledged problem among us pianists.

Grasp to activate your God-given strength!

Tendonitis most commonly occurs in the forearm, *not* in the hand, when the forearm exerts too much stress in a vain attempt to compensate for the lack of function lower down—the hand not doing its job. Let's review grasping once again:

> Step 3: Grasp one of your forearms with your other hand and squeeze not convulsively but *firmly*. Remember, *this* is the hand's strength, its most elemental function. This is the movement that separates us from the apes—it is one of the evolutionary bases of our intelligence! Why aren't you using this in your playing? Why cause yourself all these problems unnecessarily?

You will not harm your hand by developing its strength intelligently. On the contrary, you will empower your entire playing mechanism, improving your musical capability even as you reduce the risk of injury.

Through this whole series of exercises we will occasionally return to some key points as we have done here. In doing so I risk becoming repetitious, but I feel it is necessary for you to have as many opportunities as possible to grasp these ideas, to approach them from a wide variety of angles. The repetitions I include serve as opportune reminders—a review that might facilitate the development of the sensory-motor learning process.[1]

The following chapters work as a bridge to part VI, *Above the Hand: The Role of The Wrist and Arm in Legato*, and could just as well have been placed there. Although their main concern is still the glorification of your octave sound in its many guises, it seems the arm has managed to insinuate itself into the picture and can no longer be neglected. This shows again the interrelatedness of these technical elements that I have separated out only for purposes of elucidation.

---

[1] See *Moshe Feldenkrais: the Mindful Body*, in appendix III.

18 FORTISSIMO OCTAVES

Application 18.1
OCTAVES IV: SHAKE THE PIANO

Drawing fingers together to consolidate hand strength

Step 1: Place your flattened four fingers with their tips bunched together on a flat surface with your thumb stretched out to octave width pointing inasmuch as it can in a direction opposite to your fingers. Press the surface quite firmly while drawing your fingers and thumb towards each other. Your fingers are flat or even hyper-extended. If you continue this motion it becomes the tissue paper picking up motion: your fingers form a bird beak; your wrist comes straight up while your elbow falls slightly forward and in.

Step 2: Remember this move as you place your hands on an octave. Grab a white key octave and literally try to shake the piano, letting your elbow continue to relax and fall in. Watch out: stiffening your elbow will only weaken your structure, inhibiting your hand's ability to grip. Keep your elbow loose, because here you need all the hand strength and structural viability you can get!

Can you really make the piano move on its casters? Many of my smaller students end up shaking them*selves* more than the piano at first, but all eventually get the hang of it to some extent. It is not so important for you to actually move the instrument. The crucial thing is how you mobilize your whole physical self in *trying* to move it.

Here your metacarpal-phalangeal joints should rise always. Banging results from instability of structure, which in turn stems from lack of activity. This exercise aims to increase hand activity and thus actually *generate* stability. This variation on the basic grasping motion of the hand demonstrates the structural security and control needed to get an octave that sounds big but not banged.

Application 18.2
GRASPING III: SOFTEN FOR GREATER POWER

Towards healthy rather than aggressive power—natural grasping

Let's return to grasping once again.

> Grab onto any object and really grasp it with all your might. In lessons I offer students my own arm for this purpose; in fact I encourage them to try and *break* my arm. But often their initial efforts are so feeble that I will wonderingly ask if a mosquito has landed on my arm! Find a partner and practice on their arm. When you have accustomed yourself to grasping firmly, pull your partner's arm towards you while they resist your efforts. Again try not to stiffen your elbow but have the power come from your fingers *and* from higher up your arm. Paradoxically, the softer you are, the less you stiffen, the greater effect your muscular power can have.

Instantly you get a clear, graphic experience of the grasping function, and of your own eminent capability. Do you see that you really can grab, with real power! Now let's examine how this sense of healthy rather than brute power can help us at the keyboard.

Hand activation—for a free, soft forearm

I showed grasping to one student who then asked, "When I try to play loud fast octaves my forearm gets sore. How can I play them without hurting myself?" I had just given the answer experientially; but now some explanation was needed. I reiterated that when your hand is not active, its structure tends to weaken. As a result your forearm muscles stiffen, compensating for the lack of stability and power in your hand. However this is counterproductive effort on their part: originating from a state of weakness, this stiffening already puts you behind the eight ball in terms of movement. This effort of your forearm is one of compensation, of fixation rather than of real action.

Hand activation—generates structural integrity

The most important aspect of the finger-hand grasping technique is that it activates. Muscular activity is implemented before you have committed yourself to a certain fixed hand structure, before the note is even played. Thus activity not only generates movement, it also creates the conditions for good structure. The muscular activity is cause rather than effect, generation rather than compensation. The more internally active the hand, the better your sound will be and the more moveable your arm muscles remain. Note that external arm movements are a completely different matter; they can actually interfere with this process, and thus for the most part should be minimized.

Hand activation—sidesteps danger of tendonitis

Activation on time creates an ideal situation where even while we increase the power of our sound we are also drastically reducing the chances of hurting ourselves. Many students trying for Horowitz's big sound have overstrained and only acquired a case of tendonitis for their troubles. Here we provide a way for one's sound to evolve and grow without the danger of adverse side effects.

Still clear as mud? Let's try a further exercise.

Application 18.3
OCTAVES V: FREELY VIBRATING OCTAVES

Whip your hand back over your shoulder

> Step 1: Rest your hand on key, your thumb and fifth finger outlining an octave. Now, without playing anything, suddenly whip your hand straight up and back, leaving it somewhere above your shoulder. Perhaps you could pretend you harbor an intense dislike for your

teacher, who just happens to be looking over your shoulder (we certainly hope you only *pretend* to do this). Whip your hand back so suddenly that you by-accident-on-purpose smack him or her one in the face! Notice that if you leave your wrist loose as you do this, it naturally cocks itself—your hand flies further back than your arm. The further your hand cocks back the more your fingers will naturally curl.

Illustration 18.1: Natural finger curve as the arm whips back

Step 2: Do the same, but see if you can surreptitiously have your octave sound while your hand is on its way out. Practice this a few more times, not of course with your teacher-target really there.

Step 3: The same, but instead of starting from on key, begin with your hand somewhere up near your shoulder. From that position play the same octave *staccatissimo* and return instantly to somewhere near your shoulder. It's the same whipping motion, but beginning from the hand's loosely pulled back position and returning to it. The movement should be lightning fast so that it looks like your hand never leaves the shoulder area. *Keep your hand and wrist loose!*

Step 4: Try this first with no pedal, noticing how alive, full and rich the tone of your staccato is. It is a blistering, electric octave, exciting and galvanizing rather than ugly or aggressive. Then while still playing staccatissimo with the same arm movement, add the pedal. See how the initial excitement of the tone is not dampened by the pedal but prolonged, now shining on gloriously free and unhindered.

Analogous to drumstick on a drumhead

Try to make your sound as sharp and as *loud* as possible in order to make it totally free, totally resonant, totally exciting. Notice that if the movement is not quick enough, some clutching or holding or cramping up begins to occur. However, if it's *too* quick you begin to lose volume. Find the optimum speed and strength, that magic spot where the piano simply *roars* in a way to which you are totally unaccustomed! Are you having fun discovering what a piano can *do?*

Step 5: Try this move on some other wooden surface. You can tell by the amount of resonant sound your fingers produce knocking on wood how much sound you are going to draw from the piano. The special thing about this technique is that it completely eliminates strangling the sound of the piano by over-trying. The movement is completely analogous to the beat of a drumstick on the drumhead. The drummer's wrist must be ultimately supple: the rebound of the stick from the drumhead, or in this case of your finger from the key, must be completely untrammelled.

Same free attack, but now stay on key

Step 6: Finally, after all this preparation, how can you play great *ff* octaves? Simple: just intend to do this last exercise, but just in that instant your fingers should be leaving the key on the rebound, *stop.* You have already released your arm totally, you are on the way out, but your fingers just happen to remain on key. At that point, simply instantaneously decide not to leave after all!

You must really trick your mind!

Strange as it may seem, you must plan in advance *not* to plan in advance! If you know in advance that you are not going to leave the key, you are sure to seize up somehow and make a mess of the whole thing. Your thought process won't be the same. You must really cultivate all the mental processes of the 'drumhead' exercise, and only in the instant when your mission is already accomplished, when that soundboard is already singing and vibrating and roaring and dancing in sound, then and only in that instant do you decide to stay in key, and by holding onto that octave prolong its wonderful ecstatic life!

Powerful octaves: fewer movements for more sound—dispense with the classic 'arm out to the side'

Step 7: Do you see how important it is in *ff* octaves to economize your movements? Any extraneous movement, any action not related to the direct movement we learned here, only makes it more difficult for you to maintain the structure and function that gives you this amazing sound. For instance, that old villain, the classic arm movement out to the side to round out the phrase: this tends to weaken the top knuckle of the second finger, pulling it down, robbing it of its vitality.[1] If you move your elbow out to the side, you are pulling your hand *away* from the keys, depleting its energy instead of activating it! Try playing *ff* octaves first without and then with the classic 'arm out' movement. Can you clearly discern the difference in functions? Can you hear the difference in the resulting sound?

The whole rationale behind moving the elbow out to round out the sound is that a stiff arm causes a banged sound. But what is the underlying cause of a stiff arm? A weak hand! If the hand doesn't do its job the arm must stiffen in a vain attempt to rectify the problem. Thus: improve hand strength and function first, *then* use arm movements for their proper purpose: to orient the hand and to shape phrase and line, not to attenuate your sound!

Let's digress from octaves for a moment to explore the 'arm-whip motion' further.

---

[1] See paragraph 3, chapter 29.

19 REPLACING ARM SWOOP WITH COBRA STRIKE

We often see pianists raise their arms far from the board and then swoop into the key in an attempt to make a big *forte*. But this is not necessarily the free movement we just learned in the previous chapter. If you examine the quality of movement a little more closely you may detect an overly controlled aspect to it. Often the big movement 'in' will be curtailed just as the hand reaches the keyboard: the pianist arrests the movement in the instant to assure an accurate attack, and we are deprived of the big tone we have been led to expect. Two opposing muscle groups over-controlling each other will render the movement cramped and inhibited. My principle is that the larger the movement, the more freedom with which it should be done. If we can bring a real exactitude to a large, expansive movement, we reduce the need for counterproductive controlling contractions from opposing muscle groups.

Application 19.1
ARM I: THE ARM AS A WHIP

Freeing up your arm throw

Try throwing your hand at the board as you did in the previous chapter, using your arm as you would a lacrosse racquet to throw a ball, or like David's sling with which he killed Goliath. And you can kill mistakes with this—knock 'em dead! How can such a seemingly wild, almost violent movement increase accuracy? It would seem that this craziness would eliminate the little accuracy you ever had! The secret is to do it elegantly. To eliminate the opposing muscular contractions that attempt to control but actually only hinder the free flow of the movement, *causing* your inaccuracy, and instead use your mind's awareness as a control.

Step 1: Try it first away from the piano, on a tabletop. Throw your hand forward in the air with your arm completely loose; then pull it back. For the moment don't go anywhere near the tabletop but stay well above it. It's the movement of cracking a whip. Your hand will flip like the end of the whip does. Here your wrist must remain totally loose.

Step 2: Now repeat the same movement each time letting your fingers approach a little closer to the tabletop. Finally your fingertips just lightly graze the tabletop and immediately are flicked away as the movement completes itself.

Use mind over matter

At this point you may be staring to worry about hurting your fingertips. Do you notice yourself cramping up, reducing the vigor and freedom of the movement in some way in order to protect your dainty little finger pads? This is where the aim of the exercise comes in.

Step 3: Resist the temptation to employ any braking action of the muscles. Instead, even *increase* the movement's vigor, and use your *mind* to control the accuracy of the attack. You *can* focus your awareness to keep your fingers striking an exact point on the surface, *without any reduction in energy*. The focus of your mind can be so complete that when you transfer this action to the piano you can play with complete accuracy.

Fingers of steel wrapped in velvet

The feeling in the hands recalls that phrase, "Fingers of steel wrapped in velvet". The bones literally feel like steel, the flesh velvet. You can even feel the fingertips cutting into the keys with the accuracy and incision of a knife blade. This derives from the bones feeling direct contact with the key through the flesh. If your flesh is tight, your bones cannot *feel* through it. But if your flesh stays super loose like velvet because of the freedom and exuberance of the movement, it ceases to be a barrier. It becomes like water, presenting no obstacle to your bones feeling the ivories.

If this is still unclear to you, try playing the soundboard.

> Step 4: Reach under the piano's belly and using the same free, ener-
> getic movement, rap the board smartly with your fingertips. Notice
> that to make that board really resonate you must use a really vigorous
> movement, something far more dynamic than anything you would
> dare do at the keyboard. How big a sound, what kind of a resonant
> *'thok'* can you elicit from that wonderful piece of wood? You should
> make your fingertips really sting. Take it to the point where you have
> to stop because your pads of flesh hurt slightly!

I am trying to expand your universe—you must begin to see what is possible for
this instrument to do!

> Step 5: When you have really explored this, go back to the keyboard
> and see how much you can expand the volume of your *forte* by
> striking the keys in this way.

All this is preparation for something that looks completely different but grows
out of the same essential seed. Heinrich Neuhaus repeatedly mentions that pianists with small hands must take special care to learn how to play staying very close
to the keys.[1] The cobra strike gives you the feeling of sting in the fingertips, the
blisteringly alive sound that we are looking for to fill a hall. The next radical
development will be to acquire the speed and intensity of the cobra strike without any visible external movement!

---

[1] Heinrich Neuhaus, *The Art of Piano Playing* (London: Barrie & Jenkins, 1986).

20 BIG SOUND FROM A
SMALL HAND

To internalize the cobra spark feeling, first we digress to reexamine octave technique in the light of ultimate legato feel. We will take Liszt's Dante Sonata as our test piece, for it provides numerous opportunities for a whole variety of approaches to playing octaves.

Application 20.1
STRUCTURAL FUNCTION I: MINIMAL
MOVEMENT FOR MAXIMAL SOUND

Loosen all joints for a new type of legato in Liszt's Dante Sonata

Take the opening theme that follows the introductory fanfare of fate and the subsequent ominous rumblings in the bass. The right hand plays a melody in repeated octaves. For the purposes of this exercise first omit the repetitions: play each melodic octave only once.

Example 20.1: Liszt: Après une lecture de Dante, *mm. 35-39*

Step 1: Play the first octave A and while your fingertips hold on to it, release everything in your hand and arm. I literally mean everything! The joints between each and every of your bones should release, collapse, so that you barely manage to hang on to your octave. Your elbow drops, as does your wrist. The arch in your hand we have so carefully cultivated now collapses so that your palm comes perilously close to depressing the keys in between your two A's. This amplifies the relaxed feeling of your hand described later in chapter 22, *Teutonic Beef.*

Step 2: Now comes the fun part. Maintaining this 'hyper-collapsedness' and holding on to your fifth finger's A, move your arm and hand to position your thumb and fourth finger on their B flats. All your joints are ridiculously loose, yet still your fifth finger somehow manages to provide a modicum of support for the hand shift, a point of connection that gives a nominal steadiness and focus. When you are positioned well on your B flats, play them and in that moment again feel an increase in the degree of looseness of all your joints. It's not just a falling in but a sense of increased collapsing of the joints.

Keep 're-minimizing' your effort

Isn't this craziness? We just went through an extensive, detailed cure for collapsing and now I want you to cultivate it instead! But do you see the logic in it? We are so used to playing with effort that there is a constant strong tendency for much more 'trying' than you need, to come creeping back into your playing. This 'trying' reduces the degree to which you feel the difference between finger and arm function. Here your whole aim is to increase the looseness of your joints, especially the finger joints, on each attack. The looser a joint, the more it can feel the movement going on within itself — the sliding of one bone surface on the other. Your structure is more functional because 1) there is more movement in the joints and 2) because the muscles formerly occupied in hindering movement of these joints are now free to manipulate them. Here we cultivate collapsedness to increase feeling in the joints: this new ability to sense will in turn cultivate your bones' ability to sense and move to their optimal alignment.

This is medicine, therapy! With every octave you reaffirm a new feeling, a radically different approach to the sounding of these octaves. At first do this extremely slowly, until you are sure that you can succeed without any superfluous effort creeping back in. Then when you begin to increase your speed, do so only to the extent that you can maintain this new physical organization, this constant 're-reduction' of effort. Having very nicely awakened to a new technical possibility, as you begin to go faster do not go back to sleep![1] Notice how this gives you exceptionally fine control of tone and dynamic.

As you reinstate the repeat of each octave, use a subtle miniature hand flip[2] to achieve this with a minimum of movement, staying maximally close to the keys. The mournful, ghostly, ultra-mysterious mood of this lugubrious theme now begins to manifest fully in sound.

> Step 3: As this technique allows you to stay exceptionally close to the keys, can you now play the first fanfare octaves of the sonata with full power yet staying as loose and as close to the keys as you did in Step 1? This is easier said than done! Begin by maintaining the exceptional closeness and looseness we're cultivating and play with not much power. As you gradually increase your dynamic, notice the physical adjustments you must make to stay loose, close and accurate. Do not increase strain or 'trying'. Instead, increase explosiveness! It is an instantaneous movement from somewhere inside, like a strong electric shock wherein you maintain that strange 'hyper-looseness'. We are now trying to internalize the energetic vigor and sound of the *Cobra Strike* exercise.
>
> This same melody soon appears in full chords, marked *disperato*. Most of us feel desperate at the thought of how to get really great sound here! The secret is to maintain that feeling of finger sting—they really slap the keys, and manifest the same explosive energy that you created in your open octaves. But again, it is a structure-supported slap—maintaining hyper-looseness allows your bones to *feel* where their correct alignment is! Then the correct alignment of your arm behind the hand keeps you accurate and your sound focused. Relax your arm enough that it can fall

---

[1] This also serves as the preliminary exercise for Chopin's octave etude, Op. 25 #10.
[2] See *Lauretta Milkman - The Choreographing Hand* in appendix III.

naturally into correct alignment, yet keep it vital enough that the shocks of your fingers incising the keys do not knock your arm out of that configuration.

Example 20.2: Liszt: Après une lecture de Dante, *mm.* 54-56

At the first triumphant appearance of the second theme, you have the chance to combine these two techniques—the chordal melody sings above while you must stay close to keys during the glorious cascading octave runs that decorate the theme.

Example 20.3: Liszt: Après une lecture de Dante, *mm.* 103-105

In the earlier interlocking octaves (well, only the right hand plays octaves but your hands *do* interlock) you should try for the strange feeling of staying extremely close to the keys even as your forearms 'pump' and your fingers sting for blistering tone. Stay close, but think *ultra-staccatissimo* if you want your fingers to generate the internal electric activity your sound needs here.

Example 20.4: Liszt: Après une lecture de Dante, *mm. 84-86*

Increase dynamic power but stay on key, strangely motionless

You may notice that if the contractions that give power to your sound come from higher up your arm, they can be very sudden and very strong without impinging at all on the total accuracy of your finger placement. Your hand and fingers remain strangely neutral, your joints loose. They themselves do not convulse to produce a big sound. They remain on key, exactly where they need to be, the relatively passive instrument for the transmission of the powerful forces of your upper arm down, through them, into the piano. Even your arm stays strangely still, so that the power coming down through them can be so strong that you will feel sting in your fingertips just as you did in *Cobra Strike*. External movement only detracts from the effectiveness of what is now a sudden inner contraction.

Now you have completed the process of internalization. In the previous chapter we started with a movement where your hand begins somewhere near your shoulder, strikes 'in' and then returns to your shoulder. Then you struck 'in' but remained on key, internalizing 50 percent of the movement. Now you remain on key the whole time, before as well as after the attack—the movement has been totally internalized.

Here I do not contradict what I wrote earlier about the finger always being more active than the arm. Here your finger still moves externally just slightly more than your arm. To stay accurately on key we have minimized the finger's external movement as well as the arm's, thus bringing into greater prominence the role of internal upper arm contractions in producing a big sound.

For those of you with a small hand, this is the optimal way to achieve the big, powerful and electric sound that nobody would expect from you. Because you are constantly aware of the smallness of your hand and the special difficulties you encounter, two opposing tendencies have most likely been thoroughly ingrained into your reflexes. You tend to bind up your mechanism in order to maintain accuracy, and to 'try too hard', that is, to move too much, in order to get that big sound. This technique offers you a radically different solution. All that 'binding' and 'trying' has been reducing your accuracy *and* your sound. Here's your chance to maintain exceptional accuracy while developing a totally new path to powerful, magnificent, resonant sound. You'll knock 'em dead!

21 TREMOLANDO OCTAVES

Here is a way to develop freedom, speed and brilliant tone in tremolando octaves that also encapsulates much of the ground we have covered on finger/hand/arm function.

Application 21.1
OCTAVES VI: TREMOLANDO OCTAVES

Step 1: Play an octave maximizing the feeling of the arch from thumb across to fifth by trying to draw them together.

Step 2: Keeping this arch shape firm and secure, lift the outside ridge of your hand to the sky, helping of course by rotating your elbow up and out. Your whole arm rotates on the fulcrum of your firmly standing thumb, but for now your fifth continues to point down towards the key it has just left.

Step 3: Swing your arm vigorously down, making your fifth play its note with resounding, solid tone. Keep your whole structure stable and leave your fifth inert. Your fifth is structurally solid but it does not change its orientation in relation to your hand. Repeat this many times.

Step 4: Again lift the outside ridge of your hand to the sky, but this time while your hand/arm remains high in this position, raise your fifth to the sky and swing it vigorously down many times. Here you don't play a note but swing your finger in the air, individuating a maximally active finger stroke from the rest of

your mechanism that remains fixed.

Symbiosis of finger swing and hand/arm swing

Step 5: And now for the kicker: combine the two types of swinging that up to this point you have practiced in isolation, and listen to the sound this produces. How's that for alive, brilliant tone?

Steps 6-9: Repeat steps 2 to 5, but this time stand on your fifth finger. It becomes the fulcrum used to raise your thumb and the inside of your hand.

Step 10: All this has been preparation for your tremolando octave. Now simply alternate steps 5 and 9. Go very slowly at first, and only when you have explored this fully, when it has become comfortable, begin to increase the speed. The faster you go, the more concise the combined swing/rotation movement becomes, its range diminishing until at full speed it is virtually invisible. Here finger movement and arm rotation act together symbiotically, and the movement 'template' first practiced externally remains active as it becomes more and more internalized.

This process will keep you free and active— it diametrically opposes the tendency we have to tense and seize up when attempting broken octaves. You can check that you're maintaining freedom of movement by observing your triceps muscle, which hangs from the back of your upper arm. It should remain loose and flapping as you do this.

Check this technique out in some examples from the literature. How about the left hand in the first movement of Beethoven's *Pathetique* Sonata, or the tremolando octave scales at the end of the exposition of his Sonata in C major, Op. 2 #3?

Example 21.1: Beethoven: Sonata in C minor Op. 13 (Pathetique), *1st mvt., mm. 12-19*

Example 21.2: Beethoven: Sonata in C major Op. 2 #3, *1st mvt., mm. 85-87*

22 Teutonic Beef

We have been discussing the consolidation of strength and brilliance of tone in octaves. Here's a way to thicken that tone up, one that comes in especially handy for those fat German Beethoven octaves that can be found for instance all over the *Emperor* Concerto.

Application 22.1
Octaves VII: Meaty Technique for Meaty Tone

Thick, meaty tone in Beethoven octaves

> Step 1: Close the lid of the keyboard and, with your arm loose, slap your whole palm down on it. What a satisfying *thunk* that makes! Imagine that each of our fingertips had as much meat in it as the whole palm of our hand! If we could only transfer that thickness of tone to our octaves!

> Step 2: Well you can. Let's first investigate this 'slap-thunk' technique in a little more detail. This is actually a variation on the 'catching' technique described in appendix III. Slap your hand down on the fallboard again, and notice that your elbow has fallen naturally to the inside. Hmmm ... did it not? Well, it should have.... Try again and this time *let* it fall naturally. Only when you have done this can you begin to move your elbow slowly up and back out until the heel of your hand begins to peel off the sur-

face, to rise. Slowly now your palm will also come unstuck from the surface, and finally even your fingers will begin to peel off. It is at *this* point that you suddenly thunk your hand down again.

But how? Aren't large parts of your fingers still stuck to the fallboard? Well yes. This is why your mechanism must now go through a kind of flipping motion, like a fish out of water. Your hand is still in the process of leaving the surface when your arm already starts to descend again, initiating the next 'slap-thunk'. Your arm comes down suddenly, and as it descends your hand must do a flip in a hurry in order to leave the surface before your arm's momentum 'thunks' it into the fallboard again.

Step 3: To transfer this sensation to your fingers, simply soften your hand and fingers as much as you can, and play an octave imitating that feel of the whole palm *thunk*. "But *how?*" you may ask. It's not easy. Your big, fat palm of course can't actually play the notes—only your miserable skinny little fingertips get to depress the keys. *However,* if you let your palm graze the key edges, let the surface of your hand come perilously close to all the keys in between the two notes of your octave, *almost* mashing those keys down, then the tone of your octave does become a little more juicy, for two reasons. Significantly more of your fingers' flesh now makes contact with the key, and your whole hand and arm has softened, increasing its 'meaty' character and thus better allowing kinetic energy to flow through it.

I seem to be contradicting the maintenance of arch support I mentioned earlier. Not so! Appearances can be deceiving. Note that if you completely stopped maintaining your arch here it would be disastrous. You would mash more keys down than a Henry Cowell cluster! But if you relax everything as much as you can while still managing to avoid mashing any redundant keys, you'll find the optimal balance between relaxation and just enough effort to maintain a modicum of functionality in your arch. By first relaxing everything and *then* imposing this task on your hand, you give it the chance to find a really effective new organization, one that can indeed reward you with juicy Teutonic octaves!

23 THE OCTAVE ARM-SWEEP

Clangorous leaping octaves in a Scriabin Etude

Half way through Scriabin's Etude in C sharp minor, Op. 42 #5, the left hand finally gets to dispense with its 16th-note passagework and break into a passionate chordal accompaniment, clangorous open fifth chords on the beat, growling deep bass octaves off the beat. How to make this sound alive, electric and charged with a burning vibration? How to free it rather than over-control it? As a drummer must let the stick bounce off the drumhead for the skin to vibrate, so must we play those octaves. Something must be continually freeing the innards of the arm so that there is no gripping, no inadvertent dampening of the sound.

Application 23.1
OCTAVES VIII: INFLECTED LEGATO OCTAVES

Example 23.1: Scriabin: Etude in C sharp minor, Op. 42 #5, mm. 30-32

How to leave without letting go

No, this is not a love advice column; we are still dealing with music here! These chords and octaves are not marked staccato, but the leaps between them require you to be in continual movement. How can you leave one chord or octave quickly enough to reach the next one on time without playing them staccato?

Step 1: Have your arm already start traveling down towards the bass as your fingers continue to hold on to the octave-open fifth chord. A little bit of supination (rotating your hand to lie palm upwards) helps you travel further before you are forced to let go of the chord. In fact, if you continue to supinate, eventually your thumb must leave its note, then more supination forces your second finger to do the same: finally only your fifth finger is still hanging on to its initial chord tone while your hand is already winging its way down to the bass. As you do this, make sure to leave your wrist to the inside—do not let your arm lead your wrist to the outside.[1]

Arm joins to make two chords one event

Step 2: When you've finally traveled so far that your fifth has let go as well, do not immediately play your bass octave. Instead, let your hand fly *past* the bass! Then, when your fingers fall vigorously *in* to the bass octave, already be traveling back up the keyboard to the next chord. But now travel low; slide low along the board rather than winging high. Then your arm will describe a circle, and bass plus chord will be felt as one single musical event rather than two separate attacks.

Reverse the direction of the circle

Step 3: This way of playing the passage has its problems. We are rising off the pulse note and falling in to the non-pulse note. Although the bass needs to growl, we run the risk of over-accenting it. Let's reverse the direction of the circle. Still hang on to the initial

---

[1] For an explanation why, consult part VII, *Rotation.*

chord, but let your arm slide low towards the bass while your fingers are loath to leave the keys they are depressing. As you glide low through the area of the bass octave, play it and continue to swoop *up* to the outside instead of down to the inside. Now the pulse chords have the required *oomph* in their buzzing aliveness.

It actually doesn't matter which way the circle goes. Do whatever works best for you. The crucial thing is that you connect the upper and lower sounds with a one-directional (that is, circling in a flat oval shape) movement rather than separating them sonically with a windshield wiper movement that constantly reverses its direction. (About reversibility: remember I said you should be *able* to reverse at any point in time; I did not say that you should necessarily always do it in playing!)

Draw thumb and fifth together

Step 4: To give the basses some sting but not to make them overpower, draw the fifth finger and thumb towards each other as if picking up a handkerchief off a flat surface. Don't curl your fingers, but do not grip the keyboard and shake the piano as before either. Instead, use this drawing together of the finger and thumb to launch the hand into the air and direct it towards its next entrance further up the keyboard.

Arm and hand must be out of sync

All this is based on the arm moving out of sync with the hand, ahead of it. As if, while your fingers still hold the old octave or chord (or even a single note), your arm is already in position over the new note(s). This of course is physically impossible. Yet if you try your utmost to do it, to create the illusion that it really is happening, some strange alchemical magic begins to happen in your sound.

Literal and inflected legato

In the many cases where physically connecting one key to the next is simply not possible, you can still achieve a legato sound through a choreographed

gesture of the arm that fulfils the function of the supportive arm movements of physical legato. This is inflected legato. Both literal (walking smoothly along the keybed) or inflected legato can be more or less musical depending on the art with which they are employed, but without them you will surely lack the means to control what you are doing at the keyboard.

VI
HAND STRENGTH
AND FUNCTION D

MAXIMAL ARTICULATION OF THE FINGERS

24 ON FINGERTAPPING

The octave arm-sweep provided a good example of inflected legato, and there we saw clearly that as the fingers play, the arm is almost never arrested in its movement but continues to glide. In fact this is almost always true: the arm's creation of phrase shape in real or inflected legato is another basic underlying element of piano technique. But before we move on to the arm, all the careful work we have done to consolidate hand structure will be for naught unless we suffuse that structure with functionality. The structure is there for no other reason but to support your fingers in doing their job, and their job is to *move*. In chapter 18, "Fortissimo Octaves" we saw the crucial role of hand activation in healthy pianism, and in chapter 19, "Cobra Strike" we began to explore how brilliant and glorious your tone can become when your structurally supported finger enters the key at maximum velocity. How can we further encourage our fingers to activate and produce this kind of tone, even while our hand remains on key?

As we began to establish a foundational hand structure (the thumb-forefinger connection as the hand's 'pelvis'; the octave 'arch'), we were already involved in activating it as well. Our discovery of this wonderful structure goes hand in hand with our learning how to use it to full advantage. Now that your fingers have found a firm base to support their free movement in octaves, let's return to their independent work, which will come in handy for the rest of the piano literature!

Later on we will explore other ways to bring the tone of the piano to brilliant, shimmering life, but these next few chapters provide a fundamental locus for our work. You may find yourself returning to them again and again. It is unavoidable that the whole playing mechanism be involved in maximal finger articulation, so don't be surprised when again your arm crops up in the discussion, although this is not yet the section devoted primarily to its role.

Origins, definition and description of fingertapping

This curious practice gives you a graphic kinesthetic picture of the natural alignment of limbs that result from good physical organization. The alive relaxedness that this engenders is a compulsory prerequisite for the type of maximal finger articulation we will be aiming for in this section. The Canadian virtuoso William Aide writes,

> Finger-tapping is a lowly, obsessive and cultish exercise for acquiring absolute evenness and ease in tricky passage work. It eliminates excess motion in the hand and ensures intimate tactile connection with the pattern in question. I will explain the practice in its simplest application. Take the notes D, E, F sharp, G and A, for which the right hand fingering is thumb, 2, 3, 4, 5. The hand position is the natural one assumed when the arm and hand hang relaxed from the shoulder: the knuckle-ridge bump of the second finger is seen to be the highest point. Rest the finger pads on the key surfaces of the notes D, E, F sharp, G and A. The left hand taps the fingers successively to the bottoms of the keys. The right-hand fingers are as if boneless; they reflex from the keybed and return to their original position on the surface of the keys. The left hand should tap near the tips of the right-hand fingers, either on the fingernails or at the first joint. The motion of the tapping should be as fast as possible.
>
> The second stage of this regimen is to play the notes with a quick staccato motion, one finger at a time, from the surface of the key, quick to the keybed, with a rebound back to the surface of the key. This is slow practice, with each note being separated by about two seconds of silence. I am grateful to Ray Dudley for his description of this method. Ray heard the sixteen-year-old Glenn Gould practice every day, and claims that he tapped everything—passages, chords, whole pieces—that he studied with Albert Guerrero [William Aide's teacher and Glenn Gould's only piano teacher, from Gould's sixth to sixteenth year]. Ray Dudley testifies that Gould finger-tapped every Goldberg variation before he recorded it in 1955. Gould boasted to Dudley that tapping the complete Goldbergs took him 32 hours.
>
> How did Guerrero hit on this finger-tapping method? The story goes that in his early years as a music critic in Chile, Guerrero attended

a travelling circus and saw a three-year-old Chinese boy do an astounding dance full of breathtaking intricacies. Guerrero went backstage to meet the child and asked his trainer for the secret. The teacher-trainer demonstrated how he placed his hands on the child and moved his limbs, while the child remained still and relaxed. Then the child was asked to repeat the movements by himself.[1]

Resulting deep, resonant sound

And now from my diary, somewhere in 1996:

That wonderful richness of sonority which comes from non-effortful, highly precise 'incision' into the key,[2] Kemal finally found through fingertapping! He taps much more vigorously than I had imagined Gould doing it. A real *shock* is administered to the finger in question. Because the passive finger is limp, without contraction, the shock is felt much more vividly than if the muscles of the finger were active and creating contrary stimuli.

Effortless accuracy

The passive hand thus undergoes a clear kinesthetic experience of playing the note with fantastic accuracy and sound, *but with none of its normal effort*. The vigorous tap from the auxiliary hand provides better contact between finger bone and key, because in the passive hand-arm that 'not-plays', there is no effort that could interfere with the absolutely clean sensation of contact.

Quickly find ideal hand shape

Because the hand-arm is totally limp, it very quickly finds the angle, position, structural alignment most ideally suited to producing that wonderful sound.

Cure old habits

Old insidious habits of collapsing, previously masked by surrounding

---

[1] William Aide, *Starting from Porcupine* (Ottawa: Oberon Press, 1996); 32-34.
[2] See chapter 19, *Replacing Arm Swoop with Cobra Strike*.

muscular activity, contractions and compensations, are now quickly sensed, perceived and dispensed with. Superfluous contractions all the way up the arm, even into the rib cage are now felt and subsequently disengaged—no longer needed.

Active hand clamps passive finger

In ideal finger-tapping, the active, tapping hand actually tries to depress the key itself vigorously, but by seeming chance, the passive hand's finger happens to be on the key already; the passive finger gets caught between the striking finger's impulse 'in' and the key itself. The passive finger feels itself clamped to the key in the moment of striking—*ping*—and true contact is established.

It is a new way of cultivating incisiveness.

If you really *beat* the passive finger with the active, the passive hand *must* find its structure right quick!

Fingertapping builds structural sensitivity between bones.

Stimulation to new internal adjustment

When the passive hand undergoes this surprising experience of getting much better tone than it thought it could, then it quickly does some internal adjusting, finding a new position or alignment from which it can get the same juicy tone when playing on its own, without the tapper tapping!

Reorganization of biceps-triceps activity

Many superfluous, counterproductive contractions tend to happen in the upper arm. When through finger tapping one finds the new advantageous position, one sees that a completely new, different set of biceps-triceps contractions are now needed to keep the new hand position viable—that is, structurally sound yet flexible.

Do you see that here again we are dealing with special types of physical processes already referred to earlier? Fingertapping clarifies the feeling of totally relaxed joints we first sought in application 20.1, *Minimal Movement for Maximal Sound.*[3] It is through a

---

[24 3] See the last sections of chapter 8, *Arm Weight.*

combination of hyper-relaxation and super-intense stimulation that fingertapping points the way to a higher mode of control, one both more sensitive and more powerful.

Fingertapping can be seen almost as a sort of therapy, a remedial, awareness-expanding exercise, but we also need a practical way of working towards maximal articulation, one that is action-oriented. This type of preliminary sensory awareness enrichment exercise is designed to provide new information that can help you to greater success in the more pragmatic lessons that follow.

25 THE STRUCTURE-SUPPORTED SLAP

We just referred to "a combination of hyper-relaxation and super-intense stimulation"—now let's explore that quality in an exercise of extreme activity.

Application 25.1
STRUCTURAL FUNCTION II: THE STRUCTURE-SUPPORTED SLAP

Steps 1-5: Return to application #18.3, *Freely Vibrating Octaves*, pp. 108. Do steps 1 to 5, but now play just a single note with your second or third finger, let's say G, instead of the octave.

Step 6: Return to step 3, but in the instantaneous moment that you are on key, instead of one note play two in succession, let's say G-F fingered 3-2 or G-A fingered 2-3. Play them extremely quickly, as 64th notes. Do you see that to keep the sound alive you must sting but not press? Be on the way out of the key just in the instant when the pressure on it begins to be too much. By avoiding pressing you are maintaining structure. The feeling of a restrictive pressing does not come so much from increased pressure on the key as from the deformation of structure caused by the stress exerted on it. You must try to maximally sting the key, as if two successive knives are being thrown into the keyboard. If the act is too light, you will not reach maximum consolidation of structure and your sound will lack incisiveness. Too heavy, things start collapsing. If you find this too difficult, reduce the height from which your arm strikes 'in'.

Step 7: Add a change in direction on your exit from the board: if you play 2-3 exit more horizontally to the right; for 3-2 go off somewhere to the left.

Step 8: Add another note to the chain—fingered 2-3-4, 4-3-2, 2-4-3, or 4-2-3. Of course, you now start from even closer above the keys, but try and keep things as alive, sharp and vigorous as possible.

Step 9: Stand on your second finger on the note G. Raise your third to the sky and then swing it into A, staccato, returning instantaneously to the sky position. Try to recreate the feeling and sound of the 'cobra strike' attacks described above. Your arm remains as loose as it was when flying through the air, your elbow actively rising to aid the 'cocking' of your third finger, but this moving finger, still vigorously swinging through a wide very wide arc, now benefits from the stable structure of the standing finger in its attempt to play accurately.

Or stand on 3, swing-slap 2 similarly into its key. Now your elbow will fall to the inside as you cock your second finger. Whereas when you stand on 2 and swing 3 in, your elbow comes down to help the in-stroke, here there is more of a compound movement involving your elbow and wrist. Your wrist moves to the inside and down slightly while your elbow moves laterally out—the overall result is that your forearm stays basically in one place.

Step 10: Or try thumb pushups, but at high speed. Your thumb is the pylon, your second swings in with the help of your elbow. There's an aliveness in the stroke of your second finger that makes your pad *and* your sound sting! Try the same vigorous articulation standing on your second finger and swinging your thumb in.[1] What is the movement of your forearm now?

Steps 11: Return to step 8, continuing to add notes to the chain one by one. The more notes you add, the more the movement is

---

[1] As in the Scriabin Concerto excerpt, chapter 44.

transformed from a vertical 'in-out' to a vertical 'in' –horizontal 'out'. Most important, keep your fingers vitally alive and active, coiling like an octopus' tentacles.

I call all these variations where you slap 'in' while using another finger as a standing pylon fulcrum the 'structure-supported slap'. Earlier when your hand came flying in from somewhere above the keyboard, the function of your structure was also crucial—but here its role is more plainly visible.

Many of you will find this lesson bizarre or at least highly unusual, and difficult if not downright impossible! Perhaps we should examine its inner working and come to a better understanding of what is going on underneath the surface.

26 THE SOUND OF ONE HAND CLAPPING

This exercise is as different from fingertapping as is night from day. There the fingers were passive: here we will make them maximally active. We are also evolving from the structural-supported slap: we will experience a further individuation of finger and arm, a greater separation of function although by no means one that is complete. When a child grows up it individuates from its parents, yet continues to be in profound relationship to them. Increased individuation is actually just a more sophisticated form of cooperation. Increased independence fosters more effective interdependence.[1]

Arm pressure not the path to big sound

Disciples of Zen require years of contemplative effort to solve the ancient koan, "What is the sound of one hand clapping?" But the answer lies more immediately at hand (no pun intended), in an analysis of the precise finger movement needed for brilliant, full yet not overly heavy passagework. To produce a large volume of sound, many pianists use too much pressure from the arm, pressure that impinges on the natural shape and activity of the hand and finger, strangling the piano's natural resonance instead of activating it.

Of course, many times you must press into the keyboard to get the sound you want. I am not saying "never press". Far from it! But finger activity must most often be proportionally greater than the effort you invest in pressing. This will keep your hand structure in good shape and give you optimal control over your sound. Try this exercise to get a clearer feeling for this finger action.

[26 1] For more on this see chapter 21, *Tremolando Octaves*.

Application 26.1
Structural Function III: Maximize Finger Articulation, Eliminate Arm Shake

Negative effects of your arm shaking in forte scales

> Step 1: Play a scale, *forte prestissimo*. Do you feel any shaking in your arm? Take a look. Can you *see* any sign of shaking in your arm that you may not have felt? You must be extremely rigorous with yourself in this. I'll bet you dollars to donuts that your arm *is* shaking to some extent. Can you perceive it?
>
> Step 2: Rest the palm of your hand on the keys so the edge of the keyboard runs across the middle of your palm. Slide your hand back and forth along the keyboard. This effectively eliminates any chance of your arm shaking, and it is the type of smooth arm movement you should be cultivating in your scale. Are the movement qualities of your original scale and this horizontal sliding really identical or can you detect some discrepancy?

Your arm is not a finger!

Any shaking is an indication of confusion of function. In a word, your arm thinks it's a finger. It is forced to do this because your fingers aren't doing their job. They're not moving enough, and the arm is engaged in a vain attempt to save the day by adding some *oomph* of its own. But all is for naught; the result is only a further reduction in finger capability.[2]

Ultra-staccato finger stroke

> Step 3: Leave your hand resting on the edge of the keyboard, and try to point your fingers at the ceiling. The heel of your palm actually rests on the wooden rail underneath the keys. Try to touch the ceiling

---

[26 2] When your fingers really do their job, certain situations may indeed require you to add some 'arm shake' for gutsier tone. But too often we are fooling ourselves: we are shaking in compensation not augmentation.

with your fingers but leave your hand resting on the board. Relax your shoulders to facilitate ease in this.

Step 4: Begin to play the notes of your scale, and make each finger's downstroke travel not into the key but rather *through* it. That is, your finger enters from above but goes out the 'back door' (sliding off the end of the key closest to you that is), ending up nestled against your palm. Also, return each finger to the sky after it plays, and keep all your other fingers as high as possible when they are not striking a key. Thus the arc through which your fingertip travels is actually greater than 180 degrees!

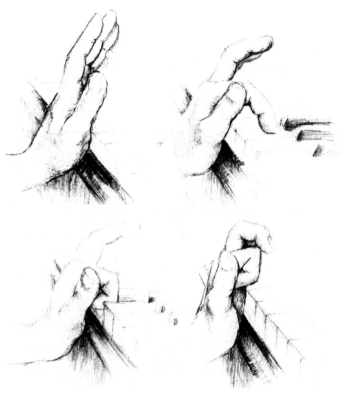

Illustration 26.1: Down from the sky and out the back door—270-degree finger arc

The greater the speed of this stroke, the more brilliant is the semi-staccato sound. It is staccato, but even if it's very short it has tone; it has a wonderful clarity and shine. It has quality!

No doubt you find this difficult at first. We are not used to this—it is a movement that requires real strength and vigour, and the fixation of your arm in space would appear to be working dead against the free movement of your finger (the worst of the old 'finger action' school). But things are not always as they seem. Although the heel of your hand is fixed, inner muscular activity throughout your arm is still a crucial part of this radical finger action.

Here's an exercise to clarify what I mean:

Application 26.2
ARM II: ARM MOVEMENT AIDS FINGER FREEDOM

Step 1: Hold your arm comfortably in midair and wiggle your fingers.

Step 2: Continue to wiggle your fingers as you move your hand, forearm and elbow directly away from and towards your body. It's the movement of a boxer doing a jab, but instead of being fisted your fingers are open and wiggling.

Did you notice that your fingers wiggled easier when your arm was in motion? Putting your arm in motion frees all its muscles to activate more effectively, even those involved not in the arm movement itself but in finger movement. Your arm is not a finger but it is *attached* to your fingers—they almost *always* work in tandem.

Now return to the previous application, trying to sense how muscular contraction in your arm helps move your finger even when your hand is immobilized. Your arm doesn't move in space, but if you allow it to hang free between its two points of fixation at your shoulder and the heel of your hand, its inner activity can still proceed unimpeded.

Application 26.3
STRUCTURAL FUNCTION IV: ONE HAND CLAPPING

Step 1: To get an even clearer idea of the free function that'll give you real speed in these finger strokes, make your hand loose; dangle it in the air in front of you. Open it as far as it will go, then *whoosh* all your fingers at once through that same 180-degree arc, so they come to rest against the palm or heel of your hand. If you do it fast enough, you'll hear the *smack* of your fingertips hitting your palm. *Voila!* The sound of one hand clapping! Notice here as well, loosening your arm gives you a juicier *smack*.

Horizontal hand/arm carriage, active fingers

Step 2: Now to conclude, go back to the piano and play a scale *staccatissimo*, using this finger movement. The arm acts only as a carriage carrying the hand horizontally along the board. The fingers alone generate the tone. But can you now sense more clearly the continued hidden involvement of your arm in your fingerstrokes? The boxer's jabbing motion of application #26.2 translates here as the arm's horizontal carriage-conveying movement. In practice we virtually never use the seemingly total separation of finger and arm function that we practiced in application #26.1. We will almost always facilitate the free movement of the fingers with some sort of arm involvement.

Step 3: Practice this until you can do it well, and then play your original scale *forte prestissimo legatissimo*, remembering the feeling of the no-shake *staccatissimo* you just practiced! No more pressing, no more harsh, ugly tone. Just a virtuosic, brilliant, bell-toned, very fast scale. As we Canadians say, 'not bad, eh?'

27 LEGATO VS. FINGER ARTICULATION: THE COOPERATION OF TWO ANTITHETICAL ACTIVITIES

Confront a contradiction for breakthrough in ability

This exercise synthesizes much of what we have discussed up until now about finger action, structural integrity and wonderful richness of speaking sound. It guides you through a concise, concentrated attempt to break through your limitations and to experience with graphic clarity the type of hand function and piano sound we are searching for. It attacks a basic contradiction head on: the more you cultivate legato, the less your fingers tend to move, and the more you articulate your finger movements, the more you tend to undermine the stability of your legato touch.

These two opposing functions, each of which tends to detract from the other, must *both* be working at peak capacity for your hand to be truly operational. To achieve the synthesis of legato and ultimate finger action so often required for optimal sound, let's turn to a passage that poses a problem to virtually every pianist, a technical thorn that almost all of us have struggled with (or will struggle with) at one time or another—the first *forte* arpeggios in Beethoven's *Appassionata* Sonata.

Example 27.1: Beethoven: Sonata in F minor, Op. 57, Appassionata, *1st mvt., mm. 13-16*

146

Application 27.1
LEGATO VI: MAXIMAL ARTICULATION
AND LEGATO

Individual finger action within block chord practice in Beethoven's Appassionata

Step 1: Set your fingers up on the first three notes by playing the solid chord B flat-E-G with your fingers 2-4-5. Stand your knuckle-hummocks up maximally high. You can also slip your thumb in to join your fourth finger on its note E, to create a completely secure structure that resembles a bird beak or the platform of an oil rig standing on its four pylons. Your fingers and hand are so secure that your elbow can relax and release in a little bit with no problem, and even your shoulder might notice that it could release forward a little more than it has already. In other words, let your elbow and shoulder become truly neutral.

Maintain structural stability

Step 2: Raise your fourth finger and play E as loud as you can. Does the rest of your structure maintain itself with total integrity and strength? Make sure there is not the slightest hint of collapsing or weakness anywhere, although your arm may breathe slightly to aid your finger articulation. Do you also feel how a small muscle just above the back of your elbow contracts strongly to help your fourth play? Try again.

How high did you raise your finger? I'll bet you any money that it was not as high as it could be. Try to literally touch the ceiling with your fingertip while the others remain embedded in their keys. Notice how this increased range of motion adds new body and *zing* to your sound. You might even feel a bit of sting in your finger pad as it slaps vigorously into its note. Note as well that if you maintain your

structure despite the increased stress exerted on it, your tone becomes very bright but not at all harsh. This is again the structure-supported slap.

Step 3: Wait a moment; confirm that everything is still secure, and then play B flat with your second finger, maintaining the same feeling of activity and security. Can you now vigorously raise your fifth (of course with a little help from your elbow) and play its G as loud as possible? All this is to be done extremely slowly, with no concern for speed but every concern imaginable for your sound, which will be better the more you maintain hand integrity. Go many times slower than you think you need to. Give yourself a chance to really change, to discover something new.

Step 4: Notice that if you take enough time between each note, you can ensure that you are maintaining your structural integrity. But now as you begin to increase the speed, your structure will tend to slip a bit, things will start falling to pieces slightly. What to do now? You can reduce the difficulty by reducing finger action. The less your fingers move, the easier it is for you to gain speed but maintain a perfect legato. This way you keep your integrity of tone, but you lose dynamic strength that is essential to the passage sounding well.

Maintain maximum finger stroke

Step 5: Let's slow back down. Now instead of increasing note speed, increase the speed and range your finger stroke to its maximum, and no longer overhold. Just maintain a perfect legato, no more. Now it is much easier, before playing each finger, to raise it to point to the ceiling. Now you can *really* raise it to the sky, but take care not to lose structure! Go very slow to do this very well. You must not allow yourself any half measures here. Even if you achieve 90 percent of the possible arc of motion of your fingertip, this is still basically a failure because you will not get any result. Only 110 percent of efforts get results here!

Step 6: Play several times one complete bar through to the next downbeat in this way. *Slowly.* Twice as slow as you think, using the extra time to double the effort with which you reach for the sky then swing your finger vigorously *in.* As you do this, again ensure that you maintain structure with absolutely no collapsing, no shaking, no signs of even the slightest momentary weakness. Is it clear? Do you hear the clear, shining, bold fiery tone that you can produce this way? Did you know a piano could do that?!

Synthesis: maintain both

Step 7: Now that you have given yourself a clear kinesthetic experience of both the technical elements of this passage, play again with maximal articulation but gradually increase your speed. You must catch the moment when your articulations begin to destabilize structure, or when your efforts to maintain structure start to impinge upon your articulation, and with your mind *simply do not let it happen.*

I cannot offer you any more magic techniques now; all I can tell you is to keep paying attention. Find a way to do it well—you have clarified all the ingredients, now start blending them! Carefully, slowly, attentively, with your feelings and your ears, not just your thinking mind. In the end your hand does not actually stand on key, but is flying very close to the keyboard. Yet it preserves all the qualities of supported structure that it had when standing. Its structural integrity is preserved by *activity* that creates effective contact; you feel well joined to the key without going so far as to stand with totally fixed stability.

When you find the way you will be surprised at how loose your arm feels. Unawares, you have been binding up your arm and reducing finger movement in order to maintain stability. But your arm must stay loose so that your vigorous finger activity can produce the required tone. In the end your fingers almost lash out like the tip of a whip or the strike of a cobra, but because your hand has learned the proper, *functional* way to maintain structure, it does not collapse nor does it bind up and impede free movement. Your arm is loose as a goose, yet your fingers are so active that your arm's looseness does not reduce their accuracy. The looseness actually *contributes* to accuracy by removing any muscular constrictions that might inadvertently hinder the exactness of your movement.

Step 8: As the most pressing problem generally exists between the thumb and the other fingers, let's take another exercise to work this aspect out. Do all the same techniques but instead of the *Appassionata* arpeggio, take a changing note pattern between your thumb, second and third fingers. Your third finger plays G sharp, your thumb A, your second finger B flat, your thumb A and so on. Keep everything maximally active, especially your thumb which will have a strong tendency to poop out, to go back to sleep.

Example 27.2: Changing note pattern for thumb-finger structure activation

This synthesis of maximal articulation with a totally dependable legato is one of the most important techniques presented here for development of your hand's capability. Learn it well!

The cultivation of maximal finger articulation should revolutionize your tone. When you do this, whatever you were doing before will likely seem colorless by comparison. In this section we have already reached a preliminary synthesis of various facets of physical technique. Now we head back to the drawing board, to separate out once again some specific functions and examine them in more detail. But feel free to return to this section whenever you need a fresh charge, a renewed influx of energetic vigor in your approach to the keyboard.

VII

ABOVE THE HAND

THE ROLE OF THE WRIST AND ARM IN LEGATO

28 ACTIVE HAND, PASSIVE ARM?

Arm facilitates physical connection between keys

Although the arm has already cropped up numerous times in our discussion of fingers and hand, it is time to flesh out our understanding of its role in piano playing. To start, we'll return to legato, the foundation of our technique, but bring a third crucial aspect into the picture. The next exercise not only gives you another experience of the strength and activity needed in the hand, but also opens a discussion on the arm's role, which although it appears only supportive, is a central part of the whole process.

Application 28.1
STRUCTURAL FUNCTION V: FINGER PULL-UPS

Few would disagree that the arm must feel relaxed to a certain extent in piano playing. But we must also discriminate: *where* in our mechanism do we need to relax, and where is relaxation counterproductive? If we fail to develop the requisite strength in our hands or if we over-relax our arms, it is all for naught—we will not be able to control the piano in the way we need to.

In piano playing in general, but especially in literal legato, there is an inverse relationship between arm tension and hand strength. The stronger your hand, the easier your arm can dispense with counterproductive tension. The weaker and less active your hand, the more your arm will tend to develop compensatory tension. Of course if you relax everything, your hand cannot control the key-

board. Thus you *need* to employ effort where it is most advantageous and not working against your goals. To this end, the more your hand activates, articulates, the more your arm will develop an empowered rather than ineffectual freedom.

Review : chain of hummocks

If your hand is strong it should be able to stand on any finger with complete security. That little hummock, the top (metacarpal-phalangeal) knuckle sticking up is the best indication that the finger is bearing full weight. Then when you play the next note you should see the second hummock rising until both of them are maximally tall. Only then can you begin to release your first note, the first hummock gradually subsiding. Thus you control your legato by ensuring that there is a smooth transfer of force from one hummock to the next.

Don't confuse your wrist with the knuckle of your second finger

A common error here is to raise your wrist instead of your second knuckle. Here's a remedial exercise.

> Step 1: Lay your hand on the keyboard without any special effort to raise the knuckle of your second finger. In fact, let the space between your thumb and forefinger collapse slightly, mashing your fingers into the keys. Move your wrist forward: it rises while your second knuckle collapses even more. This shows you in exaggerated form what you may have been doing wrong.

Illustration 28.1: The 'knuckle mash'

Step 2: Return to the rest position. This time, *stand up* on your thumb-forefinger assembly, as if your thumb and forefinger are two legs and your second finger's top knuckle is a pelvis. Make all the effort come from your second finger itself. Your arm does not push—rather your second finger *pulls* itself into standing position. There should be a complete reversal of function here from step 1 where your arm pushed to generate the movement. Now as your second finger's knuckle rises your wrist hardly exceeds it, perhaps at the most coming level with it, and your elbow naturally relaxes, gently falling in and forward. This is almost the exact opposite of that most traditional of movements, 'the-elbow-out-to-the-side-to-round-out-the-sound'.

Illustration 28.2: Stand up

Note the tendency for your wrist to take over, to make the effort in place of your finger. The whole point is to raise your second finger's knuckle, not your wrist, through an effort of pulling *by* your second finger, not of pushing by your wrist or arm. Think back to the way you used to play before you embarked on this investigation: was your wrist insidiously taking over from your finger? Does this exercise help you see it?

One thrust of this exercise, a look at the first of many contrasting views of arm function, is to experience the arm most graphically in its passive mode. Here you must feel that all your effort takes place below your wrist, and that your arm is as loose and relaxed as possible. Maximize the strong contrast in sensation between these two parts of your playing mechanism: activity and effort below, looseness and relaxation above.

This brings us to a seeming basic contradiction inherent in much of piano technique. One fundamental rule of human movement is that the larger body parts do the more effortful work, and naturally so because they are stronger, more capable. But here the situation appears to be exactly the opposite. It looks like your poor little fingers are doing all the work and your arm is just tagging along for the ride! What is actually going on here?

Indeed most often it should feel as if we *are* working contrary to that principle: although the wrist and arm are larger and stronger than the fingers, it is pianistic suicide to let them take over the fingers' work. Your fingers and hand need to do their job; your wrist and arm need to facilitate their success. Of course there are many instances (*ff* chords where you feel as if you're pushing the piano for example) where your arm feels very active indeed, but even in these your hand needs exceptional strength — *structural* more than muscular strength — to support the force of the arm moving down through it. And what about here where it *feels* as if it is just hanging, following your hand?

Though it may not be apparent, the principle still applies. Even when your fingers appear to be moving far more than anything else and your arm feels relatively passive, it actually does participate very actively in generating your sound—its hidden function may be of more import than what you perceive! Unconscious *internal* activity of the larger muscles higher up your arm always plays an important role in activating your fingers. We now examine just how the arm's hidden activity is involved in legato and in playing in general.

29 THREE ASPECTS OF THE ARM'S RELATIONSHIP TO HAND FUNCTION

The arm's functional relationship to the hand can be divided into three primary aspects:

1) In order to maintain hand strength successfully, you must also cultivate your arm's **corollary stabilizing role**. Practically speaking, your hand's structural security will not hold without support from a fairly strong contraction of the triceps muscle group way back in your upper arm. There are even muscles along your rib cage under your armpit that participate in this. Ironically, it is through a radical *loosening* of the upper arm, letting the elbow area relax and drop forward and in slightly closer to the body, that these crucial contractions in the triceps can work most effectively, free of impediment from other counterproductive contractions (such as those involved in the 'classic arm out' movement), and be perceived most readily.

Note that the 'classic elbow out' movement works *against* this function proceeding efficiently, as it engages just that part of the arm that needs most to relax in this. When your upper arm remains passive and hanging, its internal stabilizing muscular activity can proceed unimpeded, and there is no other movement that would prevent this activity being clearly perceived. The classic arm out confuses matters, engaging the muscles in some other movement than that in which they should be engaged, and reducing the clarity with which the stabilizing activity can be perceived.

2) The **smooth transition of structural support** from one standing finger to another also needs the participation of wrist and arm. Take care: if you are overholding, playing super-legato but laboriously, with your arm stiffening up, that's not it! When the transfer of structural support is done well, your arm follows your hand's lead and changes its position in space ever so slightly. You may indeed feel some effort in this, but it is smooth, easy effort because all the opposing forces are in balance. You may not even notice this happening; you may even

perceive it only as a minimal movement of the wrist. But there's a quantum difference in quality between an immeasurably small movement and no movement at all.

3) This minimal movement plays a crucial musical as well as physical role. Because of your newfound integrity of finger and hand function, your wrist and arm should now be freed to inflect the legato line by **shaping whole groups of notes into phrases** rather than having to deal with the release of tension on a single note—tension originally caused by a lack of proper support in your hand.

When your arm does 2) and 3) well, the quality of movement is markedly different from that of the 'classic arm out'—holistic, organic rather than destabilizing or distractive. Understanding, experiencing and feeling all these aspects of your arm's function in legato will be a great help in achieving a true legato sound in either physical or inflected legato. Let's take a look now at the first aspect, upper arm internal muscular activity that supports the work of the fingers by providing structural stabilization.

Application 29.1

GRASPING IV: PARTICIPATION OF HIGHER ARM MUSCLES IN FINGER MOVEMENT

I have said repeatedly that grasping is the fundamental function of the hand. Through grasping we have a simple, tangible, direct experience of the hand's innate power, and if we are attentive we can also perceive the participation of our upper arm in powerful grasping.

> Step 1: While grasping something with one hand, simply place your other hand on the triceps of the grasping arm, and you can feel the contractions. Even notice that different parts of the triceps contract to different degrees depending on which part of the active hand grasps most strongly—the thumb or some combination of other fingers. This has important ramifications for playing the piano—it means that muscular contractions higher up the arm participate in an important way in the generation of finger movement.

Triceps' stabilizing contractions feels like active work

The actual function of these triceps contractions is to maintain an alignment of skeletal structure necessary for effective finger action. Your triceps does not actually curl your finger, but it *stabilizes* the arm/hand structure. This stabilizing function is so crucial to your hand acting effectively that it can actually feel as if triceps activity *is* moving your fingers.

You can verify that this is the case very simply. Straighten your arm totally so it's not bent at the elbow as in normal playing. Now in grasping you can sense muscular contractions only below your elbow, not above it. Your triceps is now wholly engaged in keeping your arm straight; its stabilizing function is no longer involved in finger action.

Grasp, monitor where else contractions occur

> Step 2: Grasp something again with a normally bent elbow, this time observing the muscular activity not only in your triceps but in other areas as well. Place your monitoring hand on or around various parts of your grasping forearm . . . upper arm . . . shoulder . . . shoulder blade . . . collarbone . . . rib cage . . . . No matter where you touch, if you do so gently and attentively you can sense some degree of contraction—contraction that supports the generation of your grasping action. If you find this difficult to perceive, try having a friend grasp something while you monitor her or his upper arm, etc.

Supportive muscular activity is internal not external

> Step 3: Can you sense even some muscles in your back engaging in this type of structural support activity? Because there is no external movement it's not so easy to perceive. It may even be better for us if we do not perceive it, this being the assurance that we are not overdoing it! However it is also possible for your back to err in the other direction, to over-relax—of course, then your astute ears are sure to notice the deficiency in your sound.

'Functional structure'

At a certain stage in the development of one's technique, a hand accustomed to being strongly and effectively organized can gain much help from a continual and quite strong sense of contraction in the upper arm while playing. This provides what I call functional structure—not so much the support of bones but rather the stimulus to effective degrees of muscular involvement in all parts of your mechanism.

Minimize auxiliary movements to maximize efficiency—internal activity replaces external

In conclusion, this little grasping exercise suggests that although there is indeed a great deal of physical involvement, indeed of your whole body in playing, this involvement should be largely internal not external. External moves tend to *impede* the free participation of all parts of yourself in the act of playing, because if you are indulging in them you are doing something other than the task at hand. All those muscles we discovered that are involved in grasping also help generate the more independent finger movements of piano playing. If some other external movement demands the participation of those supportive muscle groups, then those groups are distracted from fulfilling their primary purpose to perfection.

30 Functionally Supported Movement: The Whole Arm as Finger

How does the internal, supportive muscular activity of the upper arm tie in with the arm's need to move? Must we dispense with external arm movement completely, or is there a way we can use it to our advantage? In this exercise you will discover how to maintain that crucial internal activity even as you engage in vigorous external movement.

Application 30.1
Structural Function VI: Isometric Arm Wrestling

> Step 1: First clasp your hands together in an unusual way. Hold your fingers at a 90-degree angle to your hands, making two bands of four fingers each.
>
> Step 2: Try with all your might to press the two bands together. Each is trying to move the other, to win out over the other—a kind of isometric arm wrestling but with the hands in midair rather than elbows resting on the table. Take care not to curl your fingers—they keep straight in order to form a precise angle of 90 degrees to your hands. Notice the intense effort not only in your hands themselves but also in your upper arms as one pulls against the other.

If this is not working so well, you might try this next series of pulling strategies with a colleague.

Ineffectual pulling, curling

Step 3: I tried showing one student[1] this 'isometric arm wrestling' by having him use the pad of his second finger to pull down against mine. At first, he pulled with his arm, but I couldn't *feel* it in my finger. If I resisted, he couldn't move me. Then he tried curling his finger: this was an ineffectual, small force that again did not move my finger. I had to find out why this wasn't working. What did I have to do to galvanize his mechanism into effective action?

Illustration 30.1: Isometric Arm Wrestling

Flatten, reinforce in order to feel

Step 4: Finally I had him flatten his finger slightly, stiffen it and consciously make his whole finger-hand-arm assembly resemble steel-

---

[30.1] The one whose 2nd finger wasn't working in Chopin's G Minor Ballade (chapter 14, *Clarification of the Thumb-Forefinger Relationship*).

reinforced concrete in its solidity. Now I could finally *feel* him. His whole arm was unified, activated and effectively moving my finger and arm. This showed him an organization that at last allowed him real contact with his instrument. Here is an example of intense effort leading to correct organization. Remember that it works best if we can maintain sensitivity even as we increase exertion to the maximum. Normally we would not stiffen so. But his mechanism was *dead*, and making him stiffen brought it to an albeit primitive functional life.

Grasping review

Step 5: If this is still not clear, perhaps grasping can help. Once again, grasp your left upper arm with your right hand. Grasp it absolutely as firmly as possible. Do you feel how your whole right arm is involved in a very real way in doing this? When you return to the piano, why don't you grasp the key with as much conviction as you did your left arm? If you do, you will really be connected. And then of course you realize: anything less than that is *not* really connected!

Now can you make the connection in your mind: the feeling of grasping with the feel of the 'banded finger'?

How does this sense of connection apply? One main tenet of the *Ruska Shkola* (Russian School) is contact with the bottom of the key. Preserve the feeling of the banded finger as you do step 6.

Whole arm as a whip

Step 6: Ensure your fingertip is firmly entrenched in the depths of the keybed—the more you use the pad of your finger rather than its tip here, the juicier your tone will be. For this your whole hand must firmly maintain its structure as it did in the isometrics. Now swing your whole arm from side to side, and around in a circle—in any direction you want. Notice you are forced to maintain strength in your hand, or else you'll fall off the key. But the more effort your hand makes, the more everything behind—from your wrist all the way up to your shoulder—tends to seize up, to contract into immo-

bility in an effort to help your hand.

Try consciously now to cultivate a completely different phenomenon. Can you free up your arm even as you grasp the key with super-firmness? The strong hand-stabilization contractions you feel in your upper arm should not impede your free movement in any way. Your fingertip becomes like the tip of a whip, and your whole hand-wrist-arm becomes like the writhing leather body of the whip leading up to the stock at the shoulder. The one crucial difference: this whip tip is attached securely to the keybed. Here there must be support from your arm for your hand's firm sitting in the key even as your arm whips about super-flexibly in space. Now *there's* a functional structure for you!

Banded fingers for ultra-lush cantabile

Step 7: While maintaining that feeling in your hand and arm but reducing the vigorousness of the movement from outrageous to respectable, play a melody ultra-*cantabile*. For instance something along the lines of the second theme from Chopin's B minor Sonata, first movement. Make sure that even as you ride from note to note and from finger to finger, the change from one finger to another does not disturb the wonderful strength of the whole banded-finger group and the strongly contracted upper-arm group. When the structure of your hand maintains its integrity through active strength rather than stiffness, then you can move your arm out to the side all you want, or in any other direction for that matter, without reducing effective contact with the key. You can 'shape' either melodic groups or individual tones as is your whim.

Banded fingers, neutral wrist position connect hand to arm

Notice also that when your banded fingers are strong enough, you no longer suffer from that overly pressed sound. As I've said before, the 'over-pressing' sound comes not from too much pressure but from lack of structural support for that pressure, from weakness in the banded fingers. This can lead to your wrist being too low and feeling pressured. If your wrist tenses you

are sunk! The force exerted down through your arm, the kinetic energy needed for a big, singing tone, can only reach the key if your structure transmits it there successfully! That force needs to go through the wrist and cannot if wrist tension blocks it. When the fingers do their job they relieve the overburdened wrist. Remember, you can play with a low wrist so long as it remains free of excess tension. There should be no weakness of structure leading to a sense of the wrist being pressed down. Strength of structure elsewhere allows your wrist to maintain its vital, strong, capable neutrality.

A 2-kg finger!

Weakness in the banding of your fingers can lead to tension not only in your wrist but also higher up your arm. If you band your fingers properly your wrist and arm and shoulder will remain free and functional no matter where you put them! And then you achieve that magical quality of your whole arm functioning as one giant finger! We always face the problem of our fingers being too small to produce really juicy tone—don't we envy those violinists who can use their whole arm through the bow stroke to make that box really vibrate! But if we had a 'finger' that reaches all the way to our shoulder, and weighed a couple of kilograms to boot, imagine what sort of tone we could produce—if this monster of a finger is successfully coupled to our instrument!

Yes, I said earlier that your arm is not a finger. Then we were aiming to activate your fingers, to prevent your arm from trying to take over their work. Here not only must they continue to work exceptionally well, maintaining their banded structure, but also to let the arm come in and enrich their relation to the key even more so.

Constant physical security to maintain phrase

In this way of playing, the arm *can* move on every note, just as our fingers normally move to create each sound. The only thing that prevents you from banging and destroying the phrase line is the *absolute security* of the banded fingers that must be constantly maintained. And of course you must have a conception of the phrase in mind as well.

Application 30.2
STRUCTURAL FUNCTION VII, ARM III: THE PHIL COHEN ARM-SWING EXERCISE

(shown to me by my highly esteemed teacher)

In this exercise we will refine the feeling of the whole arm as whip to its most optimal, efficient form of movement, enhancing and clarifying the wonderful feeling of combined flexibility and functionality in the hand, wrist and arm.

> Step 1: Bunch all your fingers and thumb together and stand your hand up on the tips of your second and third fingers somewhere near a table edge. Your wrist is quite high, a lot higher than neutral, but your elbow on the contrary hangs down low and to the inside. Your wrist is higher, your elbow more bent than they were in the previous exercise.

> Step 2: Now *swing* your elbow even further to the inside, first a little down and then up towards your body but slightly in front of it. Your wrist of course rises even higher:

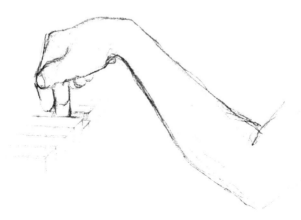

Illustration 30.2: Arm Swing I—In

Step 3: Then let your elbow *and* wrist come back down again as you swing first down:

Illustration 30.3: Arm swing II—Down

then out and as far up again as you can to the outside:

Illustration 30.4: Arm Swing III—Out

Your wrist describes a half circle, and the elbow as well. This means in fact that your forearm stays oriented almost the same in

space, always pointed forward and slightly up, while moving laterally through the same semicircle. Really swing! All my students do not swing vigorously enough at first. Or if they do, they lose structural stability in their hand. The trick is to swing with great *élan* while maintaining really good hand strength and support. *Now* you can feel the correct degree of wrist flexion.

A cure for incapable immobility

This lesson might be a disaster for someone suffering from over-movement, but paves the way towards a new facility and freedom for a student locked into immobility. If there is no strength in the connection of your finger to the key, then the weak, unstable condition of your hand will lead everything behind it, from your wrist all the way up to your shoulder, to freeze up. Contracting everything into rigidity preserves a modicum of control, but you sacrifice the much greater capability you could otherwise attain through moveability.

One of my students thought his tension was interfering with his playing. He was confusing cause with effect. I showed him how his shoulder tension was actually *created* by his lack of physical connection to the keyboard. His shoulder was freezing up in a vain attempt to compensate for the lack of connection lower down.

I needed to transform his shoulder *tension* into finger *action*. This arm-swing exercise allowed him to finally feel what he was doing. He could connect to his instrument and resonate with it, not only strengthening his hand function but also allowing his shoulders to finally let go. Now that his hands and arms were finally doing their job, his shoulders no longer had to 'shoulder the whole load'.

Step 4: Do the 'arm-swing' exercise once more, but now on each swing play a new note—your fingers walk on the keyboard. Normally you would swing in the same direction you're walking (for instance, swing in for your fourth to third finger and out for your third to fourth). Can you reverse that, and swing opposite to the melodic movement (out for your fourth to third, in for your third to fourth)? This cultivates not only arm but brain flexibility!

This 'arm-swing' exercise kills two birds with one stone, galvanizing your hand and finger into vital, active, strong control of the key, and at the same time freeing

up and dispensing with unnecessary residual contractions of your arm.

Primary movements require correct supportive activity from the rest of your mechanism

Here we see that many times it is not that you move in a wrong way, but rather that other parts of you do not support the movement in the right way. For instance, consider once again that most common pianistic arm movement, the generic rounding where your elbow goes out to the side, pulling your hand off its note or chord and reducing your physical focus and richness of tone. I often harp on about the uselessness of this movement, but the 'arm swing' provides an effective way to do a quite similar movement, even on every note, while maintaining physical and musical integrity.

31 EFFICIENT FUNCTIONALITY: THE FOREARM AS LEVER

Application 31.1
OCTAVES VIII, ARM IV: THE OBLIQUE WHOLE ARM

Economical octave leaps

Was the description of the leaping arm movements in chapter 23, *The Octave Arm-Sweep*, too complicated for you, too difficult to grasp? Let's now try a simpler, more direct octave leaping technique, one that looks entirely different to the octave arm sweep. Here, instead of cultivating it we will almost entirely eliminate the sweeping movement of your forearm.

Take a simple example.

> Step 1: With your left hand play a scale in octaves, but after each note of the scale, leap down to play an octave on the tonic note an octave lower.

Example 31.1: Scale of C major in leaping octaves

170

As you leap down, do you notice your elbow tends to travel to the outside as well? Now try something strange.

Step 2: Instead of your elbow leading your hand to the outside in a forearm sweeping motion, let it do the opposite. Let your elbow fall to the *inside* as your hand moves down the keyboard to the lower tonic octave. Also, although elsewhere I tell you in no uncertain terms *not* to swivel, now let your hand swivel, but to the *outside* a little (opposite to our habitual way of swivelling) so that on the lower octave note your thumb is a little closer to the fallboard than on the upper scale note octaves. Is it clear? Your hand swivels *out* while your elbow falls *in*.

When you do this well it magically eliminates all feeling of leaping. Observe your forearm. It seems to stay in one place! It twists slightly as you move to the lower octave—rotating so your thumb moves upward just a tiny bit. But the startling result of moving your elbow in a direction opposite to your hand is that your forearm now virtually maintains one position in space. Any lateral movement horizontally along the keys is done solely by your hand—your forearm's role in sliding along the board has mysteriously, almost completely disappeared.

My teacher Phil Cohen[1] called this the oblique whole arm technique. Here you use your arm in a way fundamentally different to the classic arm movement used constantly by pianists the world over: elbow out to the side then up, around and back in, the wrist dutifully loose and flexible. Presumably we do this to make beautiful tone, the rationale being that where striking the key directly makes a harsh sound, the indirect attack cultivated by this arm movement leads to a warm, singing tone.

As I have already hazarded, there are a number of questionable assumptions inherent in this habit. We have already said that it is not direct attack but weak structure/function that produces harsh tone, and the next exercise demonstrates this with graphic clarity. Of course, many types of indirect attack do provide us with more varieties of tone, if they are done with integrity. The problems arise when your arm movement inadvertently weakens your hand in the process.

We have also seen that often we may not even want a beautiful, singing tone. If arm movements do aid tone, is it because of relaxation or could there be some other process at work here?

---

[1] See *Phil Cohen – The Mindful Hand* in appendix III.

These issues have been broached earlier but here we will cover some new ground, further clarifying in practice aspects of the theory already presented.

Application 31.2
STRUCTURAL FUNCTION VIII: THE BIRD BEAK

Bird beak exercise renders lateral arm movement superfluous

Step 1: Form your hand into the shape of a bird's beak. Grasp your five fingertips together as firmly as possible, then point them down and let your wrist break. Your bird beak makes a pecking motion downwards. In fact, maybe your hand now looks more like a turkey's head than a bird beak.

Illustration 31.1: The Bird Beak: fingertips pressed tightly together

Step 2: Keeping your hand extremely stiff but allowing your wrist to move as flexibly as possible, have your turkey peck at some grains on the table. What other surfaces could your turkey peck? (Your forehead for instance?)

Step 3: Now let either your second or third fingertip peek out slightly from this turkey head just enough that it can play a note. You'll notice, no matter how loud you play, if you maintain this bird beak structure then the sound is resonant not harsh.

What then of the shock-absorber arm? So quickly we rendered it superfluous!

Classic 'elbow out to side' movement creates two problems instead of solving one

Do you see now how by moving your arm out in the classic fashion you may have been creating a double problem rather than solving anything! The 'bird beak' exercise demonstrates most clearly now that a lack of integrity in hand structure, a lack of support where it's needed, is the cause of harsh tone. It illustrates graphically how by moving your arm out to alleviate harsh tone, you may have been only further weakening your hand and compounding the problem instead of solving it! The bird beak stops you from doing what you would normally do, specifically, moving your arm out and pulling your second finger's metacarpal-phalangeal joint down, weakening the structure between your thumb and forefinger.

Cure an unconscious habit by consciously learning its opposite

Step 4: If you need to move the arm somewhere while playing with your turkey beak, why not move directly *forward up and in,* instead of off to the side? As if the arm is moving *through* the space between the thumb and forefinger. This is similar to swinging in and up in the previous chapter, and should *build* the feeling of support in the hand rather than impinging on it.

32 The Underlying Musical Purpose of Arm Movement

The arm as phrase generator

Our next concern is more complex and less easily solved. If not to beautify tone, then what is the true function of arm movement? As we have seen in several applications already, your arm should serve to orient your hand in space in the most efficient way possible. Twice now we have seen how the classic 'arm out' is not always the best way to do this and can in many cases be improved upon. Orientation is the arm's physical task, but it has a crucial musical one as well. All arm movements *do* affect the sound, but a sound in isolation is meaningless. Sounds only acquire musical meaning when they are linked together, and this leads us to the arm's true function, not to generate *a* sound but to shape *groups* of sounds and give them character.

Thus the classic 'arm out' on one note is useful only if we want to create the effect of crescendo or phrase on that single note. Use that arm movement to carry you through as few as two notes, and you are already into the true realm of arm function, shaping the phrase. Linking notes together. Even a series of staccato notes can be transformed into a dancing melody if the arm is consciously used to shape a phrase. You should use a distinct arm movement to generate each staccato only if you want a stodgy, heavy sound. Leave your fingers to do the staccato and move your arm through a *group* of notes, for a lighter, more aesthetically pleasing musical phrase! In general, one arm movement should equal one phrase or sub-phrase.

Even a pencil can play legato if arm helps

I once saw a documentary film about a very unusual concert pianist who is also a professional body builder. At one point in the film he takes a pencil and using the eraser tip plays a most beautiful, singing *cantabile* melody (aided by the pedal

of course). This is inflected legato taken to the extreme, providing graphic proof that a direct attack is capable of producing beautiful tone, and that in fact it is the *relationship* of one note to the next that determines tone quality.

This is why I harp on about integrity of hand structure—this allows us most easily to manage the relationship between notes. He could phrase beautifully even with a pencil *because all the other parts of his playing mechanism had already learned the organization required to achieve it*. They had already learned how, most likely through a combination of clearly defined phrase goals and cultivation of physical legato. At some point in his pianistic development his hand learned how to be as secure, solid, precise and dependable as that pencil. Once that secure foundation was in place, the rest of his playing apparatus could then learn how to connect the notes *in sound*. Now that his entire mechanism knows how, the actual tool he chooses to couple his mechanism to the keyboard becomes a matter of choice.

Legato equals phrase: only one arm movement per phrase

Let's return once again to our overholding exercise. If we take our four notes to be under a slur, then one arm movement will suffice for the four notes. If we succumb to our automatic reflex to move our elbow out and around on each note (in an attempt to produce 'beautiful tone'), then we may well have four beautifully toned notes but we quite likely will *not* have a phrase! If you make four movements you will generally end up with four phrases. Use only *one* arm move-ment to connect your group of notes into one phrase.[1] These automatic relaxing movements of the arm not only destroy phrase, they also make it much more difficult to overhold well.

Professionals fall into the same error

If you think that only amateurs and students make this mistake, guess again. I recently listened to recordings of several of our most famous pianists (who will remain nameless) playing Chopin's Polonaise in C sharp minor, Op. 26 #1. In the opening theme *none* of them phrased the rising melodic sequence of groups of two sixteenths and an eighth properly—all played the notes equally loud with no dynamic shaping and no forward lilt. Unbelievable! But examples like this

---

[1] Of course we have already considered an alternate view on this state of affairs in chapter 30, *Functionally Supported Movement: The Whole Arm as Finger*.

abound in our recorded repertory. Let's give these artists the benefit of the doubt and say that they are musical but their physical organization is working against the manifestation of their musical intention.

Example 32.1: Chopin: Polonaise in C sharp minor, Op. 26 #1, *mm. 4-8*

Try now consciously using one 'arm out' movement to shape each three-note group (the slurred groups in this example). Do you hear the resulting lilt, the phrased sound?

Application 32.1
WRIST I: PHRASE SHAPE

The transmission of forces through the wrist

In our anatomical journey covering finger, hand and arm we seem to have overlooked the wrist. The wrist is a touchy issue, providing one of the most controversial and disputable points in our discussion, and is best approached with caution and perspicuity. However I will shirk no longer from my task, but try to address the wrist and all the ambiguities of its position.

The wrist is a four-way hinge joint that has a dual function in piano playing. Physically its role is to transmit the force vectors[2] acting through it precisely, cleanly, completely. It cannot do this if it is either 'broken' or locked. If the wrist

---

[2] Forces resulting from forearm mass or arm activity moving in the direction of the keyboard, or alternately, forces traveling back *up* the arm as a result of the finger's contact *with* the key.

'breaks', the forces coming down through the arm cannot be transmitted through the wrist and on down through the hand/finger into the key. Instead they sheer off at an angle, their effect nullified. On the other hand, if the wrist is locked, the bones and force vectors may well be lined up correctly, but the forces simply can't get *through*—they're blocked at the joint by static muscular contractions.

Occasionally you'll see a third variant, the hyper-relaxed wrist. Here the degree of looseness is so acute that the forces of the arm never even make it through the wrist joint, not because of blocked-ness but simply a total lack of connection!

Another phrasing machine

The wrist is crucial musically as well: just as we can experience the arm as the instrument that carves out the actual phrase shape, so can we the wrist. In the end, the wrist perhaps most effectively generates the true legato that allows the instrument to sing because its movements are smaller, more economical and therefore more exact than those of the arm. Although I spend a lot of time harping about increased finger action, there exists a technique that would seem to be in total opposition to this. Learning the technique of phrase generation from the wrist first requires *reducing* finger movement to an absolute minimum! Here your finger hardly seems to play at all but simply remains immobile on its note. It's a special kind of legato. The feeling in the finger can best be described as if you put two or more fingers into one hole rather than in different holes.

Step 1: Take any of the slurred 3-note groups from our Polonaise example, for instance one that begins with your second finger. Begin with your second, but don't play the note—just rest your second finger lightly on its key. Now move your wrist slightly as if to inflect the small section of the phrase that flows through this note: seemingly by chance, the note sounds. This happens because a subtle force operating from the arm down through the wrist couples the finger to the keybed. You don't consciously do anything to actually play the note by moving your finger; it's as if the wrist itself plays it, not with a vertical movement but a small lateral movement. This transmits down through your finger into the key and *voila*, a singing note!

Step 2: When your wrist moves to the right it couples your next fingertip, causing *that* note's rich, juicy tone to grow out of the previous one, and so on.

Minimal movements

Here the movement of your wrist is minimal, even to the point of being imperceptible. Remember Horowitz, who I mentioned many people believe was excessively stiff, but who I firmly believe was in fact extremely free and well organized internally. I think he was using exactly this technique constantly. He just did it so well that you couldn't see it—but you could hear it! It's almost as if it's not a real movement we're talking about but an *intention*. The wrist becomes the instrument of the mind, fulfilling the mind's musical intent.

This is an effective antidote for needless over-articulation—articulation whose basis is technical insecurity rather than musical need. It also cures the conservatory habit of a 'supple' wrist—all those graceful movements in which we constantly see many pianists indulging, movements supposedly designed to avoid tension. Unfortunately this suppleness can be useless or worse, even throwing the hand out of its proper balance—it can destabilize and thus actually *evoke* compensatory, stabilizing tension elsewhere in the arm!

Step 3: There is an effective kinesthetic image that can serve as a cure for 'conservatory wrist syndrome'. At times I hold a student's forearm with extreme firmness with both my hands, and guide it in movement, but mainly only in one plane, one dimension of movement: in and out (towards and away from the backboard!). It is as if I am holding a poker and gently, subtly sticking, stoking the fire. I provide a constraint so that the student barely succeeds in moving right and left enough to play the melody, and cannot move up and down at all! If done with enough firmness (and it's probably more than you think), this practice effectively prevents all the other unconscious indulgences in movement of which the student is so fond, and gives him or her a graphic experience of the minimal wrist movement needed to sculpt the phrase accurately.

Try recreating this effect on your own, or perhaps ask a colleague to fulfill the role of physical guide and create the constraint for you.

Phrase generation from the wrist and phrase shaping with the arm are of course closely interrelated. I would say the 'wrist as phrase machine' is a more advanced technique, as it more closely approaches the *internalization* of phrase-inflection movements. However, we can each find our own most workable solution. This

technique may prove easier, more effective, useful and congenial than 'arm phrasing' to some. Master them both, then take your pick, or *combine* them in a way that gives you the musical results you want!

33 MINIMIZE AUXILIARY MOVEMENTS TO MAXIMIZE EFFICIENCY

External body efforts often counterproductive

What is the role of auxiliary movement in piano playing? What *style* of physical involvement will prove most effective, most useful? Awhile back it was discovered that your whole arm and torso participates in tone generation. This has led to more inefficiency, misguided and counterproductive effort than I care to recall! Pianists undulate their arms, sway their bodies and even rise off the piano bench for their most impressive fortes. Ridiculous! All the energy used to lift oneself off the bench is wasted energy, energy that has nothing to do with creating sound! To be most effective, the participation of all your body should be internal—no visible movement necessary! As I have said, if your torso is well aligned, floating in gravity instead of needing muscular contractions to hold it in place, its muscles become free to participate passively in activity elsewhere. There is a subtle ripple effect though the musculature of the torso—not so much an effort as a resonance, something you wouldn't even notice unless you drew your attention to it. 'Fluidity' in the torso begets more fluid, capable movement elsewhere.

Finger, arm involvement both affect tone quality

Similarly for the arm. How does, in fact, your arm participate in producing sound? What is actually going on when you try to increase or decrease the involvement of your arm in tone production? Sometimes you may feel as if you use the weight or mass of your arm to warm up the actual tone, to actually help in generating the tone. You might even state that the more you perceive your finger as generating the sound, the brighter your tone will be, whereas the more involved you perceive your arm, the thicker and heavier your tone becomes. Both these subjective perceptions are valid and valuable, but we may better master them if we objectively understand the underlying functions.

Internal generation of tone quality

Most often the arm should be joining notes together in a phrase, improving tone not by generating tone in any way but by linking quantities of note-sounds together perfectly: Here it appears on the surface that the tone is generated solely by the fingers. However as we've said, underneath there is a function going on which indicates that, although you may not perceive it as such, the arm does participate in tone production. You simply may not *perceive* it as such because the participation is an internal function not an external movement.

34 FURTHER MUSICAL IMPLICATIONS OF PROPER ARM-HAND COOPERATION IN LEGATO

Application 34.1
LEGATO VII: PHYSICAL FLOW EQUALS MUSICAL FLOW

The previous chapters addressed and resolved some of the problems associated with over-moving. Here we look at the opposite case: a student whose basic relationship to the keyboard was so weak that he was freezing into immobility for an instant on virtually every note just to maintain a modicum of control. This is what I said to him:

Successful coordination of your arm and hand will allow you to feel movement through even a single note to the next one. A note is an alive entity! It *vibrates*. It has length and not just a dying away. Your arm movement, small and precise, reflecting the very duration of the note, allows you to maintain rhythmic and musical integrity.

Control of attacks should not impede arm flow

If you play one note, move to the next but then stop before going on, all musical flow is cut. It is amazing how often we do this—we attempt to control exactly the next note's moment of attack by freezing up physically! We must undeniably control the precise moment of attack, but we must not destroy the muscular and musical flow *into* that note in order to achieve that control! No preparatory inhibition of free motion!

Here do not, in order to prepare to play each note, stop your whole arm and fix it, rigidify it. You may have been doing this with the best of intentions. You may have wanted to stabilize yourself in order to play the note precisely as you

intended. But you must find a more sophisticated way to achieve this. Yes, you must be stable, able to play the note exactly as you wish, but without stopping the movement! In other words, find a functional way to be stable.

Relearn the passage with feeling of arm's sculpting action

You must replace stopping with moving. Now you must control your rhythm mentally, all the while counting like the dickens internally, rather than physically blocking to create accents. Many rhythmic patterns are difficult! But if you try to control them by stopping your arm, you are sure to become confused. Your arm should flow physically with the flow of the music; it is your mind that monitors the flow of pulses. When your mind generates pulse your arm does create pulse as well, but in a flowing way, as the living tool of your mind. Thus like a potter carving a curve in clay your arm sculpts the musical contour.

Your arm's main function is to produce not tone but musical shapes. Thus your primary concern should be to ensure that your arm is expressing, reflecting or inflecting the musical dance in its gesture. Your arm is at once your tool and your self—through it you manifest your expression. You don't just manipulate it; you are in it. It is not inert. You live in it. You must look at what you do *through* it, not at how you use it as an inert tool.

When playing like this you almost have to learn the notes all over again, because both the physical and mental sensations are so different. The actual sensation of the distances involved between intervals changes. And as you have now physically shaped these notes into a line, they are no longer dots on the page with no relation to one another, no longer a series of isolated physical efforts, but a series of notes that has meaning. The radically different physical experience of truly joining them both through legato and through a new type of arm movement, joins them in a totally new way mentally as well. Hence new learning.

Try the following to form a relationship in your mind between the physical feeling of legato and its musical purpose. As you play a melody, try to hear the unique quality of each interval. The transition between any two notes is different from that between any other two. You may think that the melodic strands C-D-E and D-E-F sharp are identical motives just transposed, but this indicates only the limitations of your listening. The actual frequencies of vibration, the note colors themselves, are *not* the same. Not to mention the huge differences between

a minor and major second or between the various other intervals. It all depends on the exactitude of your listening.

When you begin to hear the sweetness, the charm, the pain, or one of the many other qualities with which a melody moves through any particular interval, then your musical mind will be cooperating with, and even generating your physical intention to truly join the notes in a profound, meaningful legato.

Application 34.2
LEGATO VIII: FEATHER-LIGHT LEGATO

One effective way to get a sense of legato is to press into the key very hard, in order that you *feel* the connections through all the joints that allow a true supported legato. Towards a similar end, the distinguished Russian pedagogue Heinrich Neuhaus used to lean his whole weight on the student's hand arch to solidify it![1] So far we have focused only on this firm approach to legato.

Walking without pressing

But often I'll see a student suffering from the opposite malady, overpressing, strangling the piano tone or getting a harsh, banged effect. If I show him the firm approach to building hand structure and function, it only compounds the problem—his joints are misaligned so the increased pressing gives disastrous results, and we've gotten nowhere.

In this case we need to take a radically different tactic. We need to ease off that excess pressure and find a more subtle way to arrive at effective joint alignment. This I call 'feather-light' legato.

Here you don't even feel like you're playing the note! Instead of 'playing' it, just let your finger or thumb descend down to the key bottom as if by chance, enabling you to walk on that finger (use it as the 'walking leg') *but without pressing at all. Float* instead of pressing. In the action of 'walking', your hand flows over that finger toward the next, which then descends down to *its* key bottom and so on. Your arm floats in space rather than standing on your finger. The resulting sound

---

[1] Heinrich Neuhaus, *The Art of Piano Playing* (London: Barrie & Jenkins, 1986).

is marvellously unforced, singing in the light *bel canto* style. It's a sinuous, filigree melodic quality.

Feather legato is another essential element in your pianistic arsenal. It is the first thing to acquire once your initial security in legato has been established. Consider it as the midpoint between full physical legato and inflected, arm-shaped legato. Here you maintain the complete set of physical connections essential to a true legato, but your arm has the floating feeling of inflected legato because you refrain from pressing in any way. Feather legato also relates to natural finger shape to be explored in part VIII.

Compensate for the tendency to rush

When you play in this new way there is a natural tendency to go faster. Why? Your habitual over-contraction of your arm, which unbeknownst to you had been functioning as a brake and keeping you in tempo, has now been decoupled, and so off you go rushing faster and faster. Whee! This is fun, this wonderfully delightful free flowing, and indeed you do want that flowing feeling no matter how fast or slow your tempo. Yet you also need some sort of regulating influence! For this, do not reinstate your muscular contraction! No, keep your newfound physical freedom and instead use your *mind* to control rhythmic pulse. Use the perceptive abilities of your brain to keep you in tempo![7]

Melody not the metronome

Remember when doing this to go for the melody not the metronome. This means take time when you need it to let your melody breathe, ebbing or moving forward, rather than slavishly gluing yourself to the beat.[3]

With 'feather-light' legato we conclude this section on the wrist and arm in legato. Albeit it may seem we have raised more questions than we've answered. We hope to resolve at least some of these in the ensuing sections.

---

[342] See chapter 52, *A Practical Exercise in Rhythm.*
[343] See chapter 51, *Hierarchy of Rhythmic Values Is a Practical Reality.*

VIII

ROTATION

35 FOREARM ROTATION IN LISZT

To this point we have discussed how strength and structural functionality empowers the hand and fingers both to play a true legato and to create a maximal variety of orchestral colors. We have also looked at the arm's role in facilitating optimal hand function as well at its musical function, inflecting phrase shape. But in addition to the arm's lateral motion there is another basic arm movement, one that facilitates easy resolution of problems related to navigating large intervals on the keyboard. Rotation helps you leap with alacrity.

Functional advantage of upright human posture

Think for a moment about the animals. What animal do you know that can turn to face an unseen opponent as quickly we as humans can? Other animals must deal with the sad fact that their bodies are more or less horizontally constructed, and a great deal of cumbersome effort is needed to face themselves in a different direction. However, for us it is a simple and easy affair. Upright humans can rotate their bodies instead of swivelling, and this is probably one of the main reasons we rule the planet today—our ability to turn quickly towards an attacker offers us a key advantage in self-defense.

You can rule the keyboard just as we rule the world (and we would hope even more wisely!), if you employ the equivalent principles of structural function in your hand and arm.

Types of arm rotation

The arm has two different rotational capacities. Below the elbow, when the radius and thumb rotate around the ulna they rotate the forearm alone, whereas when the head of the humerus (your upper arm bone) rotates in the shoulder socket, it rotates the whole arm as a unit. Although we will pay attention

mainly to forearm rotation, notice that if you rotate your whole arm your elbow moves in and out. Whole arm rotation moves your elbow more efficiently than lateral arm movement.

Although Matthay mistakenly saw it in even the simplest of playing movements, forearm rotation really comes into its own primarily in facilitating large stretches or leaps, and to a lesser extent in providing more efficient passage of the thumb in scales and arpeggios. A third minor aspect of rotation is a rapid forearm rotary movement in *forte* trills between thumb and finger. This third we will not consider here because the movement is not orientative: the arm remains stationary in space; the rotational movement merely takes advantage of the bipartite nature of hand structure to help increase the brilliance of thumb and finger's attack.

It is rotation in the context of lateral hand position shifts that I take as a fourth key element of physical mechanics at the keyboard.

Negative consequences of lateral wrist motion in Jeux d'Eau

The opening of the first impressionist piece of music ever written provides an ideal opportunity to investigate rotation.

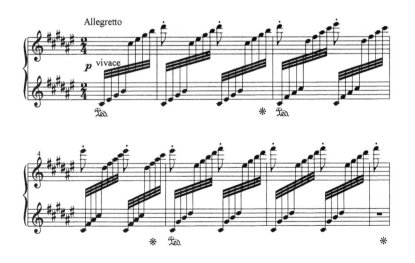

Example 35.1: Liszt: Jeux d'eau, *mm. 1-6*

Rotation offers a useful advantage in piano technique because of the design of the hand, wrist and arm. In the right-hand arpeggiation, notice that if you move your wrist laterally from left to right (as many of us do here), there are two negative consequences:

> 1) Your hand is forced to swivel and thus your thumb gets pulled away from the keyboard, towards your body.
> 2) Your fingers must stretch sideways to manage the legato. They become splayed, giving the whole process an uncomfortable, awkward feel.

This horizontal wrist movement gives a very wooden sound, but there's a way to acquire a much more fluid tone (like water!).

Application 35.1
ROTATION I: INGREDIENTS OF ROTATION

Inefficiency of swivelling

Ergonomically, swivelling the hand is a very uneconomical movement. Just when your thumb should be positioning itself to play its next note, swivelling pulls it toward you, *away* from the keyboard.

> Step 1: Stand your finger on key and swivel your hand to the outside. Notice how this pulls your thumb away from the board.

Illustration 35.1: Swivelling pulls thumb away from keys

Step 2: Try now to let your thumb, by continuing that horizontal arc of travel, to move through a complete circle and again approach the keyboard. In quick playing you don't have time for such a big circular movement—this too is impractical.

Step 3: Try simply stopping the movement of pulling your thumb away from the board horizontally and returning by the same path to the key—this is also tremendously inefficient.

Step 4: Now remove your thumb from its note by supinating your forearm while leaving your wrist and elbow inside. Even push your wrist or the heel of your hand *more* to the inside. In this way you avoid swivelling, and your thumb can now return to its key in a relatively direct arc. We have found a fluid, efficient way for your thumb to reverse its direction. This saves much time and effort and maintains musical flow. It dispenses with unneeded, extraneous movements while giving you exactly the move you do need.

Illustration 35.2: Rotation moves thumb out; wrist stays in.

Rotation necessitates and facilitates some strange stretching

But to achieve this we'll have to employ a pretty strange organization of the hand and finger.

Step 5: Lay your fifth finger on its first note, the top D sharp in measure 1 of *Jeux d'Eau*. As your fifth finger holds its note firmly yet flexibly, pick up your thumb, move it up and as far as you can to the outside. Your forearm of course rotates.

Did your wrist follow along with your thumb or even lead it to the outside? If so, your hand is still swivelling and this is your key stumbling block. As long as this happens, your forearm travels laterally to the right, pulling your thumb *away* from the board toward your body. Now if it wanted to get back to its note (the C sharp a 9th below your fifth finger's D sharp), your thumb must do a complicated three-dimensional movement—a movement that is awkward and (as we said for those poor horizontally constructed animals) cumbersome.

Keep your wrist and elbow to the inside even as thumb rotates to the outside

Step 6: Place your fifth again on D sharp, but this time when raising your thumb, as your arm rotates relax the top metacarpal joint of your fifth finger, actually pressing it down into the keyboard. The outside ridge of your hand (the part between your fifth finger knuckle and your wrist) moves to the inside, in other words to the left. This causes your wrist as well to mash itself into the keys. Your second, third and fourth fingers point to the inside, and even your elbow moves in closer to your body. You'll see the strange phenomenon of *everything* moving to the inside except your thumb and fifth, which move outward. Your fifth, although grounded in its key, seems to move to the outside in relation to your hand, which is moving in.

Illustration 35.3: Rotate don't swivel—fifth and thumb out, all the rest in

This bizarre movement yields two very interesting results.

1) Quick, efficient thumb movement back to its note

Your thumb still looks like it is quite far away from C sharp, but although you have been moving it *out*, relative to the keyboard it is still quite far *in*, because the rest of your hand and arm (especially your wrist) have been nudging it in that direction. Thus it is now actually a very quick, easy movement to get back to C

sharp! As long as your wrist and fifth finger metacarpal stay to the inside, the arc through which your thumb must travel to return to its note is on only two planes, not the more complicated three. When your wrist stays inside, your arm does not travel horizontally—it only rotates, effectively moving on only one plane instead of two.

Only when your wrist moves to the outside does your arm move laterally in an ungainly, inefficient way that works against your musical intentions. Remember, in rotation your wrist should move in the opposite direction to the accustomed and seemingly logical one, effectively eradicating the whole problem of hand swivelling.

2) 'Vertical' finger stretching more than doubles their span

In addition, relaxing your fifth's metacarpal-phalangeal and stretching your fourth finger down from your hand, towards the bass end of the keyboard, increases the distance between the two fingertips to more than double what it would be if you laid your hand flat and splayed those fingers horizontally!

Your fingers are 'up' and 'down' in relation to your hand, not their orientation in space

Are we getting confused about 'up' and 'down', 'inside' and 'outside'? Let's stop a moment to clarify. Hold your right hand out in front of you in the prone position (palm down). Let your fourth finger drop lower than the others. Raise your fifth higher than the others. Now if you supinate your forearm 90 degrees (rotate it towards the palm up position), your palm is now vertical. Your fourth is now pointing to the left, to the inside, but in relation to your hand it still points downwards. Likewise your fifth now points to the outside, to the right, but you can still see it as pointing up if you consider it in relation to your hand rather than its orientation in space.

Similarity to doing the splits in ballet

And now back to 'vertical' finger stretching. Imagine a ballet dancer doing the splits. The dancer can cheat a bit by angling the pelvis slightly to one side to make one leg point forward, the other point behind instead of both legs sticking out to the sides equally. This is exactly what we are doing here with our fourth and fifth fingers! If you really relax your fifth 'up' and stretch your fourth 'down', it's as if your hand acquires a whole extra joint. Your fifth feels as separate in function from the rest of your hand as your hand is from your forearm. Your fifth

finger's metacarpal now functions like another wrist joint—sticking your fifth
finger up corresponds to cocking your wrist. You can do ballet dancer splits to
some degree between any two fingers.

When you try this you will certainly feel a stretch. But part of this is stretching
your brain to accept new patterns. So remember: don't do it by force but by
softness. Always cultivate quality in your learning. The increased flexibility you
may thereby acquire, both physical *and* mental, will have a profound effect on
your technique in general.

A little practice

> Step 3: Still hanging on to D sharp with your fifth, and keeping your
> wrist nudged to the inside, play C sharp a 9th below with your
> thumb, and then return it to its 'cocked' or poised position.

Example 35.2: Liszt: Jeux d'eau, *cock your thumb*

If you can't stretch that interval, simulate the feeling of holding
on to D sharp by letting your fifth slide off it as you play C sharp,
but immediately place your fifth back *on* its D sharp in a sly,
subtle manner—with the smallest movement possible. Can you
find that movement?

Remember, your thumb is high and wants to go to the outside, but
it doesn't go as far as it might because you gently nudge your wrist *in*
as your forearm rotates out—as if the heel of your hand wants to
go towards the bass end of the piano. Repeat this strange movement
many times—get used to it.

Incorporation of other fingers into this movement

"All fine and well" you may ask, "but how do the other fingers fit into this? How
can 2, 3 and 4 play when my hand is in this weird vertical 'karate chop' position?"

Step 4: To find out, notice that with your thumb high and your wrist to the inside, your fifth finger is hyper-extended up above your hand as we practiced (that is, to the right when your hand is in a vertical position). If you stretch your fourth finger down below (to the left of) your (vertical) hand, you can easily play its note B. It may feel awkward at first, but take this as a sign that you need to drastically increase your hand flexibility, and here is a good place to start! Similarly 3 and 2 can play G sharp and E sharp respectively—all the time the heel of your hand leading that movement while your thumb lags as far behind as possible: Keep your thumb high! It only descends to play C sharp at the last possible moment.

Here, playing the notes in their reverse order helps to free you from your habitual movement patterns and discover the radically different organization we aspire to.

Example 35.3: Liszt: Jeux d'eau, *strange stretching*

Result: drastic increase in wrist flexibility and function

Note that through this work you're acquiring not only greater finger malleability but also a marked increase in flexibility of the wrist. When you do this technique well your wrist flexibility immediately should see a dramatic improvement. By the way, when we speak of flexibility, what is it that is actually flexible? Our bones are eminently solid—it is rather through the state of our *joints* that we feel degrees of flexibility. In effective flexibility our joints are not quite completely loose but optimally sensitive. They are still moving but *connected.*

This can have a positive effect on all your playing, but for the moment let's stay focused on our immediate problem. Remember, maximum capability means maximum variability of function. Whether we cultivate minimal wrist flexibility as mentioned earlier, or maximize it as we do here, all depends on the technical and musical context.

Step 5: Holding onto top D sharp, play the two notes C sharp and B simultaneously with your first and fourth fingers.

Example 35.4: Liszt: Jeux d'eau, pluck chord upwards

Feel like you are plucking *up*wards and to the outside and folding your hand backwards over your fifth finger, which is so loose you almost fear it will separate from your hand entirely! All the movement is up, freeing and lightening everything except your limp fifth finger. This stays flexibly on key and bears the brunt of your arm weight. It may feel awkward at first, but again do you see the implications for arm flexibility and freedom?

Thumb to the outside ahead of fingers, lags behind them moving to the inside

Step 6: Now play all the right hand notes as written.

Example 35.5: Liszt: Jeux d'eau, mm. 1-2, right hand as written

Your thumb must rise *immediately* your second finger plays. Your thumb is always trying to stay ahead, moving up and to the outside more quickly than the notes being played. Then it whips back to play the next C sharp. You will tend to raise your thumb late, leaving it low even until your fifth plays its note. Your thumb tends to be lazy. You must train yourself to react, not to lag so much in your actions.

Still swing your thumb

Do not reduce your thumb's independent action just because your arm is helping out. Keeping both your independent thumb and your arm involved to the full extent of their functionality gives you maximal possibility for color creation and control, really bringing your sound to life. Our whole discussion of rotation takes place in the context of the arm's role. But your perception is not that you rotate your arm to make your thumb rise. On the contrary, your thumb is the active agent. Lift your thumb; the rotation happens simply because it must, in order that your thumb can get to where it is going.

Anything less than a total 'thumb-up' is not it! And remember, your wrist stays to the inside. Move your thumb out *instead* of your wrist. This orientation of your wrist allows your thumb paradoxically to move almost constantly towards the outside yet all the time actually staying inside, relatively close to its note.

Improve gradually, master each individual component of the movement

You may feel that it is difficult to play the notes accurately using this movement, but this only indicates how much more flexibility—physical *and* mental— you need to acquire. Up until now I have been stressing the development of hand strength; suddenly I'm emphasizing flexibility. "What gives?" you may wonder. Don't you see, flexibility and strength go hand in hand (pardon the pun). Flexibility here is synonymous with *functionality*.

If you can't get this new organization immediately don't worry, and certainly don't go back to your old way. Stick with this new one—take your time. Just as ice doesn't melt all at once, so you must gradually melt your old habits, little by little finding your way toward really effective flexibility and functionality—as you develop an understanding of its actual movement components. Remember, this is all based on forearm rotation instead of hand swivelling, and it requires a major alteration of your modus operandi.

Your wrist is not your thumb!

In the meantime, just understand you must not confuse your wrist with your thumb! Stop moving your wrist to the outside, move your thumb instead. In this way you'll get more and more rubbery, and of course your sound will develop a harp-like quality, because this is the equivalent movement to what

harpists do on their instrument. If you still have problems, read through the next section on natural hand shape, then try this again in the light of that information.

Other instances

> Step 7: At measure 14 and following, *leggierissimo non-legato*, again use forearm rotation for lightness

> *Example 35.6: Liszt:* Jeux d'eau, *right hand, m. 14*

Practice playing just your first and second fingers, and raise your thumb on every second finger's note. This effects the forearm rotation. It's not a big movement, just a small rotation but it makes a crucial difference in what's going on. When you reinstate all the notes there will be a 'compound rotation': there is slightly more rotational movement between your thumb and fourth finger notes (C sharp and G sharp) than between your second and fifth finger notes (D sharp and A sharp).

Your arms need to be so loose to play this—like the water the music portrays. Where else can you use rotation in *Jeux d'Eau?*

Application 35.2
ROTATION II: LEAPS IN LA CAMPANELLA

Of course there are many other moments in the literature, in the left hand as well as the right, which can benefit from the incorporation of rotation. The right hand leaps (opening theme [measure 4 ff.]) and double octave stretches (right hand accompanying bell motive [measure 41 ff.]) in *La Campanella* come to mind. Consider the 16th notes spanning two octaves of the note D sharp, fingered 1-3-5-3-1.

Example 35.7: Liszt: La Campanella, *m. 42*

Here it is interesting to consider the possibility of playing legato not only from your thumb to third finger, but from your third finger to fifth as well! Do you think it's impossible?

> Step 1: Try resting your fifth on D sharp, rotating your hand to the vertical and stretching your third finger down to the left. If you have a relatively large hand you should be able to physically connect the octave. Perhaps not in performance, but in practice yes! Doing it in practice shows you the flexible rotation movement you must make even in performance to achieve the highest possible level of control, to be absolutely sure you will not miss notes.

> When you play the notes as written, on the high D sharp (marked with an eighth note in the example), your hand should be vertical, your palm pointing to the inside, your thumb and fifth finger to the outside.

> Step 2: Just as you rested your fifth on D sharp in *Jeux d'Eau* to rotate your thumb in, did you try it in the opening theme of *La Campanella* as well?

Example 35.8: Liszt: La Campanella, *mm. 4-6*

Laying your fifth on D sharp, let your fourth, third and second fingers angle to the inside while your thumb rises to the outside,

to a point directly above your fifth. Your fifth finger metacarpal and your wrist are squished maximally to the inside; your thumb is as much to the outside as possible. Play the first thumb note and then return to this position. Return here after every thumb note! In the example, the fifth finger D sharps are marked with parentheses to indicate that you don't need to play them at all, but silently take the key while returning to this strange new vertically twisted hand position.[1] Playing in this manner will increase your accuracy significantly and totally eliminate the feeling of leaping.

Is this not clear?

Application 35.3
ROTATION III: FOREARM HAND-FLUTTER EXERCISE TO CLARIFY ROTATION IN LEAPING

Step 1: Let your hand hover just above the fallboard and rotate your forearm back and forth, your hand loose and fluttering. Your fingers do not touch the fallboard yet but hover fluttering above it.

Step 2: Continuing to rotate, lower your arm gently until your thumb and fifth in turn begin to slap the fallboard lightly.

Step 3: Now here's the interesting part: slowly begin to increase the distance between the thumb and fifth strike points while continuing this movement. Do *not* stretch your thumb or fifth finger—leave them loose and flopping. Notice you are now leaping but it does not feel like it! You only feel like you are rotating!

Stay loose as you do this, so much so that you even feel your triceps muscles flapping and shaking, completely relaxed. Your elbow moves slightly in the direction opposite to your hand. As your fifth plays, your elbow goes a bit to the inside; as your thumb

---
[1] Refer back to illustration 35.3, *Rotate don't swivel — fifth and thumb out, all the rest in.*

rotates in, elbow rotates out—*slightly*. Don't try to make it do this, just observe that it does so passively as a result of the rotation.

Leaping without feeling the difficulty of the leap, without feeling like you are leaping at all, is a fantastic sensation, and very useful in many situations! Once you get the hang of it, you can increase the distance even to several octaves while maintaining an uncanny degree of accuracy.

> Step 4: Now play the *Campanella* theme using this movement. Can you get it so the thumb stroke *in* to its note and then returning to its 'cocked' position over the top D sharp feels like one move not two? There you have it.

There are countless instances in the repertoire where forearm rotation facilitates ease of motion. In general, whenever the figuration requires a lateral forearm movement you might do well to take a moment and ask yourself, can a little bit of rotation here go a long way towards making things work better?

A cautionary note: as you explore rotation you will probably go through a stage where you overdo it. The movement should be natural, unnoticeable. But as a child fascinated with a newly learned skill will employ it even in the most unimaginable situations, so might be you inclined to do in applying rotation. Don't worry; it's just a phase.

IX

NATURAL FINGER SHAPE

36 The Natural Hand in Passagework

Our logical progression from hand strength through arm function has covered some key external aspects of the piano playing mechanism. But when we looked at rotation, our focus shifted from strength and stability of structure towards more flexibility. This leads us to natural finger shape, a contrasting yet complementary dimension of pianistic capability, the fifth and final basic principle to which we turn our attention.

Granted we do need an activated, educated strength to achieve our ends at the keyboard. But cultivating natural finger shape allows us to explore the *exact distribution* of this strength—to have all the contrasting forces of the hand and fingers working together in harmony. Examining hand and finger function from the angle of delicacy and sensitivity, reducing levels of various stresses to distribute them more exactly as needed, clarifies how strength is most effective when it does not work against itself.

We'll first look at natural finger shape in passagework where it bears fundamental importance. Later on we'll discover how it can improve other pianistic textures such as chordal passages or repeated notes as well.

Chopin's Scherzo in E major, Op. 54

Brilliant passagework makes or breaks a performance of this witty work, the only one of Chopin's four Scherzi whose character bears any resemblance to the original meaning of the title. But how much of our diligent digital digging is causing us more harm than good? Are we building our scales and passagework on a technical basis that will yield brilliant results? We should be aiming for a brilliance whose tone is full and round rather than brittle, tinny or sharp, a phrasing that sounds witty because it is free and easy not contrived. Let's explore how to reduce the level of stress in our movements to improve

quality of tone and phrasing.

Example 36.1: Chopin, *Scherzo in E major, Op. 54*, mm. 66-72

Here you'll discover how any deformation of natural hand and finger shape tends to slow you down, bind you up, and harm your tone as well. Cultivating a totally natural finger shape while spraying out waves of pearl-like eighth notes is easier said than done, but it is well worth striving for. It is especially important that this particular exercise be done with a heightened focus of attention. You must become supersensitive to even the slightest twitch, every minute sign of muscular activity in your fingers and hand, if you want to gain maximum benefit.

Application 36.1
NATURAL SHAPE I: FINDING AND USING YOUR NATURAL FINGER SHAPE

Step 1: Let your hand hang by your side, limp. Notice how, although your fingers are hanging in a gravitational field, they are not straight. There is a natural curve to them, maintained not by muscle tonus but by the normal length of your ligaments. This is both the shape and the muscle tonus we will be trying to adhere to as closely as is practically possible.

Step 2: Put your hand on a flat surface such as a tabletop. There are two ways to do this. One is to flatten the fingers so that each joint rests on the surface. Or we can leave our hand in exactly the same shape as when hanging. This gives us our normal arch shape, the 'Russian Arch', or the shape we got when our teacher told us to pretend we're holding onto the tennis ball. Practice doing vari-

ous things with your hand, putting it places, waving it around, but all the time leaving it in this natural arch shape.

Remember, you do not need to hold your fingers curved—they stay that way all by themselves. That's why I call it a natural shape—that's how they stay when you're not thinking about it. Trying to *hold* them in their natural shape would be anything but natural. They would become like wood or cement, like a statue and a bad one at that because it would not be a true likeness. Your fingers are flesh and blood (albeit wrapped around bones), and retain their human, living qualities to the extent they remain vital and moveable. For this the muscle tonus must remain soft!

Natural shape means naturally soft muscles. When you leave your fingers in their natural shape they do stay soft. That's the main advantage. It's when you try to control their shape that the muscles become harder and inevitably deform natural shape in some subtle way. When we do need a stronger contraction from a muscle for a more vigorous movement, ideally it will return to its naturally soft state immediately after the contraction.

We've all imitated a tin soldier from time to time—those jerky movements, like a mechanical man. The last thing you want is for your fingers to move like that as you play. But many of us have been taught a way of articulating that resembles nothing more than this mechanical jerkiness. In other cases it is a technical difficulty that will cause you to try too hard, leading to useless muscle contractions holding you in a position and again making your fingers move like tin soldiers.

If you could maintain the position naturally you would greatly reduce the difficulty. But instead you maintain it artificially, increasing the difficulty and then having to fight against that same difficulty. You are forced to try harder and harder—it becomes a vicious circle. Cultivating natural shape aims to reverse the direction of this vicious spiral. Softening muscle tonus allows freer movement, which in turn fosters yet softer tonus and so on.

Eliminate physical spasm preparations—maintain neutrality

> Step 3: Now go to play a chord on the piano. Did you notice that your hand *did* something? That it did not maintain that natural shape and tonus but went into spasm of some sort? This is what most of us do: we *prepare* to play the piano by establishing more

tension in the hand than we need. As I said, this superfluous tension intends to maintain the shape and structure needed to play with control. But that shape can only maintain *itself*. *You* can't maintain it effectively, or rather you can, but only by consciously not trying to! Ironically, this preparation *impedes* control by distorting our hand's natural shape and structure instead of maintaining it. This distortion or deformation of form hinders free action.

When I monitor my students in this, I can *always* catch them—they always do *something!* If you are attentive you too may be able to pick up on some of your unconscious habitual efforts, little tremors or micro-spasms of effortfulness resulting from attempts to articulate but which actually spoil the whole show. You should learn to play without any of that. All those preparatory efforts that deform the hand in any way necessitate a whole other set of counterbalancing muscular activities to maintain stability of structure. All these are needless and they in turn inhibit free, effective movement.

Step 4: To trick your mind here, pretend that the keyboard is a table or something, anything except a piano! You don't go into mini-spasm when you put your hand on a tabletop, do you? When you put your hand on key, can you maintain neutrality, touch the key just as naturally as you did your tabletop? We are not aiming for a state of deadness but rather an alive readiness, a neutrality that is *capable*. When you find that state, you'll recognize a certain physical feeling—this can be felt not only in the hand but all the way up your arm as well. With practice, this state, once established in the hand, can radiate back and up, suffusing your arm and eventually even your whole body with this equilibrated muscle tonus.

Only when you do not use effort or tension to keep your fingers shaped naturally while playing can they *feel* maximally, avail themselves of the maximum amount of sensory input. In fact you cannot hold them in that shape—the very act of trying to will always deform them from their natural 'at rest' position somehow. Only by letting them assume that shape can you succeed. Constantly 'make the soft' in the words of my T'ai Chi teacher. Try to find a way to move effectively without increasing muscle tonus from its natural minimum any more than is absolutely necessary.

Lift your finger still maintaining neutrality

> Step 5: With your fingers neutrally on their keys but not depressing them, lift your second finger a little. Can you do this without disturbing this all-pervading, pleasant neutrality we are cultivating? If you become really sensitive, you can even feel certain muscles in the forearm and upper arm activating slightly to lift this finger. How high can you lift without deforming anything, without triggering any of your old, effortful actions, sudden motions? Lift and then drop back to the key surface—do not depress the key. Don't curl or straighten it; just lift it.

Drop your finger back in

> Step 6: This time after lifting it, drop your finger back into the key: the note sounds. Is everything still OK? It is possible to maintain an absolute quietness in your hand and in all your fingers that did not play. Your whole finger-hand-arm assembly maintains its form like an alive statue: still, yet not stiff. The alive readiness we are cultivating means that although everything seems externally to lack movement, the inner state is one of rich movement, or rather, rich possibility for movement.

Application 36.2
NATURAL SHAPE II, ARM V: ROLE OF YOUR ARM

Inner activations of the upper arm

> Step 1: Continuing from the previous application, leave your hand on key, and after lifting your finger, when you let it drop in, try to sense an inner 'let-go', a release in your upper arm. Maybe your elbow even drops slightly. It is counterproductive to let it drop too much, as this again will increase a sense of impeded-ness or tension. There is a neutral middle ground, a position where the little muscle activations of the upper arm and forearm can flicker

down through the arm to the finger unimpeded.

Forearm rising to lift your finger

> Step 2: What is the effect of adding a levitation of the forearm in conjunction with your finger rising? Can you do this so it does not complicate matters but rather aid your finger? If your forearm now descends in parallel with your finger dropping in, it can aid your finger: but in no way can your arm movement replace or substitute for your finger's movement. This is *not* the same as the arm pumping we investigated in chapter 26, *The Sound of One Hand Clapping*. Here you must be clear that your finger is the main protagonist. Your arm moves just enough to help and not hinder the free activity of your finger, nothing more.

Thus so far we have defined two distinct domains of arm involvement: internal and external. Internally, the forearm and upper arm muscles are either activating or supporting the actual movement of the finger, while externally the arm's movement is only adjunct to the leading role of the finger.

> Step 3: Have each finger in turn play with or without the external aid of your arm. Clearly differentiate these two.

> Step 4: Can you now return to using your arm to join a succession of notes together, all the while *maintaining the natural shape of the fingers and hand?*

Application 36.3
NATURAL SHAPE III: HAND EXTENSION AND THE ARM

Special role of the thumb

I will describe this part of the exercise for your right hand; of course you should later try it with your left as well.

When doing application 36.1, did you notice your thumb posed some special problems? Is it because your thumb is directly attached to your wrist instead of being separated by the hand as the other fingers are? In any case, instead of treating this problematic construction of the thumb as an obstacle, let's try to turn it to our advantage.

> Step 1: Put your right hand on key, and now shift your weight very slightly to the inside, lifting the four fingers so that now your arm is lightly resting on the thumb. Notice that as you did this the thumb moved in *opposition* to your hand slightly: that is to say, it moved in slightly somewhere more underneath your fingers. Your hand closes slightly while the space between your thumb and your four fingers stays open. The sensation is that your thumb wants to move to the right, but its attempt to do so simply ends up pulling your hand to the left, because your thumb is anchored in its key and cannot move in space. Now your hand stands lightly on your thumb.

Extension without deformation

> Step 2: Again using your thumb as a fulcrum, now move it away from your hand: the movement of *reverse opposition*. Because it is standing on the thumb, your hand now opens, moving into extension, but you should maintain the natural shape of your fingers! Did you inadvertently splay them or extend them? Try again, this time seeing how far you can extend your hand without deforming your fingers. Can you discover that slight adjustment, that release in your upper arm that can facilitate a wider extension of your hand without undue tension, so that any change of finger shape takes place 'naturally'?

Arm helps in this

> Step 3: To play any wider interval *legato*, it is possible to extend your hand across the span *without* distorting the natural finger shape we are so assiduously cultivating. Instead of leaving your arm and hand motionless and stretching your finger, have your arm initiate the shift of your finger. Almost your whole hand shifts as

a unit along with your arm, but your 'standing finger' (your playing finger, the finger already on key) remains behind, maintaining
connection with your anchor point. The finger designated to play
the next note maintains its natural shape as your hand and arm
shifts it to its new position.

Imagine that you are picking up a briefcase and putting it down somewhere
else. But in this case the briefcase is one of your fingers or your thumb: the
next digit to play its note. Your arm serves to orient that digit in space. Using
the playing digit as a stabilizing fulcrum, your arm can do virtually all the
work of placing the next finger on its note. Thus the tendency for your new
playing finger to distort its shape is reduced to an absolute minimum.

Application 36.4
NATURAL SHAPE IV: LEGATO REVIEW

Review legato to increase dynamic volume

Initially we cultivate a heightened delicacy of touch to learn natural hand shape.
But we will need natural shape in *forte* as well. For the development of dynamic
strength, while retaining the advantages of natural shape, we go back to the
drawing board to examine more minutiae of finger-hand function.

> Step 1: Take one finger as your standing finger, and to make this
> especially interesting, let's make it your fourth. Let's examine *how*
> you are standing on this problematic finger. By the end of this
> exercise I hope to establish that your fourth finger is no less strong
> or capable than its partners—that all your fingers really *are* equal,
> that the generally perceived inequalities stem not from the actual
> structure of the hand but from our imperfect understanding of
> that structure's function!

More weight pressure while maintaining neutrality

> How much weight can you exert on your fourth as it stands on
> key? You should be able to feel strong pressure on the key while

maintaining neutrality in the rest of your mechanism. You should feel as if you could put a 50-kilo weight on your top knuckle, the metacarpal-phalangeal joint of your fourth finger, and that finger's natural shape would maintain total integrity. Not only that, but even that this integrity would be maintained almost without muscular effort. In other words, it is the natural structure of the bones in proper alignment that bears the brunt of that weight. You should be able to move your wrist forward and up, reverse it back and down, with your appropriately curved fourth continuously bearing the weight and functioning as a fulcrum.

All superfluous effort further up the arm (and we normally employ huge amounts!) should be eradicated. Soften, let go of that extra effort in the biceps/triceps, clarify that it is your *finger* doing the work (work in this case means structural work more than muscular). All the rest of my fingers maintain their neutrality and independence. I can check this by playing another note lightly, let's say with my second finger, while my fourth continues to bear weight:

Discrimination of touches: simultaneous feather and pressure touches

Step 2: First, let your second finger gently touch its note. Feather-touch it. Do you notice how strong your tendency to do more than you need to? While maintaining the fourth finger pillar of strength, fool around a bit with the second finger's key. Can you sense the weight of the hammer by jiggling the key, sensing how the hammer floats up in the air off the key and then falls back down on it as you jog the key gently? You should feel as strong a contrast as possible between the tremendous pressure, weight exerted on the fourth finger and the delicate feather-like touch of your second. Just be sure that the pressure on your fourth clearly originates from your arm's structure and not from muscular effort. Here your fourth finger is of course the *yang* finger, your second the *yin*.

Gradual increase, decrease of pressure

Step 3: While your fourth continues to be the standing or *yang* finger, gradually increase the pressure of your second fingertip on its key to the maximum, then reduce it to a minimum again, all the while maintaining natural shape in both digits.[1] Try to perceive as many gradients of pressure as possible. The more detailed your sensation of the process of gradually increasing and decreasing weight, the more learning.

Reversibility in yin *finger's touch*

The goal of this part of the exercise is to clarify the difference between structural support (a state of stability) and movement. When we play we tend to invest too much energy in the playing finger, releasing the standing finger prematurely and lending the playing finger the quality of structural firmness too soon as well. Thus we lose our legato. If we here cultivate the quality of *reversibility*[2] we can clarify and quantify the exact amount of effort needed to move the key and not overdo it.

Towards incorporation into passagework

Step 4: Take a look at the attack of your second finger. Even if you play with a good solid *forte*, the amount of tension in the finger (take your other hand and check: touch the upper inner flesh of your second) should be a good deal less than that of the fourth, the standing finger. Reverse the direction of movement to ensure this is the case. That is, after playing your healthy *f*, observe the process of change your playing finger undergoes in order to remove itself from the key. You should not have to reduce effort drastically in order to 'make your retreat'. If you play with just the amount of effort needed, it's an easy affair to change the direction of your impulse. Continuing to stand on the fourth, expand your explorations. Trill between 1 and 2, play com-

---

[36 1] Refer back to illustration 10.8, *Sensation of the Tetrahedrom Maintained in Curved-Finger Legato*
[36 2] See the last section of chapter 5, *A Meditation on the Inner Workings of Movement.*

binations of 1, 2 and 3, always maintaining a clear and vast difference between the pylon fourth and the individuated others.

Transfer of pylon function to the yin *finger*

Step 5, the crucial final step: We are almost ready to approach some of the passagework in this Scherzo. But first, try easing off your fourth finger, allowing the next finger in the chain of eighth notes to become the pylon. Most important here is that you never for an instant lose the feeling of total contact with the keyboard. If you observe the little mounds at the tops of your fingers, where they join your hand, the hummock of your fourth finger has been exceptionally high and pronounced all through this exercise. To ensure continuous complete contact, simply make sure that the hummock of the *next* finger in the chain of eighth notes rises to an equally high level, before you begin to let the fourth finger's hummock ease off.

Remember, it is most important that the pylon finger maintain its natural shape, but this is also what we most easily lose track of.

Differentiation of yin/yang *energies between different voices*

That instant in time when a finger shifts from being *yin* to *yang* is critical. At first the transition is very difficult to manage to perfection. In mastering a perfect legato we are forced to tackle this problem head on. But there is an easier, more indirect approach through which we can familiarize ourselves with the whole phenomenon of *yin/yang* transition. The next chapter looks at this intermediate step, providing a chance for you to acquire this crucial skill under less intimidating conditions.

37 Using the *Yin*/*Yang* Finger Phenomenon in Orchestration

Yin finger retains all the structural qualities of a yang finger

Discrimination between *yin* and *yang* fingers can enrich not only the realm of singing legato and melodic inflection but of orchestration as well. The thing to remember is that a *yin* finger retains all the structural qualities of a *yang* finger, only without the pressure. There is total contact with the keybed and a legato that is perfectly felt across the knuckle-hummocks (metacarpal-phalangeal joints). The only difference is that the finger feels totally empty instead of full. And it's not dead—the *yin* finger stays vital even in its emptiness.

Take any instance (of which of course there are literally thousands in the repertoire) of two voices in one hand—one main and one subsidiary, and we have the perfect opportunity to employ the complementary opposition of *yin* and *yang* in our fingers. We will look at a few less technically demanding examples so you can achieve absolute clarity of execution more quickly.

Application 37.1
NATURAL SHAPE V, ORCHESTRATION I: SEPARATION OF *YIN* AND *YANG* IN LEGATO

Yin/yang *contrast easier to feel when no transition from one to the other required*

> Step 1: In the right hand of Schumann's *Fast zu ernst* ('Almost Too Serious') from his Kinderszenen, Op. 15, each melodic note must be held while an inner part 16th accompaniment note sounds and is released. Here you can experience the *yin*/*yang* contrast *without* having

to worry about transforming your *yin* finger into a *yang*. Your *yang* finger stands firmly all the while, generating your singing main melodic tone, while your *yin* fingers just brush their notes and then release again. However, remember *yin* must maintain its structural connection, not losing contact and not becoming rigid either.

Example 37.1: Schumann: Fast zu ernst, *mm. 1-8*

Metacarpal-phalangeal hummocks formed by function not force

I have described drawing a lobster claw on my scores reminding myself to open my thumb-forefinger oval, then later realizing how I needed to maintain not a rigid position but a function. So it is here with our metacarpal-phalangeal hummocks. They must be maintained *in the context of fluid movement all around them,* above and below them. Only then does this become a useful technique in playing. These hummocks must be formed by *function,* not force! The finger/hand/arm must find a way of moving that allows those knuckle mounds to grow and maintain themselves naturally!

Strange feeling as if triceps activates finger

The feeling that your knuckle-hummock is an isolated point of stability surrounded by pools of liquid, fluid, moving muscles can be so extreme that it really *does* feel like your triceps moves your fingers. In reality your triceps only stabilizes arm position, but everything below it is so liquefied (except the points of stability at your knuckle and fingertip), that there is nothing solid anywhere in your arm that would block the feeling that the triceps is acting directly on your finger. It's a very strange feeling. See if you can find it.

Yin/yang *in Brahms*

Let's turn now to some Brahms Intermezzi for more stress-free examples of *yin/yang* interaction.

Step 2: In Op. 117 #1, we have all struggled to have the soprano ostinato bell-note accompaniment ring with sweet tone yet still sound subordinate to the lead melody underneath it. Here again, if you've managed to find a total *yin/yang* dichotomy of function, you'll have found your voicing as well.

Example 37.2: Brahms: Intermezzo in E flat major, Op. 117 #1, *mm. 1-2*

In the middle section of Op. 117 #3 we have it even easier! Here the bell-note is the lead (*yang*) melody, the light broken chord tones underneath constitute the subordinate *yin* voice. Perhaps we should have looked at this one first.

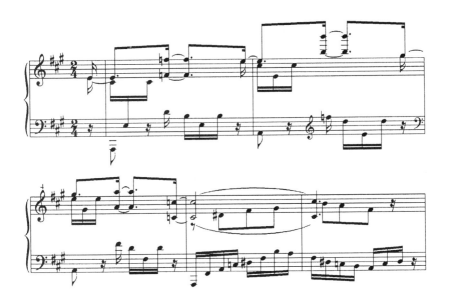

Example 37.3: Brahms: Intermezzo in C sharp minor, Op. 117 #3, *mm. 46-50*

Step 3: In this example stand on your right hand *yang* fifth finger (or left hand thumb), and walk between the subordinate chord tones like a kung fu initiate on rice paper (it must not break). You play the inner voice with a feather-legato touch, which is actually nothing more than one *yin* finger after another—there is no *yang* whatsoever. But remember, that series of *yin* fingers maintains their sense of an absolute legato connection not only from key bottom to key bottom but also across your metacarpal-phalangeal ridge.

In Op. 118 #1, the division between *yin* and *yang* is more distinct because for the most part each hand is required to do only *yin* or *yang*, not both simultaneously.

Example 37.4: Brahms: Intermezzo in C major, Op. 118 #1, *mm. 1-4*

Step 4: Basically play all eighth notes with a feather-legato *yin* touch, all longer note values are played *yang*—except the latter part of the sigh motive, which is always somewhat *yin* regardless the length of duration.

Thus notice how in the opening measures a dialogue is set up between two lead voices, the sighing exclamation of the right hand soprano answered or challenged by the strong, masculine brass of the left hand. All the while the harmony is outlined in eighth notes that run amongst the main protagonists ***ppp***. There are two orchestrational difficulties here. One is to have the soprano and baritone voices clearly *speak* to each other rather than sounding like only one voice. This is achieved through articulation, agogic delay and dynamic shaping of the sigh. The other

difficulty is to keep the eighth notes clearly 'accompanal' (hey, a new word!). They must be kept way down in dynamic *without losing clarity of voice*. It is here that *yin* fingerwork retaining physical integrity of structure can create both the necessary clarity *and* the dynamic differentiation.[1]

Example 37.5: Brahms: Intermezzo in F minor, Op. 118 #4, *mm. 1-4—practice dynamics*

Here *yin* and *yang* function are completely separated in terms of the part writing. The difficulty lies solely in the simultaneity of attacks—generally on each beat you have two *yins* and a *yang* sounding together. Again, the more clearly you differentiate *yin* and *yang*, the more effectively you can maximize dynamic differences. Notice also that if *yang*'s attack occurs a microsecond before *yin*'s (as it indeed should), it doesn't harm the sound at all.

Where else in the repertoire can you employ the differentiation between *yin* and *yang* to achieve perfection of voice discrimination? Well, how about in Beethoven for instance?

---

[1] For more on Op. 118 #1, see chapter 41, *Pressing and Holding in Legato.*

38 NATURAL FINGER SHAPE AND TONUS IN CHORDS

Beethoven's Sonata in E flat major, Op. 7

Just as natural finger shape is an integral aspect of effective passagework and dynamic discrimination between voices, it can also assure fine orchestral tone in situations such as the chordal solemnity in the second movement of Beethoven's Sonata, Op. 7.

Example 38.1: Beethoven: Sonata in E flat major, Op. 7,
2nd mvt., mm. 1-8

In this deeply expressive, stately slow movement, the key problem is not only how to keep the melodic line singing in such a slow tempo but how to maintain a truly orchestral sound. Just as in fast running passages, here in the slow, chordal orchestral chorale it is crucial to keep your fingers naturally curved—in precisely the same shape they assume when at rest.

Natural finger function leads to blossoming sound

In this way you can maintain your orchestral sound—it truly blossoms, and even in a chord of eight or more tones there is a sense of each part contribut-

ing to the total *gestalt*. Why does this happen? What is this strange phenomenon of unexpected blossoming tone?

Enlarged capacity to sense

When your fingers are free from extra tonus or effort, as I said, their capacity to feel is improved immensely. They *sense* the weight of the key, they sense the path of descent, they sense their relationship to each other, and they make a thousand micro-adjustments that could not possibly be made by your consciously guiding mind. They feel, and *they* do the job—if you let them— by not burdening them with effort that freezes them, cripples them in fact. Your mind's job is simply to monitor that you are maintaining your fingers' freedom—you are the guardian of their capacity to feel and to function to their full ability. They must be able to make these micro-adjustments that help produce a multi-dimensionality of tone. It is this that can give chords a kaleidoscopic tonal quality.

The strange phenomenon of increased sustained-ness

When you play like this, the duration of a note's tone seems to be lengthened, yet it does not actually become longer in metronomic time. It is a magical effect, and seemingly inexplicable, but it *happens!* Somehow the fingers' improved capacity to feel even the vibrations of the instrument being transmitted to them through the keys, also allows them to balance the harmonic parts in such a way that the natural sustaining power of the instrument is allowed to manifest. As well, when finger tension is reduced, your ears' capacity to *hear* is increased proportionally. There is less distractive activity in the brain, more chance for your perception to function at full capacity. 'Making the soft' also allows you to hear all orchestra parts. Strangely enough, the change in your hearing has an objective effect on your sound that can even be perceived by an impartial listener.

Arthur Rubinstein described the fundamental prerequisite for him to play well thus wise: he must be able to feel the vibration of the instrument traveling physically through his fingers and up into his body. To my mind, for this fundamental prerequisite to be fulfilled, two preliminary conditions had to be in place:

> 1) Vital, alive activity in his playing apparatus caused his instrument to vibrate in an alive, buzzing, shimmering, humming way.

2) Maintaining a naturally balanced muscle tonus throughout his body, allowing him to sense the vibrations that his activity was causing. The more specificity and exactitude we can bring to the way we feel the key itself, the more we too can succeed in this process.

Degree of sensitivity corollary to degree of color

Many fingers descending simultaneously can either make a dead block of sound that lacks individuation of color, or a block of sound that shimmers, vibrates, resonates. Your tone varies between these two in direct proportion to the degree of finger sensitivity.

Increased variety of articulation

Another benefit of this is that we can overcome our habit of using the finger as a stick that hits the key, and have it *play* instead. If your finger is softer and more sensitive there will be more dimensions to its flexibility as well. We can use a wide variety of finger strokes according to the articulative and sonic necessities of the situation. Do these now, trying to feel as clear and graphic a difference in sensation between each articulation.

Application 38.1
ARTICULATIONS I

1) The fingertip points straight down, the whole finger rises a little then the tip, continuing to point down goes *in* and down to the bottom of the key. It does not curl further but stays pointing down. This I call the hammer action of the finger.

2) The fingertip 'cat-scratches', actually curling towards the palm to make the note sound.

3) The 'cat-scratch' taken to the extreme: the fingertip travels a path that encompasses a 180-degree arc, leaving the key by the back door so to speak and ending up pressed tightly not into your palm but rather into the crease right under your knuckle. This is for extreme

staccato and fast repetitions using 3-2-1 or 4-3-2-1 fingerings.

4) The finger lies totally flat in the key, palm lower than the board, wrist maximally low but *not pressed down*. Finger rises a little, pointing straight out somewhere slightly above the horizontal and not curling at all, then the whole underside of the finger lays itself along the entire length of the key, or at least as much of it as it can cover. This is 'flat fingers', used for maximum *cantilena*, the absolutely juiciest singing tone possible.[1]

Note in these first four that your finger departs from its natural shape, and sometimes radically so. But can you at least maintain some relationship to the feeling of natural shape as you manage these departures? Can you continue to sense a softness in the flesh of your finger, to make these articulations without totally rigidifying things?

5) The finger is only very moderately curved,[2] as it is when hanging at rest. When you raise it and have it stroke into the key it maintains this slight curve—this is the most natural movement imaginable and one of the most useful, and yet it seems to be the one we use the least at the piano. It seems we always need to mess around with things somehow. I am amazed at how often I will be touching a student's hand, monitoring it, and even if it approaches the vicinity of the keyboard I can feel its internal tension increasing. There seems to be this chronic need to *prepare* to play— as if the hand was not perfectly capable of playing in its natural condition, its natural state of muscular tonus![3]

Quality of playing not hitting

Of all these items, (5) most usefully illustrates *playing* rather than hitting. To do this you must keep a relaxed finger—thus it can *feel*. Your experience is that the flesh of your finger itself does the work, rather than some other parts of your mechanism manipulating your finger somehow to make it move. Of course, muscles all the way up the arm are also involved in this relaxed, fleshy

---

[1] See chapter 47, *Flat Fingers*.
[2] For the distinction between curved and curled see *healthy finger curling* in chapter 7, *Form Follows Function*.
[3] Remember *eliminate physical spasm preparations* in chapter 36, *The Natural Hand in Passagework*.

finger type of playing, but your experience is that your finger alone does it. The sound you get from playing this way is very personal and warm. It speaks as a human voice.

But, when your finger stiffens, its own muscles maintain a type of rigidity and other muscles must be called to greater efforts to move your finger. Now you can *feel* the involvement of other parts, and they are manipulating a rigid digit that I call a stick not a finger!

Looseness prerequisite to movement, fingers move in playing chords as well

I cannot stress this enough: do not hit the instrument with a stick. Play it! For this you need movement within your finger itself. Your finger cannot have internal movement if it is stiff. Let it be in its natural shape. Let each finger preserve its independence even as they descend simultaneously to play a chord.

Application 38.2

NATURAL SHAPE VI: USING AN INCREASED DYNAMIC TO CLARIFY NATURAL SHAPE

Place your fingers on key and maintaining natural shape, play a note *forte*. Can you feel how maintaining natural shape allows the shock of impact to be felt through each joint in the progression of bones up through the structure? If your shape is really perfect, the shock will have no deleterious effect. And so your shape *stays* that way—there is no resulting deformation, misalignment or warping.

Natural shape plus an exactly placed shock dramatically increases the kinesthetic experience of the movement with no negative side effects. Joints are felt much as more alive with no increased effort. The richness of a sudden shock does *not* equal increased stress or effort. On the contrary! It allows you to feel those correct alignments more graphically, therefore to cultivate them more effectively.[4] Again, here we arrive at a flexibility that is effective, not so loose as to become non-functional.

[38 4] This is a similar process to the sensory invigoration of the fingers in fingertapping—see chapter 24.

With your finger in this state it is possible for it to move without inhibiting itself. For maximal richness in tone, even when playing a multi-note chord, use your fingers not just your arm or hand.

Application 38.3
NATURAL SHAPE VII, ORCHESTRATION II: ORCHESTRATION OF CHORDAL TEXTURES

Let's take the first right hand chord of the slow movement of Sonata, Op. 7.

Step 1: First rest all your fingers on key. Then while holding the note E with your right fifth finger, play C and G together (using thumb and third), *using your fingers*. Your second and fourth fingers remain resting on their keys neutrally, ensuring that 1 and 3 move independently of them. Can fingers 1, 3 and 5 play their chord without 2 and 4 either popping up or inadvertently pressing down their keys in sympathy? Can 2 and 4 stay truly neutral, merely brushing the key surface, resting upon it?

Example 38.2: Beethoven: Sonata in E flat major, Op. 7, *2nd mvt.—finger individuation practice*

Absence of deformation a prerequisite to effective movement

This is real finger independence, and we cultivate it for a very good reason. Notice that if you play with natural finger shape and tonus, and then don't do anything additional after the keys have been successfully depressed, your fingers stay there by themselves. Natural finger curve creates natural hand structure and function. When they stay there by themselves rather than being held

there by you-know-who, then they can still move. But when you stiffen to maintain your hand structure, it's game over! Your fingers are no longer independent, and they can no longer move (in the true sense of the word). Your orchestral tone is kaput.

Arm aids the constant miniscule shifting of the hand, increased amounts of tone

> Step 2: Now add an arm movement synchronous to your fingers'. Your arm rises and falls slightly, in unison with your fingers' movement. It is as if your forearm is a lung, filling slightly, rising as it breathes in, and floating down again as it gently expels its air. Make this forearm movement as small and as subtle as can be. Also take care that you do not get distracted and stop your fingers' individuated action!
>
> Check: are your neutral second and fourth fingers continuously resting on key? Is there never any air space between finger pad and ivory? You should be able to do an individual finger action with no help from your arm, *or* with your arm gently rising up and falling in, in tandem with your fingers. You will choose one or the other of these depending on the type of tone you want.
>
> Step 3: Arm movement can also help the shift to a new position. Remember to take care not to deform a finger in reaching for a new note. When moving to each new chord, pick up your hand with your arm and *help* your finger arrive at its note without deforming itself![5]
>
> Also take care to stay physically soft even in *forte* playing.
>
> Step 4: Your finger movements are more vigorous in *forte* playing, but they still maintain and generate your structure. If you can stay muscularly free and not rigidify, you assure yourself richness of tone. 'Making the soft' even in *forte* may at first seem impossible to you, but rest assured there is a way to do it, and the tonal rewards in discovering how are truly gratifying.

---

[385] Refer back to *hand extension* in chapter 36, *The Natural Hand in Passagework*.

Dynamic shading of chord for orchestral tone

The final ingredient in our recipe for orchestrally rich tone is dynamic differentiation.

Step 5: Your fifth finger plays E *mf* while the under two notes of the chord sound *p*. If you maintain natural finger position and muscle tonus you can do this exactly and *voila*, there's your blossoming orchestral tone!

Note that as the upper note's key must travel faster in order to produce a larger dynamic, its attack arrives a split second sooner than its harmonizing underlings. This phenomenon actually works to our advantage: the late *pp* attack of the under notes is masked by the more resonant sound of the lead voice, and the sense of orchestrative differentiation is enhanced.

Minimize movement to maximize sensitivity, exactitude

How does this philosophy apply in the opening allegro movement of Sonata Op. 7?

Step 7: Take the initial left hand repeated notes. Find a hand position where your third finger and thumb rest on E flat without depressing the key and both maintain their naturally soft tonus. Find the minimum hand movement needed to shift so that now your second finger and thumb rest on the key surface. Do all this, even up to speed, without playing anything. You have most likely been using too big a movement for these repeated notes. In this exercise, without having to play anything you are now instead free to explore the sensation of simply placing naturally soft and naturally curved fingers on key and moving very little, almost not at all. Find the arrangement of your hand that most facilitates this.

Example 38.3: Beethoven: Sonata in E flat major, Op. 7, 1st mvt., mm. 1-2

Step 8: When you have mastered this and try to play, hardly change anything at all. Just a tiny bit more movement is needed to make the key actually descend, the note sound. You should basically maintain the natural curve and minimal movement you just now so carefully cultivated.

The quality of movement we're looking for is indeed paradoxical: loose but precise, free yet exact. Only this will give you the sound you want.

Application 38.4
NATURAL SHAPE VIII: FAST, EFFORTLESS PASSAGEWORK

Drum your fingers on the desk

How about the turning figures, the first triplets in the right hand at measure 5? Do you remember in school when teacher was boring you to tears and you would drum your fingers on your desk to pass the time? Little did you know that you were then cultivating the exact qualities of natural curve and natural tonus that would later serve you so well in your endeavors at the keyboard!

Step 1: Try drumming your fingers on the fallboard now, and then open the piano again and preserve that quality of movement in your triplets. This is another way of cultivating feather legato.

Example 38.4: Beethoven: Sonata in E flat major, Op. 7, *1st mvt. mm., 5-12*

Step 2: To avoid the feeling of every individual finger working so hard, and to cultivate the effortless flow of light singing notes, try playing the triplets much too quickly. When you have found that flow, slow the tempo back down to normal but keep flowing physically—do not spoil it by over-articulating. Don't interfere! Learn this at a very soft dynamic, where it is easiest to achieve.

Step 3: Now can you keep that quality of touch while increasing your volume? Can you increase volume without increasing effort or strain? Yes, you *can* if you have fully understood the feeling and logic behind natural finger shape.

'Making the soft' physically while playing does *not* mean neglecting musical content, playing flat, lifeless phrases. Use this physical tool to better employ all dynamics, variations of touch and musical elements. To reiterate: when they 'make the soft', your fingers can *feel*. And they can join one key to another far better than your linearly thinking mind can! Let your fingers do the walking *and* the talking!

39 Maintaining Natural Finger Shape in Scales

This lesson was given to a remedial student, an adult whose problems with hand pain were so severe that he had to take time off work. I went into great detail for a number of reasons, most importantly that I not force him forward at a rate he couldn't handle. I hope this detail of description will prove useful for others as well.

'Don't swat!'

Swatting is a sudden movement that lacks control, refinement, discrimination. Swatting indicates a lack of involvement of all physical parts in appropriate proportion. It disturbs, and does not allow the hand-platform to maintain neutrality. While one finger after another in a chain of scale notes provides pylon-like support instead of the no-contact of uncontrolled swatting, the 'hand-platform' is the thing they're supporting. Remember the oil rig in chapter 27, *Legato vs. Finger Articulation*. As you move from one note to another, the 'hand-platform' moves as well. It must do this in a neutral manner, always providing the centered, effort-free point from which the fingers drop in. This will happen when the arm breathes into the position.

The system of air circulation in Chi Gung

The Chinese physio-philosophical system, *Chi Gung*, conceives an additional complete circulatory system in the body, one that Western medicine has never dreamed of. In addition to the nerves, blood vessels and digestive tract, which our anatomists have had no trouble discovering, *Chi Gung* envisions a system circulating air through all the limbs, not just the trachea and lungs! This anatomical structure has somehow escaped the attention of our medical experts! *Chi Gung* maintains there are air holes in the palms of the hands and the soles of the feet, and channels leading from these holes to the *D'an Tien*, the body's

center of gravity. Fresh air or 'gas' enters through these holes and stale 'gas' is eliminated from them.

"Ridiculous", you say, and I must admit this does seem very strange to us. But something very useful results from simply attempting to sense the existence of this non-existent system. The very process of trying to perceive something so subtle that for all intents and purposes we know it isn't there, causes a reduction of muscular effort and an increase in physical sensitivity that is in itself alone very beneficial.[1]

Application 39.1
NATURAL SHAPE IX: *CHI GUNG* AT THE PIANO

How can you put this to good use at the piano?

> Step 1: Imagine the air hole to be under your wrist instead of your palm. Then any downward forearm motion can become an out breath, all rising motion an in breath. Experience your forearm as a lung, expanding upwards and contracting downwards as it fills and empties itself of air. It is important that you don't 'breathe' too deeply! It's a subtle movement—your wrist stays very close to its point of neutrality. The smaller your wrist's 'breathing' movement, the more softening of your arm muscles is possible. Lending this quality of breathing to the series of movements discussed below will help cultivate the physical quality we are looking for.

Subtle body involvement in 'arm breathing'

Now back to the hand-platform, which in order to maintain its neutrality must be guided from above. We tend unconsciously to employ a slight effort in our standard 'elbow rounding out to the side' movement, an effort that unbeknownst to us prevents this subtle arm breathing from taking place.

> Step 2: To facilitate this subtle breathing, have your elbow relax and glide *in* rather than hold itself to the outside. Or else, when going

---

[39.1] See chapter 60, *The Masterworks as Expressions of Perfect Knowledge* for similar results from praying.

over the thumb in arpeggios, your elbow can glide forward and out, letting the finger passing over your thumb arrive at its key with absolutely no effort and no deformation of its naturally curved shape. This looks like your elbow alone is doing it, but this elbow 'let go' will happen most wonderfully when there is a Feldenkrais-like involvement all the way through your body. Your body is not trying to help; its involvement is effortless yet alive. Your pelvis won't necessarily move but there will be the feeling of subtle connection, of *alive sensation*, all the way from your pelvis through your ribs, which themselves feel involved, to your shoulders and down through your arm.

Remember, to help keep your hand and fingers in their natural curve, have your arm make something like a very slight out breath as you approach the keyboard. Approach the board in this nice way to avoid the effortful stretching that you automatically have been indulging in. (These 'visualizations' were given as an aid to activate my student's sensing function, to counteract a very high level of habitual chronic contraction.)

Application 39.2

NATURAL SHAPE X: EXTENSION WITHOUT DEFORMATION

Proximal interphalangeal joint reaches for the sky

Earlier while standing on your thumb you reached for the sky with your fingertips.[2] This was to activate your fingers, wake them up, get them moving. Now we need to refine that, because this kind of extreme reaching is causing a deformation of form we want to avoid. Your fingers were dead, but now, although you've woken them up very nicely, they're deforming themselves in your overexertions to move them.

Step 1: Instead, still standing on your thumb, reach for the sky with your top finger joint only, the proximal interphalangeal joint immedi-

[2] See chapter 13, *Thumb Pushups: The Hand as Suspension Spring*

ately below your knuckle. Try and touch the ceiling with this joint, but only to the extent you can without straining or stretching. This is a natural extension rather than a stretching. It remains a functional extension as long as all your physical apparatus *behind* the hand is participating in a released way as well. Your forearm-lung expands, breathes in, rises slightly as your proximal interphalangeal reaches for the ceiling.[3]

Opening up without 'reaching'—no deformation of natural shape

Step 2: Approaching the keyboard, now play the first note E flat in the scale of E flat major, right hand. Your third finger plays without deforming its natural curve.

Step 3: Your arm will now guide your hand-platform by moving outward or gliding, almost sinking outwards, until your thumb is touching F. Your thumb has not 'reached', it has not deformed itself in any way. Your forearm has rotated slightly to help place your thumb; this rotation as well does not deform your thumb in any way, and none of your other fingers distort themselves either.

Step 4: As your thumb plays F, all your fingers maintain that feeling of free, natural, loose curved-ness that they have when you walk down the street, and your hand maintains its natural structure.

Application 39.3
NATURAL SHAPE XI: FLUTTER-FLIP EXERCISE

Let's digress for a moment. How can we best learn to play moving our fingers but maintaining their natural shape? Here's an unusual exercise to instill the strange feeling of utterly free, seemingly contraction-less movement in your fingers.

Step 1: Hold your hand horizontally, and have the proximal phalange, the one closest to your hand, remain horizontal as well. Allow only

---

[3] For an illustration of this movement aided by an imaginary string, see application #42.3: Thumb VI—*Interdependence of Thumb and Fingers*.

your finger's tip and its middle phalange to hang down. In other words, you lightly curve the medial and distal phalanges down, but keep the proximal one straight.

Now we're ready for this weird sensation:

Step 2: Relax this finger to the point of total passivity while maintaining this unusual shape as much as you can. Use one of the fingers of your other hand to flip the tip of this passive finger. Do this very rapidly. Now the passive fingertip can flutter back and forth incredibly quickly, loosely. Flutter flutter flip flip—that weird incredibly light and empty feeling—there's no inhibition or impediment to movement in your passive finger. Leaving your finger this loose when it plays helps it keep its natural shape.

Illustration 39.1: Flutter-flip your fingertip

Application 39.4
NATURAL SHAPE XII: DON'T SWIVEL IN SCALES

Now back to our E flat major scale.

> Step 1: After your thumb plays F your arm continues to facilitate the orientation of the hand-platform in space so that now your second can drop in to note G. Here there is a crucial imperative: To get from F to G, don't swivel your hand! Here again rotation provides a desirable alternative to swivelling. Here rotation plus a certain quality of finger function cures an awkward, inefficient swivelling habit. Instead of swivelling, feel your thumb extending, opening, so that your hand-platform moves to the right but maintains its orientation in space towards the keyboard—the angle doesn't change. Instead of swivelling to the outside and reaching for the next note (a common habit), relax your arm in, your hand naturally rotates (a small movement of supination) as a result, and your thumb opens *without* your other fingers stretching. Opening your thumb facilitates a shift of your whole hand assembly to the right, while the angle between your hand and forearm does not change—no swivelling!

Illustration 39.2: Open-thumb lateral hand shift instead of swivelling

Step 2: Then play A flat with your third, B flat with your fourth, all without any 'reaching' or stretching. This is how to extend rather than stretch. Now you are ready for another 'thumb under', which again will be achieved through a combination of lateral arm glide and a small movement of pronation.

All this applies for your hand moving to the outside, away from the center of the keyboard. Thus your left hand would do this in E flat major descending.

Step 7: On the way back towards the center of the keyboard (descending in your right hand, ascending in your left), the main thing is to get your finger (either your third or fourth) over your thumb without reaching or stretching, again without deforming your hand or fingers and while maintaining optimal support in both thumb and finger as your finger plays. Again it is a combination of thumb functionality and arm guidance that can make all this possible.

Application 39.5
NATURAL SHAPE XIII: ARPEGGIOS

In arpeggios we are confronted with the same 'issues' only here in exaggerated form. The function of your thumb is even more crucial, the tendency to 'reach' has even a greater preponderance to return and assert itself. Your arm guiding, sinking, slipping, sliding, gliding will again provide the means to maintain that wonderful hand/finger neutrality, which is anything but dead or indifferent. This is a neutrality that is simply the absence of over-involvement, inappropriate or counterproductive involvement. This is a neutrality that must *precede functionality*, which facilitates and enhances the right operation of your hand and fingers.

Some swivelling now allowed

Step 1: In arpeggios as you play outwards (ascending in your right hand, descending in your left) it appears that there now *must* be some small amount of swivelling, but again reduce the tendency to swivel to a minimum by incorporating a small rotation, and help that out with a lateral arm movement. Thus you avoid an inadvertent return

to the non-functional habit you had earlier! For instance, when you put your thumb under, notice the angle at which your hand is now. Then try to keep that angle constant as your arm, through lateral movement and rotation, transfers your hand to a place where your second finger is over its note, effortlessly and without deformation. You should almost succeed.

Arm begins shift as soon as possible

Step 2: When your thumb has played and your hand is opening in order to place your second finger, it's not only your hand that moves. Already your forearm is supinating and falling in as well. Do *not* leave this compound arm movement to the last moment, but initiate it as early as possible. Then having played your second finger, begin to pronate and shift your arm as early as possible to prepare your next 'thumb under'. Don't get into a situation where you're on your third finger, ready to shift your thumb under, but you have not yet shifted your arm. Already have done it—be where you need to be before you need to be there!

Step 3: Going towards the center of the keyboard in arpeggios, notice how your arm helps you to go over your thumb, so that your third or fourth reaches its note without stretching. Then simply keep that angle as you continue on and let rotation, not swivelling, handle the other necessary changes in hand orientation. Your arm simply follows your hand's lead, travelling laterally down (or up for your left hand) the board and rotating this way and that (your elbow moving in and out slightly) to accommodate the positioning of your thumb and fingers.

This concludes our section on natural finger shape. Did you notice that hand strength and function, live finger articulation, arm involvement and rotation all cropped up in here? Natural finger shape—a continuous instantaneous 'returning to the soft'—is a quality that ideally suffuses everything we do. As you explore the rest of this book or review previous sections, always keep the soft aliveness of natural finger shape in mind. Notice how it can always improve both your facility and your tonal possibilities at the keyboard.

X

SOME OTHER TOUCH
STRATEGIES AND COMBINATIONS

40 Synthesis of Various Strands of Thought

Towards exceptional power, accuracy and color

The five main categories we have covered so far comprise at least a rough preliminary framework for a new theory of physical mechanics at the keyboard. But of course a complete theory will include many more features. This section begins to flesh the picture out, taking a look at a few special cases that can generally be related back to one or more aspects of our framework. First let's go over the essentials of T'ai Chi walking as translated to the keyboard.

Application 40.1
Legato IX: T'ai Chi Walking Review

This review of T'ai Chi walking links the most salient points on hand structure and function to the role of the arm in legato.

The essence of a stable hand structure can be discovered thus: stand on one finger so firmly that all your other fingers just dangle from your hand assembly—wiggle or flutter them with impunity. Your next finger can drop in with no pressing; you can exactly control the degree of 'attack'. Then this finger becomes the standing finger; the next portion of the melodic strand now drops in. 'Firm up, drop, shift'. 'Consolidate, shift, drop in, swing onward'. Whatever formulation works for you. Your arm facilitates this by flowing with the hand, following it passively yet attentively.

Remember the corollary in T'ai Chi, the whole new organization in walking, one that frees and empowers your center of gravity.

To review: stand with your feet shoulder width apart, pointed slightly inward so that your third toes are parallel. Sink down slightly, bending your knees but keeping your torso erect, leaning neither forward nor back. If you check in the mirror you'll probably find at first you can't even do *this* well! But it's an important point: here your torso needs to be balanced so that it does not inadvertently exert any force or pressure that would disturb proper structural alignment, just as your arm needs to maintain a balanced, capable neutral alignment in legato.

Now comes the crucial moment: lift your left foot and place it on the ground a comfortable, moderate distance in front of you, at a 45-degree angle from your right foot. Do this without shifting your weight! Aha! Your right leg should be able to function like the suspension springs on a car, bobbing you up and down a little, the weightless left foot lightly slapping the ground. Only when you feel the integrity of this position and can clearly discriminate: one foot weighted, the other free (*yang* and *yin*), then allow yourself to shift your weight. Keep your torso erect, always riding nicely on your hipbones. Don't let it lean ahead or lag behind as you do the shift.

The similarity between hand-finger, pelvis-leg

When your hand stands on one finger, the top finger joint (the metacarpal-phalangeal) can be compared to the hip joint of your leg. In walking there is a smooth transmission of weight from one leg to the other. The transmission is through the pelvis: from one hip joint to the other. In legato it can be useful to focus on your metacarpal-phalangeals and to feel the connection from key to key through them even more than in the fingertip itself.

Remember, on the keyboard, 'standing' on one finger, let's say your forefinger, you should be able to 'test' the next key with *its* finger, let's say your third, depressing the key and letting it up again, without ever reducing the firmness or security of your 'standing finger'. Then when you do play the next note, you do not begin to reduce the firm implanted-ness of your standing finger until your third finger has reached a secure state of standing and is now capable of replacing your forefinger as the standing finger. Thus as the weight is eased off your forefinger there is no 'jar' or 'bump' or break in the smooth flow from one note to the next. Your arm needs to be comfortably aligned with your hand for this to happen

well, just as your torso is neutrally erect in good walking.

Can you really drop your floating finger in while your hand and standing finger—the one maintaining stability—do not collapse in the slightest? Do you play without prematurely 'shifting your weight', without leaving the secure stance of your *yang* finger too soon? Does your arm maintain a capable neutrality that helps rather than hinders this happening?

41 PRESSING AND HOLDING IN LEGATO

You may have noticed that we have been approaching the problem of basic touch from two distinct angles, firm and delicate. This chapter aims to clarify the benefits of the firm approach, demonstrating what role it plays in the development of an overall technique. Here we see why a technique that would seem to strangle piano tone can actually improve its richness.

If you are overpressing, that is if you are pressing in a way that is detrimental to your sound, physically unaligned so that you jam yourself in some way, then you should not proceed to this pressing and holding lesson. Doing so might only compound the problem. A well-constructed arch will gain in strength the more stress you exert on it, but a badly constructed arch will crumble. If you feel your hand may fall into this second category, first you need to decouple the detrimental organization. Organize your hand properly through the hand strength and structure lessons; free it up through the natural hand shape lessons that can help your hand adjust itself to normal alignment. Only then can you use pressing and holding to consolidate this newfound optimal organization.

However, there are other cases where it is advantageous to proceed directly to pressing and holding. For instance, I had a student who was plagued with really bad practice habits: learning the notes quickly and superficially, playing very fast and brilliant with a lot of dirt, absolutely no rhythmic stability and generally leaving the distinct impression that she was not aware of what she was doing. She was a very talented young woman quite out of touch with herself. I had to find some way of grounding her. I decided to teach her a healthy way of pressing and holding, one that respects principles of movement, a way designed to improve her physical organization.

When I yell, "Don't press!" it's because I see the student's pressing is hindering him or her. What I mean is, "Don't exert stress on wrong parts of your physical mechanism in a way that hinders your sound. Don't press in a disorganized way."

Much of the time my students are overpressing and need to free up, lighten up their touch, so I do not often recommend intentional pressing. However it can be very useful in clarifying how your arm, hand and fingers work in relation to one another.

Application 41.1
LEGATO X: PRESSING IN *AU BORD D'UNE SOURCE*

Proper pressing can strengthen structure

The key to healthy pressing is to do it from the right place—to press with the correct part of your mechanism.

> Step 1: Place your fingertips on a flat surface in a circle about five to seven centimeters in diameter and assume a 'bird-beak' position.

Illustration 41.1: The bird beak for a viable arch structure

Your tips are grouped relatively close together but not quite touching one another. Your wrist is high—somewhere that's comfortable for

you. Now begin to increase pressure on the surface, without destabilizing your hand's structure. Feel even your triceps intensely involved in this pressing (to the point where your pressing almost forces your torso to rise slightly off the bench!), and notice if you do it well, your hand structure is not impinged upon but actually strengthened by the pressure exerted on it. This phenomenon reflects the nature of the arch, which as I mentioned becomes more stable the more weight that bears upon it (up to a certain point, as that depends on the strength of the materials used in its construction).

Your arm can move even while generating pressure down through your hand into the keys

Step 2: Notice as well that when your hand has found its security and functionality in this, your arm can move around behind it freely without disturbing the integrity of your hand and fingers. Elbow up, down, left, right, around—try all these while pressing strongly and really feeling the pressure coming from your triceps. Now your wrist begins to move as well, but as long as the bulk of the pressure remains concentrated in your fingertips and does not transfer to your wrist, you are doing fine.

In Au Bord d'une Source

This practice is particularly useful in Liszt's *Au Bord d'une Source* because of the two voices played simultaneously in the right hand.

Example 41.1: Liszt: Au Bord d'une Source, *mm. 1-3*

Step 3: Press and hold the first dyad (2-note chord), finding the same feeling now focused in only the tips of your fourth and

fifth fingers on their keys. Then add your thumb tip and feel your
hand structure only strengthening, never weakening for an instant!
Slowly, carefully, one step at a time add in turn your second and
third fingers, never releasing any of the others, simply adding one
more pylon to the structure until all five fingers hold their notes
and you arrive at a complete 'bird beak'. Only now when all five
keys are securely held down can you release the first two notes—
your fourth and fifth fingers now prepare and then play their
next dyad while thumb, second and third maintain totally even
pressure on the keyboard throughout the movement. This is T'ai
Chi walking, our basic legato, but in double voices. To the flighty
pianist: if anything will ground you this will!

Example 41.2: Liszt: Au Bord d'une Source, m. 1 overholding

Use the graphic sensory image

> Step 4: As you move towards actually playing this work, cultivate
> a quicker, lighter, more fluid touch, but maintain the feeling of
> security of structure and stability of function that pressing and
> holding gave you. This will create that enchanting, glowing tone
> so appropriate to this work. What we have done is provided you
> with a graphic physical sensory image of what a true legato should
> feel like. Stay with it, and hear the results in your sound.

> The magic, bubbling tone of *Au Bord d'une Source* results from
> evenness of tone, and the most fundamental prerequisite for even
> tone is that all notes sound. You would be amazed at how often
> we neglect this most basic necessity. This exercise gives you a way
> to play all the notes. It is crucial that everything sounds but in a
> controlled way so that not even one note receives an unintended
> accent that could ruin your tone-sheen.

Pressing to achieve true legato sound in Brahms' Op. 118 #1 (example 37.4, page 221)

Here phrasing the melody in octaves (initially the three-note sigh motive) is not easy. Legato fingering is the only solution, yet hand extension makes this awkward. How to manage a true legato without stiffening up?

If you press in to your fifth finger just as your thumb is leaving one note to shift to the next, you will consolidate the feeling of your fifth as the *yang*, walking finger. This gives you a better chance of controlling your melodic contour, what Neuhaus refers to as melodic intonation. The trick is to balance flexibility of movement with the pressing needed to maintain a stable physical foundation. The movement is actually similar to a thumb pushup but on the fifth finger instead of the thumb, and minimized in scope. When you really press into your fifth you will realize that whatever you were doing before, you certainly were not playing a true legato!

Ironically, here pressing prolongs and enriches the note rather than strangling it, because it affords you *contact*. You prolong the note naturally because you did not leave it hanging in midair. Pressing allows you to stay with it physically, and your ear stays with it as well—perhaps partly because the physical connection is there.

Pressing in Chopin's F minor Ballade

The opening of Chopin's F minor Ballade provides a good illustration of the difficulty.

Example 41.3: Chopin: Ballade in F minor, Op. 52, mm. 1-2

To ensure that you are really doing this touch, when your second finger plays C, make sure that your octave G's are still held down.

For a split second you see three keys depressed. Similarly, hold C as you play the next octave G. Continue like this when the inner note becomes the dyad C-B flat and so on. This is overholding taken to the extreme—here pressing counteracts the strong tendency for your fingers to let go prematurely.

Most likely you will find this an awkward and quite foreign touch at first, manageable only at an extremely slow tempo. This goes to show how far the journey is to achieve a practically competent, fluid legato. Notice that when you do succeed in holding all keys down during the transition to each new dyad, your hand feels markedly different. Its structure is secure in a new way. It is just exactly this feeling and none other that must be transferred to the actual playing tempo!

You must teach yourself the feeling well under tempo, acclimatize your hand to the new organization, and then speed up your reactions, the whole complicated series of physical impulses involved in each playing action, until they occur seemingly instantaneously.

Do you begin to perceive the synthesis we're approaching? Consolidating and pressing in to establish integrity of structure, 'slapping' and freeing to create buzzing, untrammeled vibration. As these two contradictory processes evolve, we can begin to combine them to form a totally capable technique—a technique no longer preoccupied with the physical but totally living in sound: creating it and responding to it.

42 THE HIDDEN PROBLEM IN DOUBLE NOTES: *FEUX FOLLETS*

To the average pianist the double notes of Liszt's *Feux Follets* are much more fearsome than those of *Au Bord d'une Source*, but their study can bring an astonishing fact to light. Would you believe that the two fingers we generally regard as our strongest are actually the root of the technical difficulty? The double-note trills effectively prevent your hand from moving much—the figuration constrains it almost completely to only one position. The resulting tendency is to seize up: for your arm to stiffen and your fingers to stop moving. As well, you may tend in practice to focus on those supposed weaklings, the fourth and fifth fingers, and to assume that thumb and forefinger are doing their job. Nothing could be further from the truth. Most likely your first and second are the unsuspected culprits, and it is their failure to do their job that is compounding the problem of stiffening and general lack of finger movement.

Application 42.1
STRUCTURAL FUNCTION IX: INTERNAL FINGER ACTIVITY IN LISZT'S *FEUX FOLLETS*

Play the right hand's lower voice separately

Step 1: Practice the lower voice of the right hand separately, moving your fingers maximally. Reach for the sky, really give them a workout—the energetic stroke of your finger causes the note to *sound*, to have an alive shining tone. It also keeps the internal mus-

cles of the forearm and upper arm *active*, working against the tendency (aggravated by the lack of external movement) to seize up. Note that your second finger tends especially not to play the note D (in the fourth 4-note group of 16ths—measure 19, beat 1).[1] Try returning to and doing it in this fashion.

Example 42.1: Liszt: Feux Follets, *mm. 18-20—single note practice*

Natural shape—a review

Now we come to another problem—how to move as much as we possibly can in our constrained position but stay accurate? How to keep the sound diamond-like and flowing rather than chunky? Let's review the natural position of the hand. If you let your arm hang by your side you'll notice that your fingers do not hang straight. They have a natural curve to them—the normal length of the tendons maintains this. Try to place your hand on the board without disturbing this natural position, the only position you can maintain with an absolute minimum of tension or effort. It's not so easy as it seems, because we have a tremendous tendency to make some effort when we play, to *prepare* by contracting somewhere in our mechanism. However, we must eradicate this tendency from our system if we are to have any hope of succeeding in *Feux Follets*.

> Step 2: Try to articulate the notes of your right hand's lower voice maximally, maintaining the natural shape of your fingers. You'll notice that now it is your arm that must make those minimal position adjustments. Your finger cannot distort itself by reaching for a note—instead, your arm makes an angle adjustment, and your hand shifts slightly to a point where your finger is now over its new note not having deformed itself.

---

[1] At this point you may want to review chapter 14, *Clarification of the Thumb-Forefinger Relationship,* which contains a similar exercise for the coda of Chopin's in Ballade G minor.

Application 42.2
LEGATO XI: NON-LEGATO SOUND, LEGATO TOUCH

Fast changing-note exercise—legato with no pressure gives special result

Too difficult? OK, let's forget *Feux Follets* for a moment, and do a little exercise.

> Step 1: Play a rising changing note scale—C E D F E G F A G B A C B D C etc., very quickly. Use only your first and second fingers. In order to play cleanly with control we need to play legato, yet in order to have a fluttering light sound (something that ironically does not *sound* legato) there must be no pressing in it.

Example 42.2: Liszt: Feux Follets—*changing note exercise*

Can you assure yourself: are you really going to the bottom of each key yet exerting absolutely no *extra* pressure once you arrive there? By activating your finger more, lifting between each stroke, you can achieve a fluttery non-legato sound, yet magically if you analyze it, each finger still goes all the way down to the keybed, and there is still a physical legato connection through your meta-carpal-phalangeals—the metacarpal ridge.

Note this is not a feather legato. There is a vigorous finger stroke—it's not as if you're 'not-playing'—but in the instant your finger reaches the bottom of the key, it exerts no pressure. Your tip points straight down and moves incisively, vigorously, very rapidly into the key. But at the bottom it does not press in the slightest, although it does overhold to create a perfect join.

You are trying for the type of sound you would get using a staccatissimo, 'cat scratch' (out the back door[?]) technique, but you dispense with extreme finger curling. The entire narural finger, *maintaining its natiural shape,* is raised and lowered by the metacarpal-phalangeal joint, and you achieve a similar aural effect much more efficiently.

Application 42.3
THUMB VI: INTERDEPENDENCE OF THUMB AND FINGERS

Uniqueness of the thumb

Is it still not going as well as it could? What is needed perhaps is a stronger, more functional thumb. Did you ever stop to examine your thumb and realize what a unique digit it is? For instance: where does your thumb end? (Not the tip, dummy, the *other* end!) Many of my students, believe it or not, never stopped to realize that while the base of the fingers is the ridge of knuckles, the thumb ends all the way up at the wrist!

As well, its muscle is out of all proportion to the musculature of your fingers. Take a look at the fleshy heel of your hand, the big muscle that goes from the base of your thumb's second joint all the way to the middle of your wrist joint. In total bulk this muscle is bigger than all the muscles at the base of the four fingers combined: it is the biggest muscle in all your hand!

Thumb as platform or support pylon

In playing, much of the time your thumb actually constitutes or provides the platform, the support pylon on which your whole hand rests. Even when your thumb is not playing, its active muscle tonus contributes a great deal to the maintenance of overall hand strength and functionality. When this thumb muscle is really strong and supports your hand, then your four fingers are free to either move with true facility *or* be truly at rest.

---

[422] See application 38.1, *Articulations I.*

String lifts fingers—minimal effort as if from external source

There is a completely natural movement of the finger that can be understood as follows.

> Step 1: Imagine that there is a string wrapped around your finger just above or below the second joint (that's the proximal inter-phalangeal, the joint two up from your fingertip—the first one below the metacarpal-phalangeal ridge), and this string is gently pulling your relaxed finger upward.

Robert Schumann figured this out, but then went on to prove that a little knowledge is a dangerous thing. As he perceived his fourth to be especially weak and in need of assistance, he rigged a contraption up to constantly lift his fourth finger while he practiced, and the continuous strain ruined his hand. But in one way he did have the right idea: this is indeed the natural movement of the finger. But he should have found a way to have it move itself!

> Step 2: Hold onto a note with your thumb and lift your arm slightly as you feel the string lifting one of your fingers.

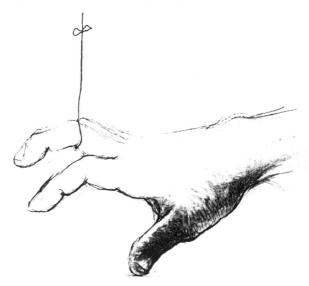

Illustration 42.1: As if a string held your finger (don't do it really!)

Then as your finger falls back into its key, your arm floats down slightly as well. There should be so little effort involved that it feels as if someone were moving your arm for you, or as if a gentle gust of wind buoys your arm. And by chance, your thumb is in its key, providing a fulcrum for the synchronous movement of your arm and finger. The whole thumb area is so strong, that the fingers and hand can relax exceptionally—even the skin on your hand becomes so soft that you can see the muscles moving underneath. This is *differentiation*—incredible strength in one place (your supporting pylon-thumb) makes possible an incredible delicacy and sensitivity in the rest of your hand.

Step 3: If you still feel a mechanical quality in the way you're doing this exercise, press even more with your thumb and liven up your finger movement. Go faster, but don't deform! For the purposes of *Feux Follets* do not let your fingertip fly up: keep it pointing downward at the key—you have no time for any larger movement.

Discrimination can transform conflict of intentions into cooperation: thumb strength can aid finger lightness, freedom

The two conflicting intentions inherent in this must learn to coexist in order for this to work. The stronger we get muscularly, the more we tend to bind up, the less we tend to move. But here, muscular strength in the thumb must not inhibit the free movement of your fingers. Your thumb needs to be so strong that it becomes capable of lending the support that *facilitates* free movement of your fingers. It's a higher dimension of strength than we normally think of, because it contains within itself discrimination—not just brute force but an intelligent distribution of forces. Cultivating this kind of strength is brainwork!

Step 4: Now play slowly any random series of notes in this fashion using all your fingers (of course your thumb still provides the firm fulcrum). Now have one 'arm breath' serve for a whole group of notes instead of breathing on each individual note.

It is a very light movement, yet there is some so-called momentum coming through from higher up your arm which gives a rich, increased tone—the tone has light in it, color. This 'momentum' is not from arm

weight but the result of ongoing internal activity higher up your arm. It can come through because the muscular effort is not the type of contraction that inhibits the transmission of movement energy. It's as if some external force were throwing your finger into the key.

No stopping—not even in reversals of direction

Step 5: Watch that you do not stop in any way between each finger stroke—the sense of continuous movement and vital equilibrium is essential to the continuing production of this alive tone. Just as a bouncing ball never actually stops,³ your finger should always be going either up or down. There is a trick in meditative breathing where you try and switch the direction of your diaphragm without any moment of holding—no stopping. Although your diaphragm cannot move circularly, if you create a circular image in your mind, you can make that feeling of your diaphragm stopping and changing direction simply melt away. Here too your fingers do not move circularly, but if their movement reaches an absolute pinnacle of precision, the feeling of stopping can also disappear, leading to an extraordinary degree of relaxation and control.

Step 6: Go back to the prestissimo legato changing note exercise. Do you do it better now? When and only when you can do this perfectly, you will finally have the sound image you need for *Feux Follets* in your ears. You achieve this by first practicing with maximal movement but then internalizing all that wonderful activity. Now you can with greater confidence return to the etude itself.

Everything must sound—dynamics as well as notes

Just as in *Au Bord d'une Source*, the magical, bubbling sound of *Feux Follets* can happen only when all notes sound. Even the omission of one note creates a hole in the tone palette and destroys the effect. Rather than speed, the sounding of all notes lightly, elegantly should be our first and foremost concern. In this chapter we focused on the right hand, but this holds for the left as well.

---

⁴²³ The two theoretical instants in time when it changes direction (at the apex of its path and when it bounces) have no duration.

For instance in measures 30-33 and similar places the grace notes are not the same. Can we hear the delightful, sprightly play between the G-F, G flat-F grace note figures that constantly shift with the shifting harmonies?

Example 42.3: Liszt: Feux Follets, *mm. 30-31*

Then at measure 38, does that strident *rinforzando* really surprise—do we really bring our dynamic up several notches, not just a few? And then do you play the espressivo, appassionato melody at measure 40 **forte** to **fortissimo** while keeping the accompanying parts **piano** (except the answering bass motive), to make it sing with real heart and once again effect a sudden change of tonal and emotional color?

Example 42.4: Liszt: Feux Follets, *mm. 38-41*

When not only all of Liszt's notes, but all his dynamics really sound, you will have found the key to *Feux Follets*.

43 Chopin's B Flat Minor Scherzo: Two Fundamental Principles Reviewed

Hand structure plus arm function to freely 'bong' the soundboard

Application 43.1
Octaves IX: Arch Function Review

Example 43.1: Chopin: Scherzo in B flat minor, Op. 31, *mm.* 5-9

Self-generating arch for better tone

Step 1: Play and hold the first *forte* left hand octave.

With your other hand (or have someone else do it), press down on the top knuckle of your second finger (the metacarpal-phalangeal joint). Your left hand resists this pressure. Press up against that downward force, *but without stiffening your wrist.* Notice that the arch of your left hand improves—because it must. If you now play the opening

octave again, maintaining this feeling of your second metacarpal-phalangeal pressing up, your sound improves instantly. The focus is better. Your tone becomes richer in quality, less harsh. You use less effort to get it, or rather your effort is displaced from external, counterproductive movements higher up your arm to an internal effort within your hand itself. Instead of effortful, sudden downward movements for big sound, you feel as if you are actually grasping the octave.

Once more, grasping review

Step 2: Yet again try grasping something with your hand and really squeezing. Do you feel how powerful your hand is?

Question: Why aren't you using that power in your octave? Answer:

- It never occurred to me.
- I didn't know how to.
- I was afraid of banging.
- I didn't know my hand was so strong.
- Other.

Application 43.2
OCTAVES X: COBRA-STRIKE REVIEW

Cobra-strike octaves for power

Well, your hand *is* that strong and you will certainly benefit from employing your God-given strength to the glory of Chopin. But we need to examine how our arm participates in this as well. Here's a variation on an exercise from chapter 18, *Fortissimo Octaves*.

Step 1: Put your fingers on key or somewhere near the keyboard and play *forte staccato*, whipping your arm up into the air beside your ear very quickly. Or try this variation: your hand hovers in the air poised to strike, and then play your *forte staccatissimo* octave, again whipping your arm back

Thus finger, hand and arm all make a maximal effort to move up, out and away from the keyboard, working directly against our customary tendency to move *down, into* the key. It is crucial as your arm whips back that you flip your wrist back and pull your fingertips back as well. Your fingers curl but the tips don't go to the heel of your hand. No, instead they touch the pad of flesh under the metacarpal ridge. All the energy moves away from the key in the instant the octave sounds. The more you can curl your fingers, tightly pressing them into those pads, the more you stimulate the reflex to *move* them, and that is what give you brilliance in your sound.

Illustration 43.1: Whip arm back to a tight finger curl

In the very instant the downward motion of your hand fulfils its purpose of causing the octave to sound, the impetus is instantaneously transformed into a vigorous, upward plucking motion. This helps you 1) make an attack that is strong yet light, as quick and sudden as a cobra's; 2) free your arm of all the contraction generally associated with trying to make a big sound. Notice how present your tone is because of this.

Step 2: Now do this with the pedal held down—note the absence of harshness. It's clean and resonant, like the vibration of a drum. It

is crucial that the drumstick leave the drumhead instantaneously so as not to damp the sound.

As we have already mentioned, harshness of sound does not come from playing too loud but from poor organization. If the hand is not strong enough to transmit accurately the force of your arm, then you end up hanging on after the attack in an attempt to regain control that was lost in the stress of the attack itself. Another way of explaining it: if hand structure is not secure then the arm muscles over-contract in order to produce the *forte*, and continue to contract after it has been produced, thus stifling the instrument and cramping its vibration. The *forte staccato* exercise is an effective antidote to this pattern of counterproductive arm contraction.

> Step 3: A similar attack, but as your arm releases vigorously upwards it doesn't move so far but somehow allows your fingers to maintain their hold on the keys. Ah! The same cleanliness of tone— it is big *and* healthy. This attack can be used for all loud chords. The same principle applies to the first D flat major chords in the left hand at measure 49:

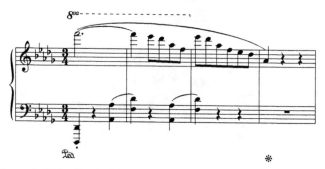

Example 43.2: Chopin Scherzo in B flat minor, Op. 31, *mm. 49-52*

> That same cleanliness of attack can now hold through a two-note slurred group. Here the initial 'in' movement continues through to the second chord (of course, without collapsing in the slightest)— only there do you release.

If we can incorporate this organization into the left hand slurred two-note group, could we apply it to the right hand eighth notes as well? Indeed we can, although again we are up against that fundamental pianistic problem, how to maintain

hand stability when finger independence is called for. If we monitor the maintenance of our hand structure as we move through groups of eighth notes, there
should be no problem, but here we must add another element:

Application 43.3
Structural Function X: Legato Review

Maintaining the sense of hand strength in passagework

> Step 1: Stand up on your fifth finger. Build a structure out of your
> hand and finger where your fifth is vertical and totally straight (no
> natural curve here, it's ramrod straight with your bottom phalange
> (the distal) even hyper-extended a bit) and your hand-platform is
> horizontal, at a 90-degree angle to your finger. Your forearm follows
> the line of your hand.

Illustration 43.2: Stand up on your fifth finger

> Step 2: When you play your fourth, at first practice not letting go of
> your fifth at all. Stand up on *both* your fourth and fifth. Make these
> two fingers feel the same as your original left hand octave felt.

Just enough wrist movement

Notice that your wrist can really mess things up here by being too flexible. Too much flexibility prevents the wonderful power of your arm from being transmitted through your wrist to the key. If it's over-flexible, your wrist moves too much and destabilizes your fourth and fifth fingers, decoupling them from their notes. Notice that when you really stand on your fingers, your wrist is relatively high: the angle between your arm and hand is negligible, very close to 180 degrees. The force vector of your forearm goes in a straight line down through your hand, and (even though your fingers are at a 90-degree angle to your hand) on through your fingers into the key. Of course you should not be stiff in your wrist! Let it move, but economically. Do not confuse a free, controlled use of your wrist with over-moving. Especially avoid the common habit of moving it down and to the outside, which can lead to loss of power and control.

> Step 3: Now continue to add fingers to this chain of supported notes, always overholding all, until you reach your thumb. Notice that between your second and your thumb it is even more difficult to maintain this feeling of support than between the other fingers. This is the point at which we all really tend to collapse. Here are two contrasting antidotes:

> Step 4: Make the four fingers into a completely firm base; swing your thumb *in*, making it go through the largest arc possible but without weakening that structure at all.

Illustration 43.3: Maximal thumb swing into key

Step 5: Construct the same base, but now rest your thumb on the key surface, and rotate your whole finger-hand structure in such a way that it pushes your thumb into the key. Here your thumb doesn't move at all—instead, your hand structure shifts as a solid unit to move your thumb into its note. The note sounds; your finger-hand structure moves forward and in over your thumb. Again of course, do not collapse in the slightest.

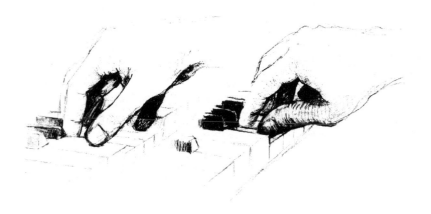

Illustration 43.4: Hand moves immobile thumb into key

Now that you have really clarified how to use your thumb without collapsing your structure, what happens when you go *over* it? If you didn't collapse playing your thumb so far you are almost *sure* to succumb when you go over your thumb to the next fourth finger!

Step 6: Try passing your fourth finger over your thumb, and playing your fourth's note. Through observation and informed experimentation, using the principles with which you've now familiarized yourself, learn to stand healthily on your thumb-fourth finger structure.

Illustration 43.5: Pass fourth over thumb

Again, note how we have been working to synthesize the various strands of thought, lines of technical strategy discussed earlier. We're cultivating a symbiotic relationship where

– Maximum finger activity (some external[1] but even more internal) contributes a great deal to maintenance of hand/finger structure and

– Maintenance of hand structure provides a secure base from which the fingers easily move with agility and power.

The synthesis of these two mutually 'opposive-supportive' functions can create the tonal qualities necessary for the dramatic power, the proud, bubbling, virile energy of this Scherzo.

---

[1] For more on the finger action needed for good sound here, refer to chapter 26, *The Sound of One Hand Clapping.*

44 Mutual Aid between Thumb and Forefinger in the Scriabin Concerto

In his late teens Scriabin injured his right hand and played only with his left for about a year. He composed a number of works for left hand alone, the most extravagant a concert waltz, which lamentably has not survived. But he also tended towards fiendishly difficult left hand figurations in his works for two hands. The recapitulation in the third movement of his concerto is a case in point.

Instead of approaching it with the dogged persistence of a chain gang we can use the opportunity to perfect our understanding of some key points concerning structure and function, looking at the interaction between two of our most consistently recurring themes: 1) rotation and 2) the thumb and forefinger.

Do not use editor's hand substitutions!

The problematic figuration in question begins at measure 170 with the entrance of the lower accompaniment motive. By the way, some editor has gone to great pains to figure out all sorts of hand substitutions designed to simplify the process of executing the text. I follow none of his suggestions! Every one of them goes against the specific sound Scriabin wanted, for which he purposely notated the distribution of notes between the hands as he did. If you extend your hands to interlock your thumbs as he notated, your tone is enriched significantly. Thus here your left hand enters on the thumb as notated.

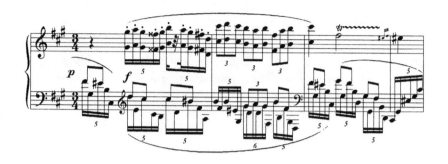

Example 44.1: Scriabin: Piano Concerto in F sharp minor,
Op. 20, *mm. 170-174*

Application 44.1
THUMB VII: MUTUALLY SUPPORTIVE PLATFORMS; ROTATION

Thumb, forefinger act as mutually supportive platforms

Step 1: When you play your thumb note, immediately feel your thumb functioning as a platform supporting the free movement of your second finger.

Step 2: As soon as your second finger plays, it returns the favor, now functioning as the supportive base for your thumb's free movement. Paradoxically, this mutual interdependence of function is what can lead to real finger independence!

Rotation

The other basic function at play here is rotation.

Step 3: Each time your thumb leaves its note, it should lift it as if trying to move, over your hand to the outside but above your other fingers. Don't turn it in and under. *Leave the heel of your hand*

angled to the inside while the cocking motion of your thumb, preparing for its next stroke, cultivates a natural forearm rotation
movement.[2]

Again we see the interrelation of several movement components—each finger in turn supports hand structure; your whole arm structure rotates to
support an increased finger activity.

---

[441] See part VII, *Rotation* and following.

45 ARTICULATIONS

Having established a wonderful ability to produce blistering, gleaming, beautifully brilliant tone, we now need to diversify. For a maximum selection of orchestral colors you will need as many contrasting articulations as possible. Here are a few specific ways to manipulate the key for exactitude and discrimination in your palette of tonal colors.

Application 45.1
ARTICULATIONS II: FEEL THE MASS AND VIBRATION OF THE KEY

Increased richness of sensation leads to improved ability control

The inherent goal of many exercises I offer is to become more aware of what you're doing, to have a more tangible understanding of hand function, to hear more graphically. A part of this process is to increase the richness of your actual physical sensation. If you can feel the key more, you can control it better.

> Step 1: Take the edge of the key between two fingers and manipulate it, wiggle it up and down. Feel the mass of the key. Sense how wide it is, how deep, how long. Feel it as a three-dimensional entity. How graphically can you sense the difference in size and mass between the white and black keys? Can you preserve this tangible sense of each key as a thing possessing mass and weight when you play many of them in rapid succession?

Partial or complete control of the hammer—both have their useful application

Of course, when you feel the mass of the key it is actually the hammer's weight you sense. Here is an exercise to clarify two distinct ways of manipulating the hammer.

Jog one arm with the other

> Step 2: Hold your left arm with your right hand, gently cradling the left wrist in your right fingers. Let your left arm be totally limp, relaxed. It should feel distinctly heavy to your right hand, almost as if you were actively pressing down on your right palm with it. Many people don't know how to relax their arm totally, and I have to tell them to actually press down a little with the arm they are cradling, just for them to release and finally for the first time to experience their own arm weight! With your right hand, jog your limp left arm up and down a bit, as if you are judging the weight of your own arm.

Jogging the key to sense hammer weight

> Step 3: Now go to a piano key and with your right hand imitate that activity, except here you will be jogging the key instead of your arm, and you'll jog it down in order to jog the hammer up. Notice that the more loose and relaxed your right arm is, the more exactly you can actually feel the weight of the key.

Grasp and jiggle—control descent as well as ascent

> Step 4: Now return to your own left arm, but this time grasp your arm or wrist rather than simply cradling it. Your thumb is above, fingers below. Now as you jiggle your arm you can control both its ascent and descent.

> Step 5: Can you recreate *this* feeling on the piano key, jiggling instead of jogging the hammer? Of course, you must jiggle gently so the hammer does not fly up off the key. Be so delicate in this that you feel as if you grasp and jiggle the hammer itself

directly, as if it is attached to the key. Do you see the difference between the techniques of jogging and jiggling?

Sensing in actuality allows absolute control

One of the most useful and distinctive applications of this little exercise is in the playing of half-staccato chords. Playing them with the feeling of jiggling assures that all notes sound absolutely equally, and allows a very exact degree of control of both dynamic and tone. Another useful application: fast repeated notes, for instance in the first movement of the *Appassionata* Sonata or the repeated notes of the Sonata Op. 7 discussed earlier. If you actually feel as if the hammer is attached to the key and not simply resting on it, you can achieve a truly exact, really *p* series of repeated notes because you really feel as if you jiggle the hammer against its string.

Application 45.2
STACCATO I: THICK-TONED, BEEFY BEETHOVEN STACCATOS

For that chunky Teutonic sound in repeated *staccato* chords: try stopping the key from rebounding fully. In staccato we normally get out of the key as quickly as possible, allowing the damper to fall instantaneously back onto the string. However if you try to *stop* the rebound of the key just before it returns fully 'up', let's say a half a millimeter from the top, you add a certain beef, a certain orchestral fullness to the tone of your *staccato*, because you now have taken absolute control over its precise duration. This also positions you perfectly to play the next chord with exact control. Do you see how this relates to the jiggling exercise above?

Application 45.3

STACCATO II: 'ARM DOWN - HAND UP' OCTAVE
STACCATOS

Mendelssohn's Scherzo a Capriccio

> Step 1: Your arm and fingers can often have quite individual func-
> tions, and in this case even opposing ones. Here instead of your
> fingers playing while your arm glides laterally, your arm actually
> goes down while your fingers rise. You are playing chords stac-
> cato. You need pulse. Your fingers and hand can give you stac-
> cato, coming sharply up out of the keys. Meanwhile your arm
> gives you pulse by moving down and in just as your fingers come
> forward and up. Thus at the conclusion of the pulse note (the
> downbeat) your wrist will be very low but your fingers high.
> Your arm moves *in*, in entirely the opposite direction to your
> fingers. They do the staccato; your arm does the pulse.

Example 45.1: Mendelssohn: Scherzo a Capriccio, *mm. 1-4, first stage of practice*

> Step 2: In the subsequent offbeat staccato chords your arm rises,
> but again it must have one smooth rising motion while your fin-
> gers play any number of staccato chords. The one movement of
> your arm rising through a whole group of staccato chords is
> used to prepare its next pulse-generating entrance. At first take a
> half bar as one pulse unit; your arm rises through two staccato
> chords. Later on when you increase the speed, take a whole meas-
> ure as one rhythmic unit.

Example 45.2: Mendelssohn: Scherzo a Capriccio, *mm. 1-4, second stage of practice*

At first you should do this exercise with as graphic a movement as possible. Your arm as far down as you can and then just a little further. Your fingers *way* up, although they remain curled not straight. The second phalange (the medial) points to the ceiling instead of your fingertip. This exaggeration ensures that you really are clear about the new physical organization and that the old habit is completely dispensed with. Later on, as you approach a performance rather than practice technique, reduce the actual size of the movement, even to the point of being imperceptible, *but maintain the new organization internally.* This ensures we will hear the phrasing that the movement was designed to inflect.

Application 45.4
STACCATO III: HARMONIC STACCATO TOUCH

Arm does have a supportive role in finger staccato

Compared to Liszt, Chopin used the wedge-shaped sharp staccato sign relatively seldom—he preferred the dot that indicates a softer staccato. But we do find it in his etude, Op. 25 #4. How can we execute this sharp staccato, yet keep our dynamic down around *p*? A special touch is required. An arm staccato will never do the job because our arm is too big and ungainly. Its size precludes its having the requisite exactitude. We need a finger staccato: how to do this when whole chords are in question?

Example 45.3: Chopin: Etude in A minor, Op. 25 #4, *mm. 1-4*

Step 1: Try curling your fingers in a special way: curl only the two bottom joints, as if you want to pull the tips back and up. Instead of touching your palm somewhere, your fingertips will almost touch at the metacarpal-phalangeal base. Also pull your thumb and your hand as well up and back. Now try playing the right-hand chords using this movement. I call it the 'cat scratch' movement.

Arm moves not to produce sound but to balance internal forces

The first problem you will run into in attempting this: your forearm will seize up! But there *is* a way to do the 'cat scratch' *and* stay loose in your forearm.

Step 2: Pluck with the bottom finger joint, but feel a slight buoyancy in your forearm. Your arm does not produce the staccato but it does perform a crucial adjunct movement. As your fingers pluck, they do come up off the keys, and your arm moves slightly to help them do this. Your arm also immediately returns them to the keys in anticipation of the next chord. But if you are clear about the function of your arm you will notice the feeling is totally different from an arm staccato, where your arm would actually produce the tone. Your arm moves not to produce the tone directly but only to place your finger where it needs to be.

Stopping the rebound of the key gives you control over staccato's exact duration

I help my students get this simply by lightly touching under their forearm and encouraging it to rise ever so slightly. This is the secret. This is what gives you magic tone here. It is imperative that your arm feels relatively immobilized so you

are not doing your usual full arm staccato, yet stays responsive and supple. In addition, organize your thinking to try to stop the keys as they rebound *just before* they reach their resting position, as you just did in those chunky Beethoven staccatos. This is how we control the end of the note as well as its beginning. As a result, another whole dimension of precision appears in our mental-physical organization and in our sound.

'Cat-scratch' *and feel the weight of the hammers*

> Step 3: Still don't get it? Take the edge of the key, the little white bit of plastic or ivory that juts out slightly from the main body of the key, between your thumb and forefinger. Jiggle the key lightly. Can you feel the hammer bouncing up and down on the inner key mechanism? Yes? Good. Thus you can judge by feel approximately how heavy that hammer is. Play around with it. The softer your arm is, the better you can feel the hammer exactly, n'est-ce pas? What do you think, 15 grams or 25 grams? 20.5? Not important to actually know the number, important to *feel* with exactitude. Now, believe it or not, it is possible to do the 'cat scratch' on your three-note chord, and have each of those three fingers feel its hammer as you play! Now there's some quality precision for you! It's exactly the right sound, the right amount of sound, and the sound is not forced.

To make this easier, for now just maintain an exact **mp** dynamic level. Later on you can reinstate the *crescendi* and *decrescendi*.

Intention to do a movement can be more effective than movement itself

I was asked, 'Is this just a practice technique or should I actually perform the etude using this 'cat scratch' technique?' As you increase tempo there comes a point where it is simply too fast to do the 'cat scratch' movement fully—your hand would go into spasm! And yet if you don't try to do it your sound will lose its vitality, the special life that the 'cat scratch' gives. You must play a sort of trick on your mind: you must continue to intend to do the movement fully, while in reality moving through much less than the full arc of the finger-tip stroke. Still *try* to move through the whole arc, but don't be pig-headed about it: *that's* what leads to hurt forearms, etc. In performance you do really

think you are doing it because it still *feels* as if you are. Only if you look closely do you see that the movement has assumed a smaller, more precise form. You must not lose the hyper-intensity of *focus* that your intention gives.

An aside: for the left hand part, learn this touch isolating it from the other main challenge of this etude, the leaps. Play the basses with your left hand but take the chords with your right. Get the exact sound you want, then transfer *that* to the left hand itself. Also have your left hand practice its chords without the basses, and even play the five-note chords with two hands still omitting the basses. First *get that sound!*

Application 45.5
CHORDS I: 'CEMENT BLOCK' CHORDS FOR A
MAXIMUM WALL OF CHUNKY SOUND

> Step 1: Play an eight-note chord *fff*. In the moment of playing, feel your whole mechanism stiffen to almost cement-like rigidity! Now as your fingers continue to hang on to their keys, gradually let everything higher up relax. You arm releases, but your hand maintains its stiffened, ultra-arched, pressing state.

> Step 2: Play another chord, but instead of taking a lot of time between chords, try to join them. Practice without pedal to see how much you can create the illusion that you are playing legato. Try to leave absolutely no air space between the chords, and yet have your fingers seem neutral as they find the next chord, as if no effort were involved. Only in the moment of playing do you again stiffen. As you increase the speed of a series of *fff* chords, can you sense that although you feel mainly like everything is just holding on continually, it is your 'inner arm' that pumps to make a massive, orchestral sonority?

Try this in the first movement recapitulation of Rachmaninoff's Concerto #2 in C minor (example 54.2, page 320). Notice that the slower tempo not only increases the tragic character but also allows for a more massive sonority, increasing monumentality. It's a simple law of physics: if the chord has longer

to sound, it will *make* more sound. This is why I spend a lot of time practicing without Rachmaninoff's staccatos, but holding on to each chord as long as possible.

There are many moments that can benefit from this. Try for instance the chords towards the end of Beethoven's cadenza for the first movement of his Concerto in C major.

Example 45.4: *Beethoven:* Concerto in C major Op. 15, *1st mvt. cadenza, mm. 30-31*

46 THE FELDENKRAIS — HOROWITZ CONNECTION

Let's digress for a moment to acquaint ourselves with two key men whose discoveries in their respective fields eventually led me to write this book.

Moshe Feldenkrais

so strong in his youth that he could grasp a vertical pole and hold his whole body out from it horizontally. He mastered judo to the point of winning the European judo championship in the 1930s and founded the Judo Club of France. His keenly inquiring mind formulated a body of knowledge derived not only from theory but also from the tangible experience of a man endowed with exceptional ability. Even while working at the Joliot-Curie laboratories in the forefront of nuclear physics research, he was also learning so much about psychology, neurophysiology, and other health-related disciplines that later on the London School of Medicine invited him to enter directly into the *third* year of their degree program!

Feldenkrais declined and, as he said much later, it was lucky he did. Had he gone the normal route, it is unlikely that he would even have *conceived*, much less accepted, his radically new ideas on human functioning. He himself said that for the first 25 years of his investigations, much of the time he wondered if he was crazy!

Genesis of a method

The genesis of Feldenkrais' method was a knee injury sustained playing soccer (or as the Europeans call it, football). When the doctors gave him only a 50 percent chance of walking after the proposed operation, he preferred to attempt a cure on his own. He lay in his hospital bed and experimented with micro-movements, experiments educated by his experience in judo, medicine, cybernetics, mechanical and electrical engineering, physics, and also by observing the sequences the

babies in the pediatrics ward followed in learning movement. He taught himself to walk again and in the process developed an extraordinary system for accessing the power of the central nervous system to improve human functioning. Through exploration of 1) the nature of movement in general, and 2) every component or degree of each specific movement in question, students of his method arrive at a more elegant, effective and capable use of self.

Moshe Feldenkrais was already in his late 70s when he came to America and began training new generations of Feldenkrais practitioners. The videos of these trainings show him walking in a somewhat careful yet extremely well organized fashion. The x-rays showed that it was a miracle he was walking at all!

Vladimir Horowitz

Feldenkrais and Horowitz. Both Russian Jews, born within a year of each other in the Ukraine at the turn of the century, and each in his own way a master of movement. Horowitz in his late 70s was still performing miracles at the keyboard with most of the power of his younger years and with ever-increasing finesse and subtlety, even as his walking came more and more to resemble Moshe's: the cautious yet enlightened locomotion of old age.

His posture reflects quality of movement

Once I showed the video *Horowitz in Moscow* to two of my Feldenkrais trainers, men who had worked with Dr. Feldenkrais himself. Their reaction was, 'Look, he moves like Moshe!' The same walking, but more important, the same eagle-like poised, exact turning of the head. Maximally efficient, minimal movement yet completely free. The head angled slightly forward yet floating. Not hanging down heavy but rather as if suspended from a thread. A head can only turn like that when it rests on top of a spine that soars up straight and long, not held up with excess muscular tension but freely standing there in gravity, 'buoying'.

This state can only occur when there is an optimal balance of muscle tonus throughout the body. Effort is minimal because there is a minimum of the unnecessary habitual muscular contractions against which the body must fight in order to move. The skeleton's structure does most of the work; the muscles, with remarkably little effort, add their aid where needed. Of course, Horowitz knew nothing of Feldenkrais Method. Part of his genius was to arrive at such a sophisticated physical organization solely through the intention to realize his artis-

tic conception. (Of course, he also practiced like a son-of-a-gun in his younger days!¹)

The video *Horowitz in Vienna*, a moving document of his last public performance in 1987, illustrates Horowitz's mastery in this regard. At age 84, because of his reduced strength, the principles of movement and organization that allowed him to perform a lifetime of miracles are displayed here in their most distilled and clear form.

His hand structure and function

He sits very low—his elbows are quite far below the keyboard rather than level with it as present day wisdom dictates. What this does is clarify the function of the knuckles: the metacarpal-phalangeal joints, the place where the fingers are attached to the hand, that I call the metacarpal ridge. In this seemingly awkward and unworkable hand position it is very difficult to play at all, unless you maintain the support structure of the metacarpal ridge to absolute perfection. When you *do* do this, you discover an astonishing fact: your fingers acquire the freedom to do anything! You can use them as tools to feather stroke, curl, 'flat stroke' (here you actually do maintain a 5 percent curl), pluck, lift and make a full muscular stroke for rich tone, or even poke for an insistent quality! However, it is extremely difficult to succeed in this, because whatever movement we make tends to undermine the security of the metacarpal ridge. We are not used to employing a strength so exact that it does not disturb the delicate and complex balance of structures in action here.

People have wondered for generations how Horowitz could play with such flat fingers: the fact is, he didn't! He only appeared to. Actually his fingers were flat only when they were 'at rest'. In the video notice that in the passagework of the Mozart, whenever he is actually using a finger to play, it does curl in to some extent. He actually maintains the old-school 'Russian arch'—it just looks as if he doesn't. In fact, this is the Russian arch in its most evolved form.

"Now wait a minute", some of you may say, "what about natural finger shape?" Indeed, when Horowitz's fingers were completely at rest, they curved slightly just like everybody else's. Observe them when he's taking a bow, for instance. But he used a more flat version of 'at rest' when actually playing. This

---

¹ For more on Horowitz and Feldenkrais Method, see appendix III, *Alchemy*.

slight extension of his fingers from the 'at rest' position probably served to enhance the activation of the playing finger.[2] The finger is slightly 'cocked', like an elastic band pulled tight in preparation for launching, and when it strikes this lends more of a *zing* to the sound.

How this cultivates finger independence

By maintaining the metacarpal ridge you are also cultivating maximum finger independence. Only when there is absolute connection through the metacarpal ridge, only when you feel with absolute clarity your legato right in those joints, will each finger be free from the others. Imagine a quadrilateral structure consisting of the keybed connecting two of your fingertips and your two fingers leading up to the bone structure connecting their two metacarpal-phalangeal joints (see illustrations 10.7, 10.8, 10.9, pp. 62-63). Between each two legato notes this structure should be clearly felt, but only for an instantaneous moment. There is no time to feel it for longer—you will bind up. But in that instant this *must* be present—it is your security and your power. It turns out that developing ultimate interdependence creates the conditions for true finger independence—they go hand in hand. When that connective structure is secure, each finger feels the appropriate help of the other. This paradoxically is the only thing that finally allows them total independence!

Internal arm contractions replace external movements to generate tone

This in turn leads to other developments. For instance, with this arrangement you can replace arm accents with finger accents! Sounds totally illogical until you realize: we tend to use *external* arm movements to add arm mass to our sound or tone. When using this technique, you'll notice that external arm movements are rendered superfluous! The *internal* workings of the upper arm become graphically clear—you can feel with actual clear physical sensation various parts of your triceps working to support various fingers in various paths of motion. Now if you curl the finger to resemble the shape of a piano hammer, lift it and let it fall straight in, with the internal power of the arm coming in behind it—it feels like an internal upper arm contraction—you get a big voiced sound. And because you are moving a lot less, you have a lot more precision and clarity of execution.

[46.2] See *Dual muscular pull: the effective balancing of opposing forces* in chapter 7.

Watch the Horowitz videos, you'll see that he is doing just that quite frequently. Granted, sometimes he sacrifices a perfectly joined legato for this bold tone, projecting each note of a melody in 'the grand manner' to the back of the hall, making each single note speak. But somehow the background rhythmic energy that always seems to be present in his playing, generating a tremendous sense of ongoing formal and phrase development, allows *him* to get away with it!

Great playing despite overmoving

This explains why he appears to be almost motionless. When you learn this internal arrangement you too will discover how to improve dramatically by eliminating your extraneous movements. That's why I say that this really is a treatise towards a new pianism. Look at videos of such great pianists as Richter, Gilels, Hoffman. You will see them doing many of the moves I am telling you to dispense with! Yet I am the first to agree, their playing was wonderful. My contention is that they played great *despite* those moves not because of them.

Of course, we should aspire in every way to reach the pinnacles of musical perfection they achieved. Yet remember that by dispensing with some of the standard conservatory training habits that they inadvertently preserved, we can accelerate our rate of progress.

47 FLAT FINGERS

The intention to curl is still present in a flat finger attack

Here's another contradiction. I have just explained how Horowitz's fingers
were flat only when at rest. But some time ago my curiosity was piqued and
I ended up finding a way to *play* with them flat! The gratifying result: I discovered some new tonal possibilities for my instrument. From my diary,
1997:

> The quest to unravel the mysteries of Horowitz's ravishing technique
> continues. . . . The other day it was flat fingers: I have noticed how in
> between movements of a work he would sometimes put his fingers
> flat on the keys with his palms all the way down on the wood below the
> keys. This form of the hand, if used to produce sound, fuses the three
> finger phalanges so they function as one big one, maximizing 'juici-
> ness'. It is the very opposite of the curled finger. I'm beginning to think
> that the value of curling the fingers lies mainly in the stimulus to
> functionality inherent therein. The basic motion of the finger is to
> curl, to grasp. But the force generated by a curling-grasping impulse
> can be transmitted even if there is no visible curling movement! Once
> this fact is 'grasped' by the mind and the reflexes, once this function is
> active and no longer subject to laziness and sleep and this has become
> the rule rather than the exception, then the function can be activated
> no matter what the finger's position.

Capable karate chops

> Then we are left simply with the question of what position pro-
> duces what type of sound. The flat-fingered, super-low hand pro-
> vides several exciting new sound possibilities. When done maximally,
> it even provides a way to 'karate chop' with integrity!

Application 47.1

STRUCTURAL FUNCTION XI: FLAT FINGERS TO INCREASE CONTACT WITH THE KEY

Step 1: Flip your wrist all the way back so the fingers point as much as they can toward the ceiling. Then lower only the pinky to horizontal, and point it forward as much as possible. Leave the rest of your hand pointing up. This brings your fingers, hand and arm into an arrangement of right angles.

Illustration 47.1: The fifth as a horizontal keyboard hook.

Step 2: Now, keeping your hand vertical and your pinky horizontal, lower your whole arm as a unit, as if you want to push your palm somewhere underneath the piano near the keyboard. Your pinky, as if by chance, catches the key as a hook would. What a sound! This is fat *and* precise, warm *and* sharp, incredibly powerful but not harsh.

Flat-fingered octaves, chords

Step 3: If you do the same thing but add your thumb to the equation, you can actually feel as if you play the octave with the middle phalange of the thumb and the *proximal* phalange of the pinky—the one closest to the hand!

Illustration 47.2: Play an octave with proximal phalanges!

Step 4: To fill in the octave with chord tones, each finger in between can swivel down and literally *swat* the key, making the juiciest of all possible tones. But watch out: notice how strong the tendency is to curl your finger into an old familiar position, in this instance thus robbing it of all its power! Leave it flat! This is indeed craziness, is it not?

Radical reorganization!

You must reorganize everything: your fingers, your hands and arms (sitting extremely low facilitates this technique's ease of employment), and most important, your brain, your conceptions of tonal and technical possibilities. In the end it feels more like you are sticking your fingers into a series of pigeonholes, playing in the keys rather than on them. But what sound! What power!

Area of contact fifteen times greater

The flat finger communicates the power of the forearm's entering motion to the key much more effectively than the fingertip alone possibly could: the actual physical base, the actual area in contact with the key is up to fifteen times greater! This can be proven very simply by this little test:

Step 5: Hold your wrist and palm below a table or the closed piano, your fingers above, and make the most powerful stroke possible into the wood with your fingertip. Note the sound, the *thwap* of flesh on wood. Now try the same thing with the whole flat finger. How about that—the sound of your whole finger is both louder and richer. Imagine all this added richness of vibration manifesting in the singing tone of your instrument!

Step 6: As a child did you ever rest your hand on your friend's head, pull your middle finger back like a slingshot and then let it go *thwap*, sending your little colleague home in tears? Try that technique now— on the *table*, not someone's head! All that booming sound coming from your little slingshot finger is yet another illustration of the untapped sonic potential right there in your hand.

Towards healthy pianistic sound for all

The adjective 'Horowitzian' crops up so often that the word has become an accepted part of pianists' vocabulary. Sometimes it refers to idiosyncrasies that arose out of Horowitz's magical personality and are better left uncopied. But many times I find the term 'Horowitzian' is used to describe qualities of playing that the *maestro* possessed in exceptional abundance, but that were not in fact unique to him alone. Two of these basic qualities of musicianship, of healthy pianism are:

- an almost motoric rhythmic impulse, a forward moving rhythmic impetus so strong that it allowed even extremes of rubato without losing its power, and

- orchestrated sound: bold, singing lead lines and subsidiary voices that are way down in dynamic yet retain all the necessary musical qualities—clarity, rhythmic impetus, shape, speaking.

"Oh, you mean like Horowitz"

I remember once showing a student 'flat fingers' so he could play a melodic line with a true, 'heart-song', voiced sound. When he finally got it he exclaimed, "Oh, you mean like Horowitz". No, I don't mean like Horowitz, I mean like any pianist worth his salt! Horowitz is no longer with us, but his example remains to show us the way. We must not copy him, but should he continue indefinitely to corner the market on the widest and most varied spectrum of pianistic sound? Would he not be the first to rejoice if healthy, well-orchestrated sound no longer remained the domain of one pianist alone?

A basic premise: the more you can do, the more fun you have!

The flat finger technique may seem strange, even outlandish to some of you. But here we have a graphic illustration of the basic thrust of my argument: the more things you can do and the more ways in which you can do them, the healthier, more capable and better pianist you are. 'Flat fingers' are simply one more weapon to add to your pianistic arsenal!

48 PEDALING

Many have said that the sustain pedal is the heart and soul of the piano, but for a long time it was not clear to me what that meant in practical terms. So when I finally succeeded in acquiring a big sound but found that it could still use more variety of orchestral color, I went searching for a solution. Along the way I finally came to understand this old pianistic adage.

Radical voicing needed to improve color of concert grand

You may think that pressing the pedal all the way down will make your sound the richest, but in reality it is the opposite. Here's another paradox: the thicker your pedal, the *less* tone you will have! You will have more volume but fewer colors, because everything is thickened. Your sound deteriorates into a mass of undifferentiated mud. It is logical that it should be this way, because the bass strings are longer than the treble, and their tendency to drown out the shorter strings is only increased by fully tromping down on the pedal.

Many seriously underestimate the problems caused by the shortness of the treble strings. Because of its basic design, the concert grand piano will tend to rob you of tone and brilliance, and you must constantly compensate for this in your voicing strategies. You should almost always bring down the dynamic of your left hand and maximize juiciness in your right. When you have mastered this it would be a shame to let all that effort be for naught, so don't thicken your pedal and spoil the good voicing work you've done.

Application 48.1
PEDAL I: 'UP' NOT DOWN

To preserve the singing, silvery sweetness in your sound that good voicing cultivates, you must take a radically different approach to pedaling. It can best be described in terms of physical sensation. When you use the pedal, don't feel as if you're pushing it down at all. Instead, constantly feel it trying to push your foot back up, and let it do that as much as possible. You actually feel as if you are constantly lifting your foot, lightening it.

Imagine a garden hose pointing straight up, and you are holding the palm of your hand above it, blocking the stream of water. The water pushes your hand up; you keep trying to push it back down. But don't push down all the way to the spout itself. Instead, maintain a balance. Even try to see how high you can let your hand go while still feeling good pressure from the water.

This should be the feeling in your pedal foot. Or it should feel as it would if, when driving a car, you did not want to push the gas to the floor but rather to use the absolute minimum amount of gas needed to keep yourself going at a certain speed.

Pursuing the metaphor of piano and automobile, notice that the sustain pedal of the piano actually resembles the clutch more than the gas. (If you've never driven on an standard transmission you're not going to get this.) Just as releasing the clutch gradually engages the transmission, releasing the pedal gradually couples the dampers to the strings. The key word here is 'gradually', reminding you that it's to be done with sensitivity.

Lighten your pedal to open your sound, increase variety of color

In any rich, pedaled pianistic sound texture, the lighter your pedal the brighter your tone will be. In the end you will virtually never use full pedal but always be playing with ¾, ½ and ¼ pedals as well as degrees in between. This opens up a new sound world, where each individual voice becomes more discernible from its neighbors, and all their colors become more distinct as well.

Often in our addiction to pedaled sound we fail to take advantage of the special emotional qualities inherent in thinning it out. For instance, if you want to create a feeling of loneliness, isolation, emptiness, play passages that would nor-

mally receive pedal with none. For instance in the first page of Scriabin's *Vers la Flamme*, if you use pedal only in the instants when you must join two harmonies, the sound of totally dry chords fading slowly into the ether has a totally different emotional impact and meaning than if you pedal them fully. Think about it!

Example 48.1: Scriabin: Vers la Flamme, Op. 72, *mm. 1-6*

And of course, there are exceptions to this rule. When you simply want maximum mass of sound, in some cases you can help yourself a great deal by going to the opposite extreme. Consider two points in Rachmaninoff's Second Concerto—the opening eight measures of the first movement and the climactic recapitulation of the third movement's second theme. Try playing these passages on one full pedal. Just tromp it down and leave it there for the duration. Don't worry: in the first case, your carefully managed crescendo (can you really play so the listener perceives, measure by measure, the following clear dynamic progression *ppp, pp, p, mp, mf, f, ff, fff*?) will mask the blurring of the harmonies, while in the second the orchestra covers you so much that there is no way the over-pedaling can be perceived. Here by changing your pedal you only cut your sound in half.

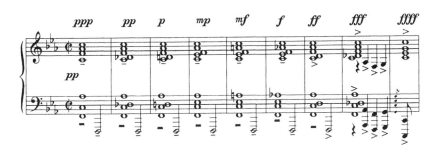

Example 48.2: Rachmaninoff: Concerto in C minor, Op. 18, *1st mvt., mm. 1-8—do you really have nine dynamic levels?*

Example 48.3: Rachmaninoff: Concerto in C minor, Op. 18, *3rd mvt., mm. 431-434*

Horowitz's pedal technique

As in just about everything else, with regards to pedaling Horowitz presented a special case. I had the opportunity to observe his pedaling at close hand, sitting on stage in Massey Hall, Toronto, in 1979. His piano was voiced so brightly that for *any cantabile* passage the left pedal would automatically go down. As soon as he released the left pedal he had exceptional brilliance and power at his command, but there was no way he could play a sweet *cantabile*—there was too much metal in the sound!

Even the way he placed his foot on the pedals I have never seen elsewhere. He contrived a way to depress the pedal that feels more difficult when you first try it, but actually cultivates this feeling of constantly trying to lift it up rather than tromp it down. It also dramatically increases your physical sense of the distance between the pedal's position when raised and when depressed, thus augmenting the number of half-pedal shades available to you. Rather than placing the ball of his foot directly on the pedal, he would leave his foot resting on its outside edge by the side of the pedal. The outside ridge of his foot always lay on the ground, and only the ball of his big toe, not of his whole foot, rested on the pedal. Thus his pedaling movement was a rotation of the foot sideways, not a vertical up and down movement hinged at the heel as most of us do.

You need not only more strength but greater sensitivity as well to pedal like this, but it gives you much greater command over what you're doing. When mastered, this physical arrangement helps you enter that magical world of $\frac{3}{4}$, $\frac{1}{2}$ and $\frac{1}{4}$ pedals, where the heart and soul of the piano dwell.

49 TOGETHER!

I haven't counted up the various practice techniques scattered throughout this book so far, but surely they number in the dozens. Suppose hypothetically you're stuck on something—you just can't play it right and you've tried everything! Don't lose hope, there's one I haven't mentioned yet which always works! And it's the simplest of the lot (but that doesn't mean it's so easy to do).

Application 49.1
STRUCTURAL FUNCTION XII: HANDS TOGETHER

You may not have noticed this, but it is highly doubtful that your hands are really together. "No way", you say. But I'm serious, and I can prove to you that trying for a greater degree of togetherness is always a fruitful line of work. The proof is very straightforward, actually—suppose your hands *are* together to let's say within one tenth of a second. Then try for a hundredth of a second! If you can succeed to a within hundredth of a second, try for a thousandth! There's always room for improvement.

Increase togetherness of hands to improve your sound

What may not be so obvious until you discover it for yourself are the amazing sonic improvements possible to achieve this way. There is a direct relationship between togetherness and tone quality that is not arithmetic but geometric. That is, if you succeed in having your hands play twice as much together than they did, their tone will improve not twofold but fourfold. This is true all the way down even to let's say one two thousandth of a second.

The reason is very simple—it's physics. Let's say you play the octave A 440 (A above middle C)—A 880 (that is, the A that vibrates at 880 cycles per second).

The first harmonic which they share is A 1760, the second E 2346, the third A 3520 and so on. If the attacks of your two notes are out by 1/1760 of a second, the first partial or harmonic that the notes share will not vibrate in phase. This will reduce quality of piano tone. You may think I am splitting hairs, but this is a verifiable phenomenon. Try it out for yourself!

Trying for togetherness uncovers insidious habits of overmoving

The other wonderful aspect of this is noticing why they are not together. You are probably indulging in all sorts of unnecessary movements. You may think you've gotten rid of those nasty over-movements, but even if a 1 percent vestigial trace remains it is enough to throw your hands out of sync. You may be lifting a finger to give a note extra articulation, not noticing that you are also making its attack a hairsbreadth late. You may simply be lavishing so much attention on one hand that the other gets lazy and fails to keep up. You may discover that your two hands have differing ideas on the nature or degree of rhythmic impulse required. In a chord, the differing structures and strengths of your fingers might be causing them not to descend together. There are literally thousands of possibilities. Use your ears to ferret out your remaining bad physical habits.

Develop your powers of observation

- **You must develop your attention.** These tendencies must be overcome by sheer power of concentration. First and foremost, you must observe.

- **You must develop your hearing.** In many cases I must simply sit with the student and stop them every two notes or two bars to point out that they think their attacks are together but in fact they are not. They simply did not hear the lack of togetherness.

- **You must develop your powers of sight and kinesthetic sensation.** Take two keys and have them descend slowly, making sure they are together in every micro millimeter of the descent. They hit the keybed simultaneously; they are really one. A better, more perfect marriage could not be envisioned even in heaven itself. Are you really cultivating this degree of accuracy in all your playing? Check it out—you stand to gain a great deal.

50 Questionable Contradictions

One thing you may have noticed wading through this confusing labyrinth of techniques and ideas is that some principles seem in direct contradiction to others—that an idea appears somewhere in my text and a few pages later I'm just as vehemently urging you to do exactly the opposite! Well, you're not going crazy, you did indeed notice this. Here are a few of the most glaring examples:

1) *"Don't press! Pressing strangles the free vibration of the soundboard"* disagrees with "Press and hold to consolidate structural security and strength of sound."

2) *"Don't swing your elbow out to the side (the classic conservatory movement). This reduces your contact with the key, especially by pulling your thumb away from its note and weakening the structure of your thumb-forefinger metacarpal-phalangeal ridge. It also tends to cut your phrase into little ever-so-expressive bits"* contradicts "swing your whole arm on each note while maintaining solid key contact for gloriously rich, singing tone."

3) *"Don't break your wrist. Don't let the force vectors sheer off at an angle, but keep the forearm and hand at a more or less neutral angle to each other. This avoids jamming, and allows the power of your arm to go down through your wrist into the piano instead of veering off somewhere underneath the piano"* seems to oppose "in rotation, let the heel of your hand stay to the inside as your thumb goes to the outside", which is in effect breaking your wrist.

4) *"Your arm is not a finger"* would certainly seem to negate, "Make your arm a 2-kg. finger"!

But do you see that there is wisdom in all of these? You *can* press, as long as you don't strangle tone. Indeed, often we will first practice pressing and holding to

consolidate our feeling of contact, and then sophisticate this basic touch so we don't stifle tone. Tone must not be choked but yes, it must be maintained. Similarly, you can let your elbow out as long as you take care to maintain the structural functionality of your hand and wrist, thus avoiding all the possible negative side effects. And in rotation your wrist indeed must break, but not to the point of jamming. Sometimes we need to accent finger/arm individuation, at other times their cooperation. It all depends on the musical context. To produce a kaleidoscope of sounds we need a plethora of pianistic approaches. Many of these will seem to be in radical opposition to each other, but it stands to reason: a Bach Sarabande has little in common with the closing octaves of the Tchaikowsky B flat Concerto—they're light years apart.

Once again, as Feldenkrais said, if you know what you're doing you can do what you want. You should be able to do any of these well—press or not press, swing or not swing, break or not break—and to understand when to use each. Only you can decide, based on the musical context and your own organization, what to do in a specific situation.

Each of these seemingly contradictory examples was given to a student at a specific time to address a specific problem. While reading this book you are your own teacher, so you must be able to observe yourself intelligently, to evaluate where you're off—to see what's missing. Then choose the exercise that helps you. And remember, trust your own curiosity!

When new knowledge appears it is fresh and alive, but after repeated transmissions through the generations it tends to pass into stale, mechanical repetition. This is the almost inevitable state of affairs. So, once more I append this cautionary note: do not do these physical exercises mechanically. Stay curious, and always relate these physical practices back to music. Listen to yourself! Live in the music! Respond, react! Always know the reason you're engaged in a specific physical technique—always relate the physical back to both your thinking and your feelings. Because ultimately, you're honing locomotion to evolve your emotions.

This brings us to the end of part one, where we focused purely on the physical. Of course we are far from having exhausted the subject—in fact, we have barely scratched the surface. I have only presented some basic ideas in the hopes that they stimulate you, point the way towards your own exploration and development. As we now consider some aspects of musicianship at the keyboard, keep in touch with the physical sensations you have been cultivating. Keep aware of them; let them 'remain in your system' as an aid to the fulfillment of your musical tasks.

SECTION II
THE MIDDLEGROUND

SOME GENERAL ASPECTS
OF MUSICAL CRAFT

XI

RHYTHM

51 HIERARCHY OF RHYTHMIC VALUES IS A PRACTICAL REALITY

The starting point for our physical approach was hand structure and function in legato. This provided us with a foundation. Our musical discussion also needs a foundation, and this is best taken to be rhythm. It may sound strange to say, but one fundamental quality of rhythm is that it is *not* metronomic. The metronome would seem to give us something fundamental to healthy rhythm: absolute evenness of attacks in time. But remember, this is only an indication, not the end product!

The astonishing fact is that healthy rhythm will always *diverge* from metronomic regularity for two key reasons: 1) the nature of phrase breath (to be discussed in part XI) and 2) the discrimination of levels of rhythmic hierarchy: the difference between strong and weak beats. If you have the type of metronome that can click strong and weak beats, set it now to let's say, three-quarter time, one strong and two weak beats. At this point you may be surprised to hear me assert that your metronome is no longer rhythmically accurate!

Your metronome is now *distorting* a bar of three-quarter time into mechanical regularity, but *real* three-quarter time is not like that! In a rhythmic bar of three-quarter, the second beat will generally come infinitesimally before the metronome, the third beat ever so slightly behind it. This is an example of *aural entasis,*[1] and any good musician is doing it constantly (although perhaps not consciously), no matter what the time signature. This is one of the key elements giving music its human, speaking quality. This also separates real music from the mindless mechanics of electronic drum machines and all the other horrors of 'techno' pop.

In other words, hierarchy of rhythmic structure is not something that only music theorists should worry about—it most definitely manifests in reality! Downbeats and upbeats are not the same and should never be played as such, not only

---

[1] See chapter 3, *Background, Middleground and Foreground: A Plan for Work.*

in terms of dynamic differentiation *but of their placement in time*. Although this applies to all time signatures, perhaps waltz time affords us the best chance to grasp the essence of this idea.

The three beats of a waltz are by nature unequal

There is a practical reason why each beat in a measure of waltz time is unique and dissimilar. There must always a slight pause between beats two and three, because the dancers need a moment of suspension to help them slide through beat three, then swoop still further on down through beat one and on up to the next moment of poise.

There is nothing worse than three beats in a bar completely undifferentiated. The listener cannot hear properly, because there is no basis for discrimination. As well, these rhythmic discriminations form the basis of control for the performer. Both player and listener must feel that sense of lifting the dancers and whirling them around the floor. Three must always lead into and through one. There must always be that rhythmic *élan*—if you're just typing notes you're wasting your time (and mine!).

The pulse that locomotes your dancers is not created by dynamic accent so much as by a feeling of push. Try pushing someone, literally placing your hands on their shoulder or back or chest and giving them a gentle but firm shove on each downbeat. It is not a rough push but it lets the person being pushed know in no uncertain terms that *this* is the movement the music is generating. Now try and play, lending this feeling of push to each downbeat. This can be done in any meter, not only in waltz time. Notice that the feeling of push can be drastically improved through a slight waiting before the beat. This is what makes it a push rather than a hit—there is a sense of control in it. Now we are really grappling with the complexities and contradictions inherent in rhythmic inflection. Beat three must be delayed to help you move *into* beat one, but beat one must be delayed in order that we feel that *push!* Yet it *is* possible to achieve both!

The push that the musician senses as she or he plays should be such that the dancers actually *feel* it—they feel buoyed by that impulse, as if your physical push can be felt in the musical sound, lofting and lifting and whirling them around the floor. Do you know how to waltz? Why don't you enroll in a dance class and learn! Through experience and feeling you will come to understand this in a useful way.

Phrase entrance, exit are also components of rhythm

Here is another strange assertion: phrasing is a key element of rhythm. I say this because each phrase entrance, no matter on what beat of the bar, lends a certain rhythmic impetus, a kind of impulse to that moment in time. Every phrase must have an *entrance*. This entrance is not necessarily accented yet it defines the beginning of the phrase in a way we can feel, and creates a sense of pulse as well. If this pulse does not receive a dynamic accent it can still be felt, solely by the sense of a gesture, of entrance.

There must also be a freeing at the end of the phrase, a physical release. Even a little three-note slurred group becomes one musical entity rather than three separate notes when both entrance and exit are attended to. Charming music must be played with charming inflections!

Hemiolas must be felt as well! This means that micropauses must be inserted before all three beats of a hemiola, thus lending to each of them a virtually equal stress. You must ensure that listeners *get* the rhythmic variation of a hemiola. Almost poke them in the eye with its insistent quality, but of course elegantly, not harshly.

We might even say that pulse equals phrase, phrase equals pulse

I was exhorting a student to improved rhythmic practice in Bach's D minor prelude from the WTC Book II, but wasn't getting any results. Even with an explanation of micropauses, rhythmic stability and differentiation of beats,[2] I was hearing no music, just notes. Here's where we can explore the interrelatedness of rhythm and phrasing. In the end, I say that they are the same thing. Why?

Example 51.1: Bach, Prelude in D minor, WTC II, *mm. 1-5*

---

[2] See *Nuts and Bolts: Rhythm* in appendix III.

Pulse will not be felt unless the notes in between are phrased

For pulse to have its ultimate or real musical life, the notes in between each pulse note are just as important as the pulse notes themselves. These must not only be even, but also have phrase value. One way to achieve this is to imagine each group of four 16th notes under a slur, and to play the four notes of the slurred group either in diminuendo or in a *mezza-di-voce* pattern, crescendo-diminuendo. Imagine the slur as a violin bowing, and really perceive the difference in sound when the four notes homogenize into a single musical unit of expression rather than four individual events. As you already know, if you refrain from moving your arm up and down on each note, you vastly improve your chances of succeeding in this.

Examples 51.2A, B: Bach, Prelude in D minor, WTC II, *m. 2
(four-note slurred groups)*

Alternately you might separate the pulse note from the following three unaccented notes, putting only the unaccented group under a slur. In either case it is by attributing a phrase value to a rhythmic pulse that you give it musical content.

Example 51.3: Bach, Prelude in D minor, WTC II, *m. 2
(beat notes separate, three-note slurred groups)*

Looking at things from the other end, there is always one note in a phrase, a point of orientation around which the phrase organizes itself. This note will always be inflected in some way that increases its rhythmic weight. We may separate out phrase and rhythm from one another in certain stages of practice, but the sooner we realize their interrelatedness and incorporate both into our practice strategy, the sooner we will reach a true foundation upon which we can base our interpretation.

52 A PRACTICAL EXERCISE IN RHYTHM

Pulse: the lifeblood of any musical performance. Let's discover if you have really mastered this phenomenon by going back to the simplest of all rhythmically generative patterns: the Alberti bass. By dividing the notes of this little four-note pattern between the hands in various ways you may be able to increase not only your physical facility, but also your flexibility of thought and ultimate mastery of rhythm.

Application 52.1

PULSE I: DIVIDE THE HANDS TO EXERCISE YOUR BRAIN

Alberti bass split between the hands to increase brain flexibility

Step 1: Start by taking the beat note with your left hand, the other three notes with your right. Give the beat note a good, healthy *oomph*, while playing the other three offbeat notes extremely lightly. Don't play them staccato but use the 'finger dropping in from the platform hand' technique (feather legato) for an extremely light and exact sound. When you have achieved a degree of perfection you may want to increase the arc and activity of your right hand finger stroke for more speed and energy, but maintaining a distinct difference in quality between the two hands. Do not use any side arm motion in the downbeat: the *oomph* or push must be a direct transmission of arm, hand and finger motion to the key. Keep your left hand quite stiff,

even try the bird beak shape—poke or peck the key with slightly loose wrist and the whole compact mass of your arm. Try doing this on a tabletop or other surface. You should create the most graphic difference possible between the sound and feeling of the two hands.

Example 52.1: Rhythm Step #1—*left hand on beat, right takes three offbeat notes*

Increase dynamic without increasing speed

Have you ever noticed that the louder a note, the quicker the descent of the key, and the sooner in time the note sounds![1] Thus whenever we increase dynamics we should compensate for this strange phenomenon with an infinitesimal waiting before the attack. This is the surest cure for rhythmic hysteria and lack of control.

For instance, notice here that as you increase the loudness of your left hand, your movement becomes quicker, causing the note to arrive too soon. Not only that, but in your attempt to make a louder sound you may tend to get internally excited, and jump on the note, causing it to sound even sooner. This is one of the main problems in rhythm: how to adjust or compensate for these phenomena that cause one to rush and lose precision of attack?

Micropauses for graphic, tangible pulse

Step 2: You must insert a micropause before each strong beat—the stronger the beat, the larger the pause. This is brain work, and useful for several reasons. Inserting the micropause adds an element of mental control to a process which otherwise can be distressingly unconscious, automatic—we tend to take rhythm for granted. Also, the instant of mental clarity afforded by the micropause allows you

---

[521] See *Nuts and Bolts: Rhythm* in appendix III.

to monitor any imbalance in your physical system that might have
built up during the previous rhythmic group, and to re-equilibrate.
Thirdly and most important, the pauses allow the hierarchy of rhythmic structure to be heard more clearly by the listener. There is a
tremendous heightening of perceptibility, the interplay of beats and
offbeats becomes tangible, not only heard but also felt in a much
more profound way.

Example 52.2: Rhythm, Steps #2, 3—*left hand on beat, right takes three
offbeat notes*

Pulse: precise muscular control of the moment of attack

It is most useful to think of pulse not so much as a dynamic accent (volume of
sound) but rather as precise control of the moment of attack. This is achieved
through the distinct activation of various parts of the musculature further up
your arm.

Distort pulse proportions (a la Parthenon) for an even more visceral rhythmic feel

Step 3: If you insert just enough of a micropause to keep you in time,
this is already a great thing. But by lengthening the micropause even
further we enter the realm of heightening rhythmic effect through art-
ful distortion of the succession of pulses: another type of rhythmic
entasis. Just as in our Parthenon example concerning the proportional
relationships of note durations in phrasing, we can enhance the audibility of pulse by overdoing the micropauses. Applying aural entasis to
pulse opens up another wonderful new realm of musical creativity for
us to explore. Before moving on to variations on this exercise, try to
do the initial one again, noticing what effect incorporating the principle
of rhythmic entasis to a greater or lesser degree has.

Cross hands over

Step 4: When you have mastered a really tangible, visceral, meaty rhythmic feel with this first pattern, now reverse the hands. Cross one arm over the other and let your right hand take the bass downbeat while the left takes the offbeats. It's not so easy! Achieving the same level of accuracy requires no small amount of effort on the part of that grey matter in your cranium!

Example 52.3: Rhythm Step #4—*right hand on beat, left three takes offbeat notes*

Master more variations for more brain flexibility

Step 5: But this is just the beginning. Now try different note patterns, and after mastering each new pattern taking the beat with your left hand, again switch your hands to take the beat with your right. For instance, if you played C-G-E-G before, now play C-E-G-E. Do each of these variations to perfection. You will increase the flexibility—*of your brain*—immensely!

Example 52.4: Rhythm Step #5—*new note patterns*

Step 6: Now change the downbeat note. For instance, play E-C-G-C, or E-G-C-G, or G-C-E-C or G-E-C-E.

Example 52.5: Rhythm Step #6—*change downbeat note*

Step 7: Try some of these again, but changing your fingering. Here the possibilities are virtually limitless—but we're *still* not finished!

Vary not only the note sequences but which hand takes what notes

All these you've done with one hand taking the beat note, the other hand the three weaker notes. Now we can mix up *that* pattern!

Step 8: Let your left hand take notes one and three of the four-note group. Give a lesser stress to note three but let it still have slightly more sound than notes two and four.

Example 52.6: Rhythm Step #8—*left hand takes first and third notes, right hand takes second and fourth*

Step 9: Or play an 8-note group: C-G-E-G-E-G-E-G, with your left hand taking only the first note. Step 10: Then with it taking notes one and five.

Step 11: Then notes one, three, five and seven.

Example 52.7: Rhythm Steps #9, 10, 11—*variations on how many beat notes taken by your left (or right) hand*

Step 12: Or a 16-note group, following the same logical progression.

Always maintain an incredibly clear difference in sound between the beat and offbeat notes, as if the one piano is actually two instruments. And it goes without saying, always maintain absolute rhythmic stability as well. Doing this requires—guess what?—brainwork!

Try making up your own variations. Try finding variations which *you* can do but which discombobulate your friends! Quite simply, the more of these you master, the better musician (musical craftsman!) you become.

53 Creative Work with the
Metronome: Pulse

Rhythmic pulse must be generated from within rather than imposed from without. Thus many people including myself do not advocate constant practice with the metronome. That infernal machine can suck you dry of any inspiration, spontaneity and humanity. But here I suggest a way of working with the metronome that respects the idea of rhythmic generation and even capitalizes on it.

Application 53.1
Pulse II: Mastering the Metronome

Become the master, not the slave of the metronome

Instead of listening to the metronome passively, struggling to synchronize your musical pulse with the machine's, try playing a game with your perception.

> Step 1: Imagine that by playing the note or chord, *you* are causing the metronome to tick! Create it in your mind that it is really so: the downstroke of the key, the impact of the key hitting the keybed, sends the electrical impulse to the metronome that makes it tick. This completely changes the order of things: instead of doggedly trying to align your playing with an often all-too-foreign outside irritant, now you are the master, the generator of the impulse, the intention.

When we feel harassed by the metronome-master we are distracted from the process of music making: we too become reduced to machines. Working in this new way leads to a healthier, more human rhythm. There's a hidden reason why:

Mentally, physically relax prior to pulse note

In order to successfully play this way, you must be mentally and physically prepared in advance to generate each pulse. There must be a moment of relaxation prior to playing the pulse note, in order that you are free to hit the beat exactly on the mark. If you try to control the attack through tension you have no hope of success. Any tension creates a constraint that invariably deforms the attack somehow, making it inaccurate. Ideally, you will use the entire of group of unaccented notes prior to the pulse note to cultivate this quality of relaxation. Thus this group as well acquires a better quality—more evenness and flow. Try this:

> Step 2: In running 16ths in four-four time, play the three unaccented tones a little faster than the metronomic speed. This facilitates the relaxation needed to make them really even, flowing and unaccented. It also leaves you with a little time before the pulse note. In this extra split second you can gather your awareness, sense and plan the exact instant you will play the pulse note, leaning on it slightly, *pulsing* it so that it is entirely in sync with the metronome. If done exceptionally well, the attack of the pulse note obliterates the sound of the metronome, literally drowning it out!

Here we kill two birds with one stone, establishing a rock-like firmness of rhythm while also creating in a natural way the micropauses described earlier.

XII

PHRASING

54 CREATIVE WORK WITH THE
METRONOME: MELODIC INFLECTION

Chopin described rubato as the left hand keeping time while the right hand played freely. This description has the seed of truth in it, but also has led to much confusion. For one thing, it seems impossible! How can the hands stay together if one is in time but the other is not? The method of metronome practice described below may shed light on the crux of the matter. We will work with the soloist's opening theme from Rachmaninoff's Second Concerto, first movement, as its structure provides an ideal opportunity to investigate the phenomena not of rubato but of melodic inflection.

Here we will discover the practical meaning of the basic principle of musical declamation mentioned earlier: long notes longer (played slightly slower than notated), short notes shorter (played a little more quickly). Remember, this musical practice need not be done in a gross way. Lengthening or shortening by only a few microseconds may be enough to create the effect of aural entasis we seek.

Slower tempo lends tragic emotional tone to Rachmaninoff's Second Concerto, first movement

Rachmaninoff marks the tempo of this movement Moderato, with the half note equal to sixty-six. Most pianists take a faster tempo, perhaps following Rachmaninoff's lead: both his own recordings have significantly faster tempi. However these performances were recorded in the days when you could only fit four minutes on a record side, and the recording engineers required Rachmaninoff to quicken many of his tempi to fit a certain section of music onto one acetate! So much for the relevance of the documentary evidence!

In any case, following his original tempo indication allows for a much more expressive reading, and the movement's tragic overtones begin to see the light of day. A quicker tempo destroys all possibility of the tragedy unfolding.

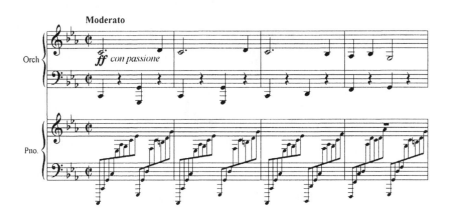

Example 54.1: Rachmaninoff: Concerto #2 in C minor, *1st mvt., mm.* 11-14

Note that at the movement's climax, the beginning of the recapitulation, he marks a new tempo, *Maestoso (alla marcia)*. Again, the tendency is to follow the *alla marcia* and play it in a vigorous march tempo, ignoring the fact that *Maestoso* would indicate an even slower tempo than the opening. Rachmaninoff clearly intended a tragic march, with dark, almost funereal overtones.

Example 54.2: Rachmaninoff: Concerto #2 in C minor, *1st mvt., mm.*
245-248

At one point in the film *Richter: Enigma*, the tolling of massive Russian church bells segues into the opening chords of this concerto—I can think of no better example of the monumental, tragic emotional impact of this music than Richter's performance here.

In one lesson I was using the metronome to steady a student's vacillating tempo, but we quickly noticed that if the melody was played keeping in time with the machine, it lost all its poetry. Here was an opportunity to use the metronome not dogmatically but in a way that would heighten musical effect. This next exercise can be done without the left hand's accompanying figuration—just work with the melody alone.

Application 54.1
PHRASING I: THE METRONOME AND FLEXIBILITY IN PHRASING

Ahead of or behind the beat, nevertheless always tied to it

Step 1: At measure 55 the soloist finally takes over from the orchestral melody.

Example 54.3: Rachmaninoff: Concerto #2 in C minor, *1st mvt., mm. 55-58*

When rising from G to A flat, the temptation is to delay the A flat, thereby making it more 'expressive'. However by doing this

we lengthen the initial eighth note G, going against our basic principle of long notes longer, short notes shorter, and bogging the melody down. Things very quickly become heavy and long-winded if you keep up this type of inflective strategy. Instead, move *through* the G, bowing *up* into the long note A flat, giving it some impetus and allowing it to soar. Quite simply, if you wait between G and A flat, you kill the A flat.

You can shorten G either by delaying its attack or even by allowing A flat to sound *before* the downbeat has arrived. Standard conservatory training most certainly forbids this type of freedom, but isn't this exactly what Chopin describes? We are trying to develop a rational set of rhythmic strategies that when employed will lead to an intelligent, noble rubato—one that deepens not cheapens expression.

Step 2: Following along this train of thought, at measure 56, try delaying the quarter notes F-G-A flat. In other words, lengthen the note A flat (measures 55-56); heighten its singing expressive quality by extending it, drawing it out. Don't worry about the metronome—after the downbeat of measure 56, waaaaait almost until the halfbeat ticks before playing the note F. When you finally allow yourself to play that F, swoop up; begin to make up the lost time by moving the rising line forward. Thus although the note G will still sound after the metronome's halfbeat tick, it is already closer in time to the beat, and by the time you arrive at the half note B flat you will be back in time, or again even slightly ahead.

Step 3: Now again lengthen the long note: draw out the half note B flat (measure 57) and delay the sounding of the A flat quarter note until after the metronome's halfbeat clicks. Speed up the quarters notes A flat-G to arrive on time or even a little early at the A flat whole note (measure 58).

Unfortunately it takes several paragraphs to describe in words what takes only a few seconds to occur in time. Perhaps a visual image can show more effectively the proportional distortions involved in this type of aural entasis. In the following graph the metronome clicks are marked at regular intervals while the notes are displaced either to the right or left depending on their

relation to the beat. Notice how clearly the visual displacements allow you to 'see' the phrase shape that you are trying to create. Your eyes can literally 'feel' the breathing of the phrase, its ebb and flow.

Example 54.4: Rachmaninoff Concerto #2 in C minor, *1st mvt., mm. 55-58—melodic departures from metronomic regularity to breathe life into phrase*

Be careful; overdoing this type of shaping can very easily lead to musical disaster. In this graph I have heightened the proportional differences to make them clearly visible, but in actual time your departure from the beat might be less blatant. It's all a question of degree and of taste—what effect do you want to create? Are in you in total command of all the resources needed to create it?

Have you gotten the hang of it? Continue now to inflect the whole theme following this rubato strategy, at first still using the metronome as your accompaniment. Then turn it off and reinstate your left hand. Why not leave the machine on? Didn't Chopin say the left hand keeps time? Yes he did, but in practice it turns out that not even your left hand should keep absolutely metronomic time. It stays a lot closer to the beat than your right hand does, but not entirely in sync with it. Your left hand does keep time but in a flexible, human way.

Do you find the complaint rising within you that this amount of detailed work kills artistic or emotional spontaneity? I beg to differ: we are working to lend integrity to your spontaneity, allowing you to enhance expression by following rather than contravening the basic rules of declamation. Look closely: there is a whole magnificent world of spontaneity awaiting you in the *degree* to which you delay a note or flow through it. There are literally thousands of ways to do it that don't go against basic laws! Learn those laws, observe them, learn to use them to your advantage. This can become a wonderful stimulus to artistic maturation! Even spontaneity can be educated, and so it should.

Mozart's Sonata in B flat major K.333, 2nd movement

Phrase structure in this slow movement is very similar to that found in our Rachmaninoff example.

Example 54.5: Mozart: Sonata in B flat major, K. 333, *2nd mvt., mm. 1-4*

Here a group of shorter note values almost always leads to a longer note on the downbeat. The lack of accompaniment figuration in the first few bars allows you to stretch and then move with extra audacity. Try really overdoing it just to expand your horizons a little! Do this to give yourself a graphically strong experience of freeing yourself from 'metronomicity' and opening the door into the world of melodic breath. When Mozart introduces an accompaniment at m. 8, try to maintain this graphic sense of breath you have established.

Example 54.6: Mozart: Sonata in B flat major, K. 333, *2nd mvt., mm. 9-13*

The difference in your phrasing should be so marked as to destabilize you at first. It requires a really radical adjustment in your thinking!

Chopin's E minor Nocturne, Op. 72 #1

Similar to our Mozart and Rachmaninoff examples, this nocturne's melodic structure consists mainly of longer notes on the downbeat, shorter notes leading to them through the latter part of each measure. In this example I have indicated by words instead of spatial proportions the type of push-pull phrasing we're aiming for. Which type of graph helps you more? It all depends on your thinking style. Some will react more immediately to the visual image of the spatial proportions while for others the verbal commands you should be telling yourself in the moment will be more helpful.

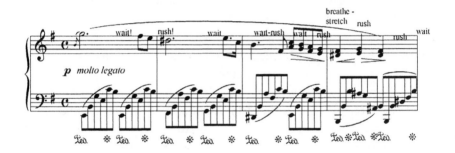

Example 54.7: Chopin: Nocturne in E minor, Op. 72 #1, *mm. 2-5*

First practice the right hand alone with the same stretch-and-pull breathing strategy. Again notice how you must stretch *more* than you thought, and to rush forward almost *criminally* to really, definitively break out of the straightjacket of metronomicity. Dare to be audacious here; and so discover how to bring the tragic, lonely quality of Chopin's melody to life.

When you feel you've really mastered this, do you see how Chopin's regularly flowing accompaniment can indeed be played flexibly enough that it can follow the singer's lead?

Chopin's Scherzo in B flat minor, Op. 31 (again!)

Finally, the scherzo discussed earlier provides us the opportunity to attack one more exceptionally clear-cut case of metronomicity: the falling chords at measures 17-22.

Example 54.8: Chopin: Scherzo in B flat minor, Op. 31, *mm. 17-22*

Do not play them in time! Note that m. 17 has a quarter note and two quarter rests while measures 18 and 19 have a half note followed by one quarter rest. This gives us a clue as to how to proceed. Wait a moment in the two quarter rests of measure 17: slightly lengthening their duration emphasizes the fact that there are two of them. Then purposefully rush slightly through measures 18-20, arriving unexpectedly soon on the F of measure 20, like the Tasmanian devil bursting unexpectedly into a room then glancing around to see where he's gotten to. Your slightly premature arrival on the upward appoggiatura F of measures 20-21 gives you the perfect excuse to now lengthen it, and what, given the musical context, could be more appropriate? It gives the Tasmanian devil time to sight his prey, and for you to feel the tension of that appoggiatura fully before you finally *pounce* on the G flat of measure 22 as our devil would on the unlucky Bugs Bunny! Thus in measures 17-19 make the long *rests* longer, the shorter rests shorter; then in measures 20-22 return to lengthening the long note.

This practice of bringing rhythmic character to life should be constantly at work in your playing. The next chapter continues to explore this essential part of musical craftsmanship.

55 Plasticity in Phrasing: Expression without Bombast

Repeated agogic accents an unevolved expressive strategy

There is a way of being expressive where I . . . pause before an important . . . word and lay a . . . stress on it. It is a common way of being expressive at the piano as well: pausing before the downbeat note and then stressing it. 'Tah', it comes out sounding, and *voila*, you're so musical!

Well it's not really so simple. Laying an agogic stress on every downbeat serves to cut the phrase into little pieces—bar by bar we laboriously slog our way to the end of the piece. One such accent and we are enchanted—so expressive! Two or three and it is already starting to wear a bit thin. By the tenth we're looking at our watch wondering when is this going to be over? This is one standard way of being expressive that is relatively unevolved. There is a much deeper, wider, more passionate way of expression which follows the whole shape of the phrase rather than cutting it into one bar or half-bar sections.

Application 55.1
Phrasing II: Don't Cut Phrases, Complete Them

Rachmaninoff's Etude in E flat minor, Op. 39 #5

The melodic structure of this magnificent etude affords us a wonderful opportunity to investigate the phenomenon of melodic life. Here longer notes often occur not the downbeat but following it—the group of quicker note values moves not to the downbeat but *through* it. Note that Rachmaninoff did not include phrase markings in his opening theme as he does for the

second theme, measure 26 ff. The only indication he gives at the beginning is *molto marcato*, implying that indeed a trumpet-like articulation of each melodic note is called for.

Example 55.1: Rachmaninoff: Etude Tableau in E flat minor, Op. 39 #5, *mm. 1-5*

And yet the melody must remain melodic and not bombastic: how?

> Step 1: Try singing the melody of this etude, on purpose making a big agogic accent on each downbeat. Note how the music grinds to a halt on each stress.

Example 55.2: Rachmaninoff: Etude Tableau, Op. 39 #5,
mm. 1-11 with agogic stresses

Cut it or care for it—what is your relationship to the life of a melody?

A melody has a life of its own. The tone of every note, after its initial attack, has a continuation. Each note has a beginning, middle and an end. As a note flourishes, lives its short life, it develops momentum. Even if there is no crescendo in the note, there is an accumulation of energy, of total number of vibrations through the note's duration, which if sensed, can serve to launch the melodic line to the next note, so that one note's energy connects itself to the next. This is the nature of melodic flow, and we must be careful about interfering with that flow—it is not to be done indiscriminately but only when the expressive structure can benefit from such an intervention.

As the long phrases of this etude develop, as the process of melodic spinning out progresses, the momentum and movement increases in power. We do not increase in speed, yet there is a mounting intensity that results from the accumulation of flowing melodic vibrations—the melody is an alive thing that carries you along more and more. By being agogically expressive on every downbeat note, we effectively cut this momentum—we emasculate the music's melodic power. Just as the melodic wave begins to develop some power, and this is an emotional power not just vibrational—it is passion—we cut it off and must start again from zero.

> Step 2: Now try singing the melody again, but this time smoothly, with no agogic stresses—you'll notice that it feels much better. You're no longer strangling the melody to death! And notice that if you consciously restrain yourself from speeding but hold back your tempo, almost broadening it, this as well increases melodic power.

But something is still wanting—we've eliminated the flaw but we did not yet inflect the melody in any way. We need to find other strategies we can use besides agogic accent to be expressive, techniques that do not go against the melody's inherent expressive structure but heighten its expressive passion, enhance the mounting flow of energy.

Sing to create pure musical image, then translate it to piano

I asked you to try singing the melody in these different ways instead of playing it on the piano for a very specific reason. We must learn to think not "how to play the piano", but rather "what is the nature of music?", "how to express this music", "what are the rules of musicianship?" By divorcing yourself from the piano for a moment and turning to the most natural of all musical instruments, the human voice, you can deal with these issues more directly.

> Step 3: Sing the melody once more, this time following the phrase shapes indicated in the example below. I have put an arrowhead on the end of each phrase mark to indicate how it should feel as you sing it. Bow through the whole phrase, gliding through the down-beat and not letting anything interfere with a smooth arrival at the goal note of the phrase. Sensing an entrance, an impulse *in* as you begin the phrase will help as well.

Example 55.3: Rachmaninoff: Etude Tableau, Op. 39 #5,
mm. 1-11 with shaped phrases

Dynamic and rhythmic direction for phrase life

A melody has natural peaks and slopes. You can see the contours visually on the page. The melody of this etude characteristically moves across the barline. Thus here it is exceptionally counterproductive to make agogic stresses on the barline. Melody consists of note values which can either get faster or slower or stay the same. If we follow the rule of inflection, then long notes are played infinitesimally longer, short notes shorter—that is, we exaggerate whatever quality the note has rather than distorting it.

> Step 4: Thus if there is a series of even note values, exaggerate their evenness. Certainly do not cut the group of regularly flowing notes in the middle! The group of notes with unchanging note values generally has a goal—you must not interfere with its reaching that goal. In this etude the downbeat note is often this goal note. If you use the even melodic flow towards that downbeat to buoy the music, to loft the melody to the goal note, the sense of passion and intensity increases dramatically. Instead of using agogics for your expression, use dynamics and rhythmic direction. A crescendo to the goal note with no agogic cut will very quickly unleash the juices of passionate expression in large quantities!

Example 55.4: Rachmaninoff: Etude Tableau, Op. 39 #5, *mm. 1-2—counterproductive phrasing strategy*

Example 55.5: Rachmaninoff: Etude Tableau, Op. 39 #5, *mm. 1-2—advantageous phrasing strategy*

Cut neither the phrase nor the actual physical forces coming down through your arm

You must feel as if you are actually lifting the listener up. Make a real crescendo, which means start softer! To avoid a pressed crescendo that is also ugly, do not leave your wrist too low. You risk creating a lot of strain on the wrist joint: the energy that should be going directly into the key is going down somewhere under the keyboard instead, creating strain in the sound and on your wrist as well.

> Step 4: Press your splayed fingers against a wall as we did earlier, keeping your hands arched, and now lean on them, really—with all your weight. But first have your wrist go in a different direction from your hand and fingers—of course the energy is dissipated rather than focused. Do you feel what tremendous strain this misalignment creates?

> Step 5: Now line up your forearm, wrist, hand and fingers—really align them well and see how your force goes *through* them into the wall now! Hercules, watch out! Learn to use the copious energy of your body and arm mass effectively by aiming it in the right direction!

Soloistic expressive rubato—for the accompanying orchestra: verboten!

> Step 6: While the melodic long note sounds, the repeated chord orchestral accompaniment surges underneath. Several strategies should be employed here. Do not try to make the accompaniment expressive in an agogic way. As soon as the repeated chords begin to speak *espressivo*, they draw our attention away from the melodic long note. We don't want that now, do we? The *espressivo* also disturbs the sense of rhythmic flow. Not only does the accompaniment distract because of inappropriate expressiveness, but also because the smooth energetic momentum of a developing melodic note is again being interrupted by its subordinate partner.

When you do little *accelerandi* and *ritardandi* in the under parts, any orchestral feel is lost. No conductor could possibly conduct all those rubati, and even if he could, he would only be destabilizing the soloist instead of supporting her or him.

Step 7: Try having two pianists play this—one takes only melody, the other only the accompaniment. When the accompanist indulges in expressive rubato do you feel how this strangles the soloist's melodic line? When the accompanist tries *not* to mess with rhythmic flow, doesn't the soloist feel buoyed, helped by these surging vibrating chords? Why yes, of course! Can we feel the flowing, wave quality of the repeated chords yet not infect them with a false expression? Aim not for metronomic regularity, but just enough ebb and flow to give the repeated chords life: the life of *an accompanist* not a soloist. This difference is crucial. A natural flow and surge can contain much more real expression than a mannered rubato does. When this is done well, whole pages of music take on a tangible shape because you haven't obscured the forest with a bunch of trees.

Step 8: Don't play the repeated chords with rubato, and don't rush them either. Remember, long notes longer: if you rush the repeated chords you only succeed in shortening the long melodic note that they are accompanying. You must flow forward without *rushing* forward! This subtle ebb and flow is best done with dynamics, not rhythm! Rushing the repeated chords draws our attention away from the melody just as expressive rubato does.

For more on orchestration in Rachmaninoff's Op. 39 #5, turn to part XII.

Breaths between phrases can be counterproductive

Not only should we avoid over-cutting phrase flow, but we should also manage the delineation between phrases with care as well. How much should phrases be joined or separated in time? It all depends on context. The moment that joins two phrases is rich in possibility for various types of musical inflection.

More often than not we take a breath between phrases in order to articulate them, to clarify their place in the musical structure. But sometimes the composer arranges his musical structure so that phrase delineations are naturally felt without any need for further inflection on the part of the performer. Liszt's *Jeux d'eau* is a case in point. Here our performing strategy should be to join phrases more than separating them with breaths.

Example 55.6: Liszt, Jeux d'eau, mm. 32-43

Application 55.2
PHRASING III: CONNECTIONS BETWEEN PHRASES

Liszt's Jeux d'Eau

> Step 1: For instance, at measures 39-40, the join between intro-
> duction and first theme, we tend to wait before the first note of
> the theme, articulating the beginning of the new phrase and sec-
> tion. This causes the music to stop dead in its tracks. Any water-
> like flowing effect we may have succeeded in creating is quickly
> dispelled in a moment of musical aridity! No! You must join the
> two formal sections not separate them. If you want their nature
> as two distinct sections to be felt, it is best to slowly lengthen the
> expressive syncopation of measures 38-39 instead of stopping
> dead at the end of the measure to breathe. In this way it is possi-

ble to articulate two phrases even as you link them together agogically. The melody must arrive like a blossoming newness. Ease us gently into its opening note; do not poke us in the eye with it!

Step 2: More on the syncopated figure that precedes the first theme proper: Be sure to put a micropause before the syncopations at measures 36 and 38, and then lean on them, lengthen them to heighten their length effect. The resolution of this figure is a note of shorter duration. Lengthening it would go against one of the fundamental principles of the art of rhetoric—longer, short notes shorter—whereas shortening it has more than one advantage. By respecting this note's 'short' quality you also allow it to seamlessly join the introductory material to the first theme proper (measures 39-40 again), killing two birds with one stone.

Liszt has also built in a natural phrase breath at the end of the introduction by slowing down the sequence of attacks. At measure 34, the flowing 32nd notes suddenly stop and we find ourselves in 'water droplet' chordal quarter-note writing. Here the cessation of activity alone provides all the structural breather we need. Adding a breath-pause before the entrance of the first theme is certainly a case of overkill—the music grinds to a halt. No, this music must flow like the water fountains of its name, and this strategy applies for virtually all the phrase connections in the piece.

Lengthen long notes

This shows how in *Jeux d'eau* as in the Rachmaninoff etude, the consistent application of our basic principle of rhetoric will accomplish a great deal towards keeping things flowing and naturally expressive. If you want to be expressive in a supple, subtle way, don't lengthen a note of shorter duration—this distorts the natural time proportions of the melodic structure. Instead, lengthen a long note: that's what they're there for, to be expressive. The shorter note values should serve as connecting links to the longer notes, which can sing, soar, breathe—if they are given the time.

If you breathe on the short note leading to a long note you go completely against this principle. You add expressive value where it is not wanted, and rob the long note of its rightfully deserved full length. Instead, cultivate respect for the structural relationship of long and short: heighten the effect of these proportions

instead of deforming them. Do not bring the music to a full stop just when it needs most to flow. You may occasionally want to go against this principle for a specific expressive purpose, but take care: do with extreme perspicuity! Know what you're doing and why you're doing it!

Soft wrists for limpid staccatos in Jeux d'eau

> Step 3: The water droplet chords preceding first theme proper (measure 34 again) also require a special loosening of your wrist. A plucking motion in which you draw your hand back, cocking your wrist is not needed here—that would tend to give us too aggressive an articulation. The languid, gentle character calls for the wrist rather than your fingers to come up as you pluck. Again, here is an opportunity to develop flexibility of thinking, not just of movement. Pluck each chord 'wrist up', with a loose, limpid hand, until the syncopation at measures 36 and 38. Then really fall in, letting your wrist fall more than your hand. And up again for the resolution of the syncop, measures 37, 39.

A higher type of control

If you are one of those 'safe' pianists, playing very correct but controlled, this will open up your tone color. This is control, *but on a higher level.* The control is derived not from physical contraction or holding but rather from the mind and ear choreographing a movement which guides the fingers in exactly the right path to play a supple melodic line with a specific character. The melody blossoms, lives and breathes rather than being stifled. Now there is no need to compensate a wooden sound with an artificial rubato—expressive content is derived naturally from the buoyant suppleness of the line.

Melody in octaves: wrist flexibility while maintaining finger contact

> Step 4: Later on when the melody appears in octaves or chords (measures 64 ff, 144 ff, 198 ff) you will need flexibility in your wrists for a different reason. Here you must clarify which parts of your mechanism perform what function.

Example 55.7: Liszt: Jeux d'eau, *mm. 64-67*

Example 55.8: Liszt: Jeux d'eau, *mm. 144-147*

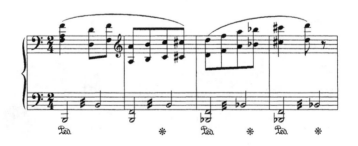

Example 55.9: Liszt: Jeux d'eau, *mm. 198-201*

There must be lots of release in your arm/wrist even as your fingers play *tenuto*. If your arm does not feel secure in its connection to the keyboard, it will not release and free itself up but

continue to strangle, stifle your sound. Only your fingertips can provide your arm with this crucial contact. Your fingertips will press into the key more or less depending on the type of tone we want, but remember, for the sound quality demanded by the character of *Jeux d'eau*, only your tips must press, not your arm. Motion *into* the key is generated through the arm, but not pressure *on* the key. Instead, release any tendency towards pressing from your arm even as your fingertips maintain secure contact. Thus here you can afford to loosen up your arm/wrist on every octave melody note, as long as your fingers continue to hold each octave to the maximum time limit. Keep loosening until you hear the tone blossom.

Note as well Liszt's pedal markings. They would seem to indicate that he wanted something that was far from full pedal, that you should rely rather on your actual touch to produce that special singing, blossoming tone.

This is the practical differentiation of function. Here we see clearly *why* your finger needs to hold on while your arm/wrist is releasing.

56 Gesture in Phrasing: A Detailed Examination

Other elements in legato besides the physical

Some of the simplest preludes and fugues provide excellent opportunity to ascertain if our legato is everything it could be. We may be connecting from the bottom of one key to the next, but is this perfect connection reflected in our sound or is a further element needed to have our physical legato *sound* gloriously legato? Many times we physically connect and yet the melodic line still proceeds 'plunk plunk plunk', because we depend solely on the fingers. This of course cannot work. This chapter and the next will consider three additional ingredients—two mental-aural-musical and one physical—that are needed to have your legato become everything it can be.

1: Dynamic inflection

There's a danger in stating that a melody should always be in either crescendo or diminuendo. We tend to overdo it if we try too literally to 'inject' these hairpins. The dynamic shadings can easily become forced, arbitrary. And yet it is true: a melody's flexibility, its very life depends on these subtle qualities of growth and subsiding of sound. Any singer knows this (except the modern day power singer, the *can belto* specialist who thinks that louder is better, and any other type of expression is only for weaklings!), and if we try to imagine a singer's sound as we play, our instincts are to move with the natural melodic surges. So we must constantly, consciously shape—always a little louder or softer.

Clues: violin bowings and vocal phrasing

It's a question of degree. One of the best aesthetics for melodic inflection can be found in renaissance and baroque violin bowings. The old bow was

very different in structure from our modern bow. Because it was less powerful, the old bow stroke produced a 'zing' sort of sound, a natural crescendo-diminuendo that even acquired its own specific name: the *mezza di voce*. Singers of that era then picked up on this and used the *mezza di voce* to give expression to their melodic lines in a way quite different to the long-phrased, Romantic style more familiar to us today. Cultivation of *mezza di voce* led to an increased sensitivity to the subtle possibilities inherent in the ebb and flow of melodic contour.

This is true even in Mozart. Take a look at an urtext edition of his sonatas. There are virtually no long phrase marks. Occasionally you'll find a slur covering two bars (never more), but for the most part the slurs are restricted to a measure or less. This reflects Mozart's background as a violinist. Quite simply, in his piano music he indicates phrasings exactly as he would bowings to the violinist—thus it is the logic of the violinist's bow that governs his piano phrases. Here we see how this Renaissance/Baroque phenomenon carried through even to later historical eras.

Thinking in terms of violin bowings, of melodic gesture, we are more likely to shape in an expressive way without overdoing it or forcing it. We must sense the aliveness of it—each melody has its own unique shape and thus requires its own unique inflection: a dynamic shaping which is suited to its own specific content. This dynamic shading can be done in finer degrees of difference if we don't think crescendo—diminuendo mechanically but follow the evolution of the melodic structure as a living entity. And it is of course inextricably linked to a subtle rhythmic ebb and flow—it tends to come more naturally when done in tandem with the rhythmic micro-alterations described in the next chapter.

2: Refinement of physical movements

Similarly, the amount and quality of physical movement needed to phrase successfully is largely a question of degree. If I overmove it is counterproductive. I never move gratuitously, in order to 'produce tone'. I never move on a single note unless I want it declaimed, purposely spoken in a way that breaks the phrase. I most often move *through* a group of notes, joining them in melodic flow.

I will also refrain from pressing my wrist down. It is difficult to maintain a state of physical neutrality while maintaining the standard low wrist position I most

often encounter in my students. Slightly higher, towards the true neutral where the line of the forearm goes straight through the hand to the finger, allows the arm to float and to contribute to melodic tone—the supple ebb and flow of the dynamic level.

Stop wrong moves, not all moves!

We must analyze all the things that could possibly go wrong with this. When I have a student curtail her gratuitous generic movement, sometimes she stops moving altogether! There must virtually always be *some* movement, the degree of which is dictated by the musical line. However, most of our movements in this regard are too gross, because we try to do them with the analytical, thinking part of our mind. Our reflexive movement organism hasn't yet learned the fineness of it. When you approach the level of subtlety needed, you might measure the movement of your wrist through a phrase in just micromillimeters.

But even moving a tenth of a millimeter a second is completely different from not moving at all. That tiny difference in amount makes all the difference in the world to your sound. Your tone improves drastically when musical movement is reflected exactly in your physical movement. It's all in the way you move. There are literally hundreds of movement options that are at odds with the musical direction or shape, but a quite few that indeed express the exact shape of a phrase in elegant choreography.

Replace generic moves with exact melodic choreography

Conservatory training cultivates a few generic arm movements, the most common of which is the elbow out to the side. The goal of these movements done constantly and automatically by thousands of students the world over is to improve tone, eliminate harshness and relax, but they achieve nothing of the sort! If your physical movement goes contrary to the musical movement you are bound to increase your physical tension and the harshness of your tone as well, not decrease it. The only thing you decrease is your musical organization. If you want to improve the tone of your melody, improve your physical inflection of its specific and unique musical content! Choreograph it! Your tone loses its lustre, gets harsh the very instant you move contrary to the melodic contour instead of aligning your movement to it.

The difficulties of polyphonic choreography

This is why playing polyphony is so difficult. Simply keeping track of the notes of the various melodic strands is a relatively easy affair, but following the exact contour of each melodic part takes a lot more awareness: it is brainwork! It is very easy to make generic movements, any one of the many old moves already stored in our physical memory banks. But it's a much more complex exercise for the mind to follow and inflect even one exact melodic contour and cultivate that special blossoming of tone that results. Multiply this by two or three simultaneous melodic shapes, each with its own unique blossoming tone, and you have your work cut out for you. It's not so easy! When one hand must deal with more than one voice, you must find a compound movement of the wrist: one that can inflect several contrasting melodic shapes simultaneously!

Do your sigh motives really sigh?

Although each melody is unique, there are some general rules to be followed. For instance, do you sculpt your sigh motives enough to make them really speak? The diminuendo needed to make a sigh expressive is likely more radical than the one you're doing. Again, following the exact shape of the sigh with your wrist helps inflect the musical content of the sigh in your sound.

The easiest way to avoid harshness of melodic tone is of course to be in continuous diminuendo. Piano tone is constantly dying away; by being in diminuendo we easily blend one note into the next. However if you follow this principle unswervingly you very soon run out of gas—you can't get any softer! Finding the places where it is advisable to swell in tone is one of the key strategies you need to develop in your evolving skills of melodic inflection.

For instance, syncopations provide a convenient opportunity for increasing your expressive intensity while maintaining respect for musical content. Any louder note following a softer note will most likely create some degree of accent—can you find syncopations and other places in the melodic line that could benefit from an agogic stress, which need the extra attention? For a gradual swelling with no accents can you ensure that there is no bump by managing a perfect physical legato, especially important in crescendo?

When the composer calls for a stronger dynamic, can you maintain the same flowing physical organization and not succumb to the 'bang' syndrome? The

louder you play, the more likely you are to try too hard, thus weakening your physical structure somehow, producing strain instead of tone. There is a way to play even *ff* without losing the basic physical ingredients of phrased sound. You must consciously cultivate it!

Instead of passively maintaining a legato touch and observing the melodic flow, you are actively participating in shaping its expressive ups and downs, living them, generating them as a vocalist would, letting your movements shape its contours as they come. Of course, there is also the danger of being too involved or rather involved in a wrong way: Do not press; do not over-try; do not give way to an inner tension triggered by some emotion. Expression is not derived from your inner tension; it is generated by the contour of the melody itself.

All this is to the end of overcoming a certain stuck-ness, a certain limitation. You may have conceived a really beautiful phrasing in your mind: do you bother monitoring whether it is actually sounding that way in practice? You cannot rely on your instincts to do this for you: you may not have trained them well enough to succeed in such a job! You need to know *how* to shape for the most beautiful tone possible and to be actively involved in doing it. Your involvement is not some generic indulgence in gushing emotion but the enactment of a certain task that allows the composer's intended emotional tone to find its voice.

It is possible to have good head, hands and heart. But if your head does not guide your hands in an informed way, how successful can you be? It is the connection or relationship between head, hands and heart that makes the whole musician. Intelligent generation of the phrase through your wrist can make you a musician instead of a note-reproduction machine. Done properly it effectively joins your head to your hands, and it is this that facilitates the blossoming of your heart's expression in sound.

The art of phrase inflection is a technical tool—a skill you need to acquire and practice. Mastering this particular skill brings truly bounteous musical rewards. If you can already conceive of and sense subtle differences in shades of emotional tone, this technique now allows you to manifest those nuances in sound.

57 Towards a New Mode of Awareness in Playing

Remember that the exercises using a lot of muscular effort to obtain a true legato touch are only a step towards a legato we can use in performance. The excessive amount of effort involved provides a stimulus that is one effective way of waking up your hand—literally thousands of sensations come alive that were dormant.

You will understand the skeletal structure of your hand when you can feel it. Using a certain force directed towards a specific, precise goal is one way to line up the bones of your hand. As soon as the exact alignment of the bones falls into place, you can let the effort go—the structure will remain. The more your structural connection to one key can be maintained with perfect solidity and minimum effort, the freer you are to play the next note precisely as you wish.

This all relates to *yin* and *yang*. Remember, *yang's* strength is bone-derived, not muscle-derived. The following exercise demonstrates this with exceptional clarity.

Application 57.1
Legato XII: Refined Legato Engenders New Process of Phrase Intonation

Play a dyad with any two fingers that are not adjacent to each other. Hold the notes firmly. As finger two, three, or four fills in the dyad to make it a triad, try and find the sensation of slipping a sheet of paper into an envelope. Your fingers on the triad's outer notes are the sides of the envelope; your inner finger is the sheet. Paper would seem too thin and malleable to serve as a structural material, but it is just this quality that has it serve as an

344

optimal image—an envelope holds its contents securely despite its lightness and flimsiness.

This is not quite the feeling of feather legato I describe elsewhere, but an alteration or refinement of our original T'ai Chi walking legato to make it more amenable to our musical needs. When you find this exact quality it will open up the possibility of a new subtle dimension of musical expression, incredibly rich in its diversity. You now have a practical physical means to control the flow of musical attacks to the very millisecond.

3: Micro-adjustments in rhythmic flow

How to move a phrase forward without rushing? How to broaden a phrase without loosing the sense of basic pulse? Just as in dynamic shading, here as well it's all a question of degree. A sense of rushing is not derived so much from any change in speed as from lack of control. If your pulse and the way you carve out the phrase are secure, you can play as fast as you like and even accelerate without it sounding rushed.

By cultivating this touch you can refine things even further. If speeding up the flow of attacks by one tenth or one twentieth of a second per note disturbs and creates a sense of agitato, now you can remove the bumps in your melody by accelerating only a hundredth or even a five hundredth of a second per note. This opens up countless possibilities for minute variations of speed and articulation between each two notes in the melodic line, imitating the myriad subtle nuances of human speech.

The general problem with trying to make a phrase move forward is the tendency to press it forward, to force it somehow. This touch gives you a sense of poise in which you can feel exactly when the next attack should come—you are waiting for it, and then just when that moment is about to arrive you might slip the note in a tiny bit ahead of time. Voila! You've avoided a bump in the line and that stodgy note-by-note feeling, yet you did not alter the basic rate of pulse flow by any significant amount. But always when you slip notes in ahead of time there comes that moment when the opposite is needed—the melody now needs to breathe, to relax a bit. Again your sense of poise comes to your aid, allowing you to broaden in just the precise amount that the phrase expands without losing pulse and flow.

When you lengthen a note, there is a moment when the next melodic attack *must* arrive—if you wait any longer you'll really cut the melodic line. I call it the 'half-life' of the note.[1] When you prolong a note slightly beyond its notated duration, it has a chance to soar and bloom—the listener does not expect it, and just a modest lengthening is enough to create that blossoming effect. The longer duration comes as a welcome surprise. Ah! We have a chance to really feel the note, experience its speaking. But at a certain point if you don't move on, the note dies. Its 'half-life' is spent; it cannot be drawn out any more.

Order, precision, exactitude

Return now to the musical examples of chapter 54, pp. 321-26. Can you find just the right amount of rhythmic inflection, the one that suits *your* taste? These ways of altering the flow of rhythmic attacks tend to sound banal or mannered only when they are overdone, implemented in a gross way. We lack the control to do them in just the right amount. It's a question of order, precision, exactitude. These processes might take place several times per second. You might think that the effect of such micro-alterations might be lost on an audience perhaps too far away to perceive them. But paradoxically the opposite can happen. Your attention to detail, your heightened ability to manipulate microscopic increments of time opens up the audience's listening as well. In the end they perceive the music with a heightened awareness—your cultivation of this mode of expression evokes in them a heightened ability to listen.

Free your playing from a conventional aesthetic

Bringing these techniques of micromanipulation to the art of melodic inflection infuses it with a refreshing richness. In the end you don't do it with your thinking. This touch couples your ear to your sensing mechanism, which works much faster than your analytical mind. The emotions work fastest of all, and they can make even dozens of subtle alterations per second if you provide them with the physical means. That's why I say that this touch can free you from your automatism, from all your habitual ways of shaping a phrase,

---

[1] The atomic half-life of a radioactive substance is the time needed for the element's radioactivity to diminish to half strength.

conventional formulas that were inevitably instilled in all of us through our training. It joins your ear to your hand, allowing you to sense both aurally and tactilely exactly what the melody wants to do. How it wants to speak at that given moment in time. This is true interpretation, the bestowing on a melody its own life rather than imposing on it your own ideas about it. In the end you can arrive at an entirely different way of playing, one based not on adherence to an imposed aesthetic but to absolute laws of musical shape and content.

Neuhaus says somewhere that a pianist must be someone "who has something to say to others." In this way of playing, I personally may not have anything to say at all! *Mozart, Beethoven* et al. had something to say. It is my job simply to unlock the secrets of their utterances. To manifest what *they* had to say in my playing, I must be able to feel—but *my* feelings are not of such great interest to an audience—it's *Beethoven* they want! I must feel what the composer felt—my feelings function only to bring the composer's emotional experience to life again. I won't be communicating my feelings *about* Mozart or Beethoven's music. No: my feelings simply function as a sensing antenna, transmitting the composer's feelings that generated the music in the first place.

XIII

ORCHESTRATION

58 ORCHESTRATION: THE HEART OF THE PIANIST'S ART

We should be orchestrating at the piano all the time. Everything we have discussed so far aims to empower our orchestrations: to make them clearer, more graphic, more dramatic, more effective, more colorful. Orchestration and tone color have cropped up at many points in our discussion already. Look back, for instance, to chapter 37, *Using the* Yin/Yang *Finger Phenomenon in Orchestration*, chapter 38, *Natural Finger Shape and Tonus in Chords*. This subject is so vast that an entire volume would be required to do it justice. Here we must be content to consider a few key points—the challenge is yours to explore and expand on these in your own playing.

Application 58.1
ORCHESTRATION III: ACCOMPANIMENT'S LEAD ROLE IN CREATING OVERALL DYNAMIC LEVELS

Let's first turn back to Rachmaninoff's Etude Tableau in E flat minor, Op. 39 #5 for some tips on dynamics in orchestration.

> Step 1: From measure 18 onwards the melody often sounds in full four-note chords or octaves. Play all four parts of the chord as if each is a lead melodic voice. This gives you an orchestral sound. Do not do normal top note voicing! Try out Application #58.2 for a physical solution to this.

Example 58.1: Rachmaninoff: Etude Tableau in E flat minor,
Op. 39 #5, *mm. 18-20*

Step 2: When we reach *ff*, let the repeated chords come up in dynamic level. We modify our normal practice of subduing the accompaniment, because this would rob us of *ff*. We cannot crescendo in the melody itself because we have already been trying for as full, singing sound as is humanly possible. Thus it falls to the accompaniment to help us out. It creates the crescendo by swelling up until at the peak of the crescendo it almost (but not quite!) drowns out our lead voice(s).

Example 58.2: Rachmaninoff: Etude Tableau, Op 39 #5, mm. 22-24

Generally, in any dynamic from *mp* to *ff* your melody should remain in the area of a full-throated *forte*. It is through your accompaniment that you have tremendous leeway in creating the impression of changing dynamic levels—anywhere from *ppp, p, mp, mf* and *f* through to *ff* and *fff*. This of course all depends on

your absolute control of dynamic differentiation, which in turn depends on your physical and aural capability—we'll be sending you back to section one before you know it!

A few further pointers

> Step 3: When we reach the second theme at measure 26, remember again: no rubato in the left hand figuration. Instead flow naturally through the tied notes, joining measures together instead of cutting them.

Example 58.3: Rachmaninoff: Etude Tableau, Op. 39 #5, *mm. 26-27*

> Step 4: When the main theme returns in the left hand thumb at measure 53, play all thumb notes *ffff!* By now you should be capable of organizing your thumb to do this successfully. Have you ever come across a teacher who recommended using your fist to achieve the trombone-like orchestration required here? Instead, I recommend you find a way to use your thumb to create just as bold a sound as your fist would, but with finer control. Develop your technique to develop yourself! And here too, keep the accompaniment chords (now in the right hand) an expressive *mf* but flowing—none of that rubato garbage!

Example 58.4: Rachmaninoff: Etude Tableau, Op. 39 #5, *mm. 53-56*

Remember that the very construction of Rachmaninoff's melody lends itself to this natural ebb and flow. The long notes of his melody almost always occur at the beginning or middle of the bar, the even-flowing eighths always leading across the barline.

Application 58.2
ORCHESTRATION IV: A SIMPLE APPLICATION OF GRASPING IN ORCHESTRATION

Here we look at how the fingers' role in grasping can be utilized to improve orchestral tone.

Step 1: Play a four-note chord C-E-G-C. Normally the top voice receives primary voicing, and the lower octave secondary. This voicing is necessary for the lead voice to have color. But there's a hidden tendency for the two inner voices to become pale, lose their vitality, to fail to make their contribution to the overall orchestrational color.

Step 2: As you play and hold onto the chord, draw your second and third fingers towards your hand in the basic grasping motion. Don't curl them. Leave them hyper-extended so the pads can give you richer color. Your fingers will press into the keys and slide on them towards you a little, and their knuckles still rise a little into their hummock shape. Notice the blooming of the inner voices—now there's a fully orchestrated chord!

Application 58.3

ORCHESTRATION V: ORCHESTRATION AS RHYTHMIC MEDICINE

In these chapters of section II we are working with the ideas of sound, phrasing and rubato in a specific way. One implication that seems to be emerging is that good orchestration is an effective cure for unhealthy rubato habits. Many pianists indulge in a type of rubato that can only be described as contrived, gratuitous, mannered or rhythmically warped, simply because they are not doing what they should be doing in terms of orchestration. Just as overpedaling is commonly used to cover up lack of security in fingerwork, mannered rubato attempts to leave an impression of expressivity when a great *sound* is what would really touch the listener's heart. When you throw your concentration fully on doing your job in terms of togetherness of attack, playing to the true bottom of the key without excess tension, and creating tangible, obvious dynamic differences between your orchestral parts, you simply won't have any brain power left over to indulge in your normal bad rhythmic habits. Then the surprising thing occurs. You are now giving all your attention to craftsmanship and none of it to expression, but your playing has become more expressive! It now *speaks*—fancy that!

I am not telling you to neglect the subtleties and myriad expressive possibilities inherent in the art of shaping a phrase. I *am* saying do not neglect the foundation of pianistic craftsmanship that will render this practice indeed an art and not a travesty!

Let's return to Rachmaninoff's second concerto, at the first movement's second theme, measure 83 ff.

Example 58.5: Rachmaninoff: Concerto in C minor,
Op 18, *1st mvt., mm. 83-87*

The right hand melody is played in octaves or full chords. We can orchestrate the chords by conceiving them in parts. Hearing the melody as being played at the octave by let's say first and second violins will give us a different sound than if we hear it as octaves on the piano. There must always be a sense of duet between different orchestral voices, even if the second voice only doubles the melody at the octave. If in addition we conceive the interior harmonies to be provided perhaps by some combination of woodwinds, the whole right hand gestalt takes on a wonderfully rich shine and resonance. You may of course voice the inner lines down in dynamic, but not so much that they lose color. You have likely been overdoing it in this regard, voicing them too far down.

Technically you can achieve full color in each voice by holding on to each melodic chord with your fingers as long as possible even as your arm is moving through. Here your arm both mirrors the alive, moving nature of that chord's sound and moves you into the physical position for the next melodic chord. Do you notice how much hand strength you need to do this well? It's not easy!

But that's only the first half of our orchestrational work here. The left hand must be conceived as an emotionally laden countermelody, not just an accompaniment. Imagine that your cellists are all real Slovenes, Slavic souls that love to soar to the heights of ecstasy and plumb the depths of sadness and despair. They love to paint all that emotional experience in sound, and they also have an absolute perfection of technique with which to do so. Imagine the soulfulness with which they would play that countermelody. Look how much expression is inherent therein. See how it soars up to the expressive appoggiatura at measure 84 and falls again in surging waves. Play your left hand alone until it can give the utmost in singing, soaring, expressive melodic content. But take note, it must have the utmost in expression without exceeding the bounds of its accompanal role. Cultivate a perfect legato to keep yourself rhythmically healthy. Again, notice that you need a great deal of strength in your hand not so much to get a big sound as to get a sound that has high quality in terms of legato, orchestration and musical craftsmanship.

Now when you play all the parts, do not let your left hand lose that richness of expression. If you manage to maintain the full sonic and expressive content of each hand when putting them together, you are orchestrating not only sound but also emotions. And do you notice that the effort you invest in creating that wonderful sound effectively foils your tendency to indulge in your previous inappropriate rubato habits? *This* is really playing the piano!

SECTION III
THE BACKGROUND

TELL A STORY

XIV

EMOTIONAL CONTENT

59 EMOTIONAL CONTENT IN COUNTERPOINT? YOU BET!

Bach Prelude in B minor, WTC Book I

Counterpoint: the art of inflecting voices through articulation and stress so that they sound as independent entities engaged in conversation. If this work is played all legato, the interplay of the voices is lost in a wash of tone—it may sound beautiful but the essence of the contrapuntal writing has been lost. This exquisite prelude is written in the style of a trio sonata, two upper voices in quasi-canonic writing accompanied by an obligato bass. Our first preparatory work involves playing the right hand part with two hands.

Example 59.1: Bach: Prelude in B minor, WTC Book I, *mm. 1-5*

Do not neglect subsidiary voices

In fugue playing we are taught to bring out the subject and subjugate all the other voices. However, this strategy, if overdone, in no way fulfils the requirements for contrapuntal playing. Oftentimes I will hear a fugue played such that each recurrence of the subject comes booming out while all other details of counterpoint are lost in a wash of background color. This technique of maximum voice differentiation works excellently in situations such

as the voicing discussed in chapter 37, *Using the Yin/Yang Phenomenon in Orchestration.* But it not only fails to fulfill the obligations of the contrapuntist but actually works in direct opposition to the realization of contrapuntal goals.

The word counterpoint comes from the Latin *punctus contra punctus*, literally "point against point" or "note against note", which in practical terms means "melodic line against melodic line." If all subsidiary parts are relegated to a subservient role they cannot fulfill their contrapuntal function. They no longer sound 'against' the main melodic strand. As we will see here, a melodic line has structure. Inflection of that structure in performance will make it speak, and as each line is speaking in a different way at any given point in time, the contrast between their respective structures will allow us to hear them as individual entities. But for this interaction to happen we must hear the structural aspects of each melodic part, not only the main one. This requires an interpretive strategy quite different from simply bringing out the main voice.

Inflecting melodic structure makes it speak

We practice each individual voice of a fugue separately not simply to learn the notes, but to uncover and imbibe the essence of its melodic structure. In this practice we must evaluate the function of each and every note in the melody. There is no such thing as a neutral note! A note can receive a stress (either preparing or articulating a dissonance, strong rhythmic pulse or a syncopation), or not (as when resolving into a consonance or flowing through to the next articulated note), but unstressed notes are never merely neutral. They each bear a specific weight in relation to the notes around them.

It even speaks with emotion!

The next miracle in all this: when you begin to invest in a series of melodic notes their full structural values, lo and behold they begin to acquire expressive power! You did not think at all about expression, and yet here is a melody now sounding with emotional power! How can this be? Very simple: that's the way the composer planned it. Did you really think that Baroque music was dry and intellectual? Far from it—there is as much passion to be found in Bach as in Beethoven, Chopin, Liszt or Rachmaninoff, because Bach was just as passionate a human being. Just because his passion takes a different musical form in music doesn't make it any less potent.

Application 59.1
MUSICAL STRUCTURE AND
EMOTIONAL CONTENT

A melody's emotion is inherent in its structure

Let me illustrate this. For instance, shortly after the opening of this prelude there is a little three-note falling figure in eighth notes (measure 3). Now remember, we said that no note is neutral. Therefore this motive will either be in crescendo (if we want the goal note to be especially expressive) or, perhaps in this case more to our purpose of a delicate, pathetic hue, in diminuendo. This diminuendo turns the three notes into a sigh figure, lending it a certain expressive quality. We have said that music must speak. If you are not sure how certain notes want to speak, look to the melodic or harmonic structure. The answer is right there. Inflect the structure and you have already inflected the emotion as well.

Detach leap to better articulate syncopation

Thus the opening leap F sharp-B must not be played legato but half-staccato—*portato*. I must actually be able to hear in the musical sound the physical gesture of pressing into the F sharp in order to leap up from it and land on B, just as a diver launches himself from the springboard. The stress that the B thus receives allows the syncopation of the suspension motive to be felt. Leaning on that B gives the following moment of dissonance poignancy and power—it is not empty. Then as this melodic strand falls down through A to G sharp, we are in diminuendo— the A does not receive an accent because it resolves the tension of the dissonance.

Second voice is doing something else—that's why we hear it as a different voice!

Meanwhile the second melodic voice (which you are now playing with your left hand) enters on C sharp, which is dissonant to melody #1's B. This C sharp provides the dissonant element of the suspension structure. As melody #1 is falling through the consonant A, melody #2 is leaping to its syncopation, the high F sharp, consonant to melody #1's A. This consonant syncopation prepares a second suspension figure, the dissonance of which is provided by melody #1's G sharp.

Constant fluctuation of structural intensities

And so it goes, a continuous fluctuation between dissonant tension and consonant relaxation. This is a phenomenon that can only occur between two voices—it is something foreign to homophony—or rather, when it does occur in a homophonic texture, it is the contrapuntal element of homophony. Your purpose in practicing the two voices of the right hand part with two hands is to make it easier for you to perceive and inflect all aspects of the structural dance between them.

Strategies to inflect counterpoint

Thus we see that this prelude is not just a bunch of beautiful sounds! We have found specific ways of heightening the impression of two voices in conversation. Three such strategies are:

- The clever juxtaposition of legato and staccato/portato
- Placing stresses on dissonances and the approach to a dissonance, and
- Relaxing the dynamic as the melody flows into a consonant tone.

Only when you have mastered with two hands every detail of the contrapuntal conversation in the upper parts should you attempt to play them with the right hand alone. Still do not add the left hand obligato—ensure that your right hand alone can really do its job, that you have implanted in your senses, your listening, your understanding, a real practical ability to inflect the interplay between the voices in an alive way.

Left hand 'bowings'

Now we can add the obligato left hand. Knowledge of Baroque style will lead us to conclude that this also must not be played legato. The *viola da gamba*, precursor to the cello, would have played each note with a separate bow stroke. Thus we need a detached touch that, although not entirely staccato, approaches a real staccato in lightness. Played too staccato it becomes cheery and we lose the emotional tone of pathos or melancholy, but played too legato it loses emotional and stylistic delicacy.

In studying virtually any of Bach's works, the issues discussed here should of vital concern. Of course, fundamental musical and pianistic issues still apply, but here we approach the essence of Bach, his magnificent mastery of

the expressive possibilities of counterpoint, the special reason for our returning to him again and again. Just as he mastered the compositional process of expressive counterpoint, so must we be able, through variations in articulations and dynamics, to recreate its inherent expressive power in performance. Thus through the study of his works we can develop not only our intellectual capacities but our fluency in interpretive emotion as well.

60 You Must Be Willing and Able to Live Emotionally When You Play

(written 1994)

I have been privileged to experience several peak emotional experiences directly related to music. One was playing the slow movement of Rachmaninoff's first sonata and experiencing it as the expression of a love relation. I remember tears flowing all the way through my performance even while I managed to maintain clarity of execution and perception. Rachmaninoff captured that sweet spiritual communion between man and woman that reflects everything that is also between man and god. He put it in sound—all the colors, the emotional tones, the darkness of disagreement with its emotional turgidity, the sweetness of resolution and reconciliation, the light interactions of interchanges, intercourse, conversation.

I grasped the emotional content of this music partly because I happened to be going through an intense relationship at the time. Simultaneously I was presented with the very same content in the music and in my immediate life experience. How could I miss it? The question is, how to take advantage of this correlation between life and art, how to use it and not let it slip through one's fingers, another wasted opportunity. And how to recreate at will that process of recognition even when life does not happen to be presenting the same material to you on a silver platter?

I was cultivating the feeling of each key with precise, sensitive finger movements and supporting this with the quietness of my arms, ribs and mind, quietly observing. When the emotional realization came it coursed through me, made me cry, but I maintained clarity. I didn't convulse my rib cage, nor my arms, nor my consciousness. And my piano made a sound I have never heard anywhere.

Another time something similar happened with the Schumann Fantasy Op. 17. If through distillation of my own personal love experiences I can understand and express Schumann's similar experiences with Clara, distilled into his compo-

sitions, then what is going on? Both of us have accessed a human archetype. We experienced something that exists in every person's genes. Whether or not a particular person experiences this in actual time depends on many things, but I believe the blueprint is there in the gene map. That is why my connection to Schumann can be so accurate, so strong.

Access the same archetypes that moved composer to create masterworks

When a great pianist plays at his best I feel that she or he accesses direct human experience archetypes encoded in our genes and expresses them through the schematic of the composer's notes, which the composer arrived at through the same process of divination. Your conscious self must understand the nature of these emotional, experiential *facts* which exist implicit in the music and which wait to be expressed through it.

When you listen to a musician play, do you get a sense of the level of his or her emotional maturity? This is a completely practical, even mechanical question. Can you sense quite tangibly the degree to which he or she has the wherewithal to activate this process of manifesting emotional templates?

Conceive a program to activate archetype

You must be willing to and capable of living emotionally when you play. To take another example, I was teaching Chopin's second Ballade to someone who just couldn't *get* it. So I gave her a program. Actually it started through a technical question. Her octaves couldn't *sound* because she couldn't play them legato so I said, "Imagine you are a mother. There's a wild, crazy flood engulfing your town, you're in a small rowboat, your child is dragging behind it in the water":

Example 60.1: Chopin: Ballade in F major, Op. 38, *mm. 47-48*

'He's 12 or 13 years old, already quite heavy, and you are holding onto his arm. If you let go he's gone, drowned:

Example 60.2: Chopin: Ballade in F major, Op. 38, *mm. 63-64*

'Do you *understand?* Hang onto those octaves with that kind of desperation! Do you remember the film *Ordinary People,* the scene where one brother loses another by drowning because he couldn't hang on? Bring that utter panic, the pain of that scene to this passage. *'Mama! Save me! Don't let me go!'* " I was almost yelling at her just to give her that desperate energy she needed to play those chords and octaves with a real clinging, screaming legato touch:

Example 60.3: Chopin: Ballade in F major, Op. 38, *mm. 69-71*

'Then as the torrent subsides, the absolute grief: 'I let him go; I couldn't hang on. He's gone, gone, I couldn't do it' ":

Example 60.4: Chopin: Ballade in F major, Op. 38, *mm. 71-74*

As I was explaining all this to my student, *I* lived it totally. My *student* was crying. But can you imagine, she still couldn't play the octaves legato!

It's not that the music must mean absolutely and only this particular program, which I conceived on the spur of the moment. But if you at least attempt to divine what was in the composer's mind, you have some chance of bringing an appropriate level of emotional intensity to the passage you're interpreting. Give it a maximally basic, maximally intense program, which demands the utmost exactitude and vividness of expression. Then play, and evaluate whether your playing does justice to the program you have appended. In this Ballade, can I the listener *feel* that mother's anguish and despair when you play? In order for you to achieve this, all technical resources need to be fully worked out. The finishing point for many pianists in their performance preparation here becomes the point of *departure* towards a real interpretation.

Unfortunately this particular student couldn't play legato octaves if her life (or the life of that mother) depended on it. But the 'life' of that mother literally *does* depend on it, because the spiritual essence of that fictional figure will only exist if those octaves *are* legato and phrased and intense and a dozen other things as well.

A new view of art and emotions

We are dealing with archetypes, and the archetype must *sound* in the interpretation. This process is similar to that which Gurdjieff describes in his discussion of art:

> There are figures of gods and of various mythological beings that can be read like books, only not with the mind but with the emotions, provided one's emotions are sufficiently developed. In the course

of our travels in Central Asia we found, in the desert at the foot of the Hindu Kush, a strange figure which we thought at first was some ancient god or devil. At first it produced upon us simply the impression of being a curiosity. But after a while we began to *feel* that this figure contained many things, a big, complete and complex system of cosmology, And slowly, step by step, we began to decipher this system, It was in the body of the figure, in its legs, in its arms, in its head, in its eyes, in its ears; everywhere. In the whole statue there was nothing accidental, nothing without meaning. And gradually we understood the aim of the people who built this statue. We began to feel their thoughts, their feelings. Some of us thought that we saw their faces, heard their voices. At all events, we grasped the meaning of what they wanted to convey to us across thousands of years, and not only the meaning, but all the feelings and the emotions connected with it as well. That indeed was art![1]

When you live with a composition long enough, you begin to understand it with your *being*, if your being is evolved enough to grasp these essences. The masterpieces of our culture are masterpieces because they have emotional archetypes embedded in them. How did those archetypes get there? I suspect the composer had access to whatever universal energy created those archetypes. Or maybe he simply lived a full life and put it in sound.

---

[1] P. D. Ouspensky; *In Search of the Miraculous: Fragments of an Unknown Teaching* (New York: Harcourt Brace & Co, 1949) 27.

61 THE MASTERWORKS AS EXPRESSIONS OF OBJECTIVE KNOWLEDGE

(written December 2000)

The nature of actions derived from being

Imagine that our DNA contains not only the design for the millions of chemical processes that create, out of a few basic elements, the miracle of a living being, but also the design for our behavioral and experiential processes—that the templates for certain actions and thoughts exist in our genetic material. Imagine that by a process of meditation and quietening within the physical-thinking self, we can facilitate the activation of these templates in us. That all the complex realm of human emotional experience is a body of knowledge, the templates of which we share in our very physical substance. That by this process of quietening we can pass from an externally derived acting (created by our mind that thinks it knows how but can only do so artificially, copying actions seen elsewhere), to actions more genuine in character because they are accessed from internal templates, internal being. By going so far *in* that we become sensitive to the physico-chemical structural nature of our being, we discover a mode of acting that is at once, paradoxically, both most personal (derived from our most essential self) and impersonal in that it was generated from templates of behavior common to all humanity.

Masterworks derived from being

Suppose that one thing separating the great composers from the others was their greater ability to access this other mode of functioning and to incorporate material from those templates into their compositions. If so, then perhaps the aesthetically pleasing aspect of their works, the aspect we most immediately notice, is not the most important. Perhaps these works contain, through re-creation of the process of sensing within all the way down to the molecular level, the possibility

of the performer and listener accessing that mode of existence, accessing their own *being*. Perhaps one's purpose in returning to these works and interpreting them again and again is not only to entertain onlookers but also to subject oneself to a process of learning and change, a type of strict improvisation designed to access the 'templates' of human emotion, experience and action that exist in our genetic material, and to share them with the listener.

Kemal Gekich describes it this way: "It's as if that information exists inside of us in a kind of tunnel. You just have to enter that tunnel and then partake of what is there. But this is not so easy because the tunnel is very narrow and difficult to get into."

Similarity to prayer—leading one towards being

Seen in this light, the interpretation of these works could be likened to the process of prayer. In the early 1990s *Time* magazine ran a cover story on the resurgence of religion in America. The article touched, among other things, on the nature and value of prayer. It mentioned the opinion that the act of praying, for example, for someone's health or to save a people from some natural calamity, could have an actual effect on the situation in question. But nowhere was there mentioned the inherent effect of prayer on the pray-er, the one doing the praying.

By focusing on God, the pray-er (perhaps inadvertently) moves in the direction of this going within, this becoming sensitive to the nature of one's being in the physical sense, literally sensing oneself. The prayer may be a supplication, but the unacknowledged effect and primary benefit of the prayer may have little to do with whether God grants one's petition or not.

The process of prayer brings the person closer to awareness of one's essential self. This is a self that will act not according to subjective morality, which may vary dramatically from one culture to another, but according to objective morality, those modes of behavior derived from the templates mentioned earlier, behaviors in accordance with the fundamental nature of our being. This is the practical benefit of spiritual practice. Prayer *feeds* the pray-er. It has been said that all prayers can be summed up in this one: 'Lord, please make two and two equal five'. But perhaps the real purpose of prayer is not to beg or extol that things be different, but to attune to things as they are.

An interpretive process at the piano that accesses being

I believe a great musician playing or composing at his best manifests this same process of attunement. I remember listening to a colleague perform the Rachmaninoff etudes. She is a good pianist who of course possesses her own set of mannerisms, as each of us does. This time she surprised me—her playing was qualitatively different. It was as if she personally disappeared. She devoted so much attention to inflecting Rachmaninoff's phrasing, his sound shapes, his expression, that there was no room left for her own mannerisms and they simply vanished.

And yet this was anything but impersonal playing. It was passionate, emotional, dramatic, expressive, and touched more deeply than her playing normally does. She accessed the templates of the music itself instead of imposing her own mannerism-templates that would serve only to divorce her from musical content. I believe that here she happened upon the real process of interpretation, what interpretation should be.

I believe that if another pianist playing the same works went through the same process of going so far in to the composer's 'head space' that this depersonalization took place, both performances would share that special *quality* of real interpretation but each would also bear the personal stamp of the interpreter—the two performances would be recognizably different. This is a strange phenomenon: my colleague's innate musical wisdom, derived from those commonly shared templates, is genuine, related back to the source, yet still bears her personal stamp. It is not the personal stamp of her mannerisms but of her *being*. Thus the coexistence of personal and impersonal. The interpreter serves as a channel for the source, coloring the material not with mind-imposed distortions but of *being*-derived enhancements.

62 Real Piano Sound Can Generate Emotional Content

Divining music's true meaning can lead you to divine the type of sound needed to most ideally express that meaning. But the process can work in reverse as well! Cultivating real piano sound and a phrasing that is free of distorting mannerisms can actually help you divine the music's program and emotional content in unexpected ways. For instance, in a lesson on Liszt's *Vallée d'Obermann* I was not satisfied with the change in character from the first few phrases in the bass to the subsequent answering melody in the treble.

Example 62.1: Liszt: Vallée d'Obermann, *mm. 1-4*

Example 62.2: Liszt: Vallée d'Obermann, *mm. 9-12*

I told my student to imagine two singers, a baritone and a soprano, on the opera stage, to better create that quality of real communication and interchange between the voices. Then it occurred to me that perhaps Liszt put these two voices

in the baritone and soprano ranges for exactly that purpose—to portray the relationship between man and woman. This opened up a whole new profound dimension of feeling in the interplay between the voices.

Aspects of Liszt's interior life expressed in composition

Later on, when the second theme appears, my student's sound was too open, too thick, not ethereal enough.

Example 62.3: Liszt: Vallée d'Obermann, *mm. 74-78*

So I told her, "This is heaven; imagine little tinkling bits of heavenly light; try and make that in your sound." She still couldn't get it. I stopped her and asked her what she knew about Liszt. Did she know for instance that in his youth he was reputed to be one of the greatest womanizers in Europe (although he said that it was always they who were chasing him!). Did she know that later in life he took minor holy orders? Thus we see right there in the biographical data a fundamental contradiction in his character. Two opposing forces pulling him in opposite directions, one down to earth and carnal knowledge, the other towards heavenly union with God. And all at once, Liszt's thesis for *Vallée d'Obermann* becomes perfectly obvious. It is not *Vallée d'Obermann* he's portraying but what went on in the valley, or perhaps what went on in his own soul while he was there, or even when he was just thinking about it. His aspiration towards heaven, his sense of the divinity of existence in conflict with his deep human feelings, the emotional intensity of a love relationship.

Thus after that heavenly second theme there is the transition to the storm—it has been thought that this section portrays a real natural thunderstorm. But how much more emotional punch can you lend to these virtuosic passages if you see them as the battle in his own soul—his carnal nature and that 'blasted woman' pulling him back down to earth, away from his momentary ecstatic experience of heaven!

Example 62.4: Liszt: Vallée d'Obermann, *mm. 120-121*

Just as the composition has a structural logic that is complete, a whole unto itself, so does our program. Notice when the 'heaven' theme returns after the storm, what figuration does Liszt use? Gone are the delicate hues of a pristine, heavenly vision. Now he employs a much richer, warmer figuration very much reminiscent of his *Liebestraume*, his love dreams. Here is resolution—now carnal love is suffused with spiritual light. Instead of a battle there is now synthesis between heavenly and earthly love that builds to a magnificent ecstatic climax.

Example 62.5: Liszt: Vallée d'Obermann, *mm. 170-171*

The wonderful thing is, all these insights grew out of that little request to my student to make the baritone and soprano voices sound like singers! When her sound improved, the real character of *Vallée d'Obermann* began to sound, and these further ideas just started suggesting themselves. Once the seed of a programmatic idea had been planted, the fertile ground of good piano sound and healthy orchestration nourished its growth.

XV

A FEW LAST THOUGHTS

63 TALENT AND CRAFTSMANSHIP

One mistake in judgment I have often seen some of the most talented students make (and which I confess I myself made when I was younger): to believe that because I possess a natural talent, I can get by on that and do not need to invest so much energy in the development of craftsmanship. The line of thought goes something like this: "If I practice too much I will spoil the spontaneity of my performance."

Unfortunately, people who think like this are living in a dream. They commit about the most serious and foolish error one can, because exactly the opposite is true. The more talent you possess, the more you are *obliged* to develop your musical and pianistic craftsmanship to the utmost. Just look at it logically. Even if a person with little talent practices his program into the ground he will end up with only a passable result, but at least he has reached the maximum of his potential, and he has committed no crime.

A more talented person may play better even with much less practice, but if he does not fulfil his potential his sin is far greater than his less gifted colleague's. For a greater talent, there are far more creative possibilities to be explored, and a more perfect skill in craftsmanship is required to fulfil these. The more talent one has, the better the vehicle needed for its manifestation. Talent is only raw material, and we the public are not interested in listening to that. We want the finished product, and that you get only through a process of refinement. Plain and simple, the more raw material you possess, the more complicated and extensive is the process of perfection you need to undertake.

Craftsmanship provides the means by which talent can find its full expression.

64 PROFESSIONAL DEFORMATIONS

At the recital of a colleague recently I noticed a curious dichotomy. His Beethoven Bagatelles Op. 126 were wonderfully original, with marvelously effective dynamic discriminations between voices and witty, blatant, very Beethoven-ish *sforzandi*. Later on in the program was an impressive *Dante* Sonata (Liszt), yet here I noticed a certain hysteria, a rushing forward to create an effect of excitement rather than a considered plumbing of the depths of emotional content and drama inherent in this music. It was virtuosic but in the shallow sense of the word. This puzzled me. How could he be so much musically in command at one point and then seemingly so much at the mercy of a certain set of habits shortly thereafter?

The Beethoven was newly learned but the Liszt he had learned back in his student days at Moscow Conservatory. This was even more of a puzzle: shouldn't the Liszt interpretation have been more mature and worked out than the Beethoven? Theoretically yes but in practice not necessarily so. In fact, another process altogether was at work here.

Maturity and habit

My colleague is a mature musician and a very capable pianist. He brought the full force of his talent to bear on his Beethoven interpretation. But the Liszt was a mixture of his mature musical ideas and old Conservatory habits. Although the Liszt theoretically should have been more mature it contained traces of the young, energetic but as yet unrefined enthusiasm of his student days.

Even the greatest pianists can suffer from this syndrome. Can you find recordings of Rachmaninoff, Horowitz, Richter where their performance seems to reflect the vogue of the day (that past day when they learned the work) more than their mature musical thought?

In Horowitz's case there was an additional professional deformation. As time passes I find myself noticing more and more but liking less and less his 'hysterics'—the manic bursts of electric energy with which he galvanized and seduced his audiences. But let's face it, Horowitz was thrown on his own resources at a very young age, and early on he probably figured out that this was one of the most effective ways to enlarge his paycheck!

Try listening to his recordings discriminatively: at any point in time, is it Horowitz's deep ability as a pianist, musician, and even philosopher that you hear, or might it be this 'money-making machine' aspect of his arsenal?

65 RECORDING

The microphone is your friend! The recording process tends to evoke fear, trepidation and musical constipation more than eager expectancy, but the mike can be the biggest help to clean, musical playing if you approach it properly. Just remember, the microphone hears all, and God grant that your ears should be so perceptive as that mike!

Raise exactitude of hearing and execution

One of my students decided to make a demo tape. We went back over some old repertoire she resurrected for the session. Simply knowing that she will sit in front of the microphones, and that it was my job to make her sound good, galvanized my hearing and thought processes and gave me the added energy input to raise the level of exactitude in her playing.

We spent a long time on one fugue subject alone. I started by correction: "too *staccato!*", then when she had corrected this, "too strong pulse accents!" When she fixed that up it was then "no direction to the melodic movement"—and so we would go around in circles. She could never get it right, correcting one flaw but losing command over other musico-technical elements in the meantime.

Necessity to formulate conception in advance

Finally I played the subject precisely and exactly the same way 5 times in a row, then said to her "How did I do that? You keep making one error or another because you did not *conceive* the exact sound of the subject in your mind before you started to play. You have no mental template to which you can match your actual playing! So of course there is no consistency."

She tried again, and suddenly she was listening in a totally new way. We were all listening differently! There was real attention. Her mind was involved in creating

the fugue subject, because now a process of *generation* had been invoked. We were involved in verifying that her conception was fulfilled in sound. Then I said to her, "the microphone listens like this. It hears all. It can be your friend because it can teach *you* to hear just as well as it does!"

What could be simpler? Many times her hands are not together. But she doesn't notice! She had better remember that the mike *will* notice even if she doesn't! I believe this is the hidden but true basis for fear of the microphone: subconscious awareness that you haven't done all your musical-pianistic homework! By knowing what awaits you and preparing for it, you can turn the fear of the microphone into something positive, healthy, akin to the fear of God, instead of falling into a fear that paralyses your creativity in performance. Just keep in mind who is your best help in time of trouble: God for morality, the mikes for musicality.

66 Playing an Acoustic

Many of the techniques I offer for improving both quality and sheer quantity of sound will seem like a case of overkill in your practice room, teaching or recording studio. You will realize their full value only when you try them out in a large hall.

Since the advent of recording our hearing has undergone a radical change. Although I say the microphone is your friend, in one sense it has not been a friend to the art of pianism. The microphones have actually totally eliminated the need for a big piano sound, rendering for instance many of Horowitz's hall-filling techniques grossly overblown and ugly. But you should have heard the same effect in the large concert hall for which it was intended! What magic!

I heard Horowitz for the first time sitting in the second balcony of Salle Wilfred Pelletier in Montreal (the only recital he ever gave for which his paycheck bounced!). I was about 50 yards from the stage, so far away that his Steinway looked dwarfishly small. But when I closed my eyes his sound was so tangible that it seemed I could literally reach out and touch it. I have never experienced anything like it.

I suspect that he learned to create this effect in the years he was touring all over the Soviet Union, playing one cavernous hall after another. Perhaps fate offered him the chance to benefit in this way from valuable experience.

The larger the acoustic, the more extreme your voicing

If you get a chance to practice for even ten minutes in a large hall, jump on it! Try out the techniques for extravagant voicing and big sound you have been reading about here. You'll quickly discover that what in your practice room you thought exceeded any boundaries of aesthetic quality, barely reaches the *minimum* requirement for healthy sound in a big hall. When you start to use your instrument properly and really fill the hall (some refer to this as project-

ing your sound), you may happen upon the strange feeling that it is not the piano that is your instrument so much as the hall itself. Don't listen to your instrument directly but rather to the sound of the piano that comes back to you from the hall.

It's a wonderful feeling when you find it. It affords you the opportunity to perceive the sense of crowdedness in your sound—you hear what is not clear. What I mean by crowdedness is the sense that there is not enough space between each voice, that all the different sounds keep bumping into each other rather than each voice of the orchestral complex having its own space in which it is clearly audible, clearly perceptible and differentiate-able from the others. To repair crowdedness you can now start to maximize dynamic differences between voices and thin out your pedal even more than you had been doing previously.

At a major competition in the Great Hall of Moscow Conservatory, I heard many competitors make the piano sound like a little tiny instrument in a big huge space, whereas some succeeded in making it sound like a large, healthy tone-producing instrument in a decent sized space. Tactful voicing and intelligent use of the piano's resources made such a difference that even the way we perceived the proportions of the hall itself was altered.

Many pianists never exceed level one; most are satisfied to reach level two. But there is a third level possible, one that requires even greater extremes of voicing, more intensive varieties of color. It is very difficult to achieve, because these extremes make great demands on a pianist's mental and physical resources. For instance the more extreme your projection of a solo voice, the more difficult it is to avoid unwanted accents and maintain a perfect legato. But the reward of success is one of the most profound experiences a pianist can offer an audience. It is difficult to describe objectively. It is as if every listener in the hall not only can hear the sound of the melody speaking to them but can even feel it. The intensity of the melody becomes not only aural but *physically vibrational*, touching the heart in the most tangible, direct way possible.

Much of the expression we try to create through our habitual, mannered rubato sounds incredibly cheap when compared to this, for me, real emotional content, real contact created through intensity of vibration.

67 Feeling Emotion in Performance

Emotion and physical tension

When you feel emotion do you feel tension in your body? When you feel emotion as you play, do you feel excess tension somewhere? Does your breathing change? Do you move in a certain way that you wouldn't if you weren't feeling that emotion? There is a very strong tendency to associate the feeling of an emotion with increased tension in the body. This is of course disaster for a musician, because the excess tension prevents him or her from hearing accurately, sensing accurately, moving accurately, or even feeling emotion accurately! The body tension also renders the emotion a generic emotion—all those emotional feelings start to take on a similar hue. Beethoven's emotion begins to resemble Bach's emotion, which resembles Liszt's and so on. Even sad and happy start to bear a resemblance! It all seems so emotional—but it's not, really, is it? Isn't this kind of superficial generic emotion really something closer to hysteria?

Some recommend that we try not to feel emotion in performance but to keep our heads clear—just to plan what we want to execute and do that successfully. Others recommend going with that feeling: that's what gives a performance life, that's what makes it human. I would say, learn to dissociate the emotion you are feeling from the physical tension that it usually triggers in our body, often in your chest area. This way you can have your cake and eat it too—you can simultaneously have your clear head and feel what you are feeling.

Another consequence of this ability to separate: each emotion takes on its own unique hue. The emotion unpolluted by the physical interference is free to be fully and exactly what it is and nothing else. You become a lot calmer. You learn to differentiate emotion from hysteria. The feeling your performance communicates becomes deeper and more meaningful.

And, as every good actor knows, if an emotion is felt, there is a resultant specific body tonus that is a direct result of that specific emotion. This is a completely different psycho-physiological process from the generic hysteria described above: physical resonance rather than interference. This phenomenon can be used to tremendous advantage in performance, because the body tonus resulting from a specific emotional state has a direct influence on your sound. In other words, if you exist in a feeling state of fear, fear will be in your sound. If you're feeling joy, the 'joy' tonus of your body will directly help make your sound joyful, and the same for sadness or any emotion.[1]

In his autobiography, *My Life*, Chaliapine describes a tenor singing a very tragic role but 'overdoing it', the result being general hilarity in the audience instead of the reaction the tenor intended. Afterwards Chaliapine went backstage and found the tenor crying. "I am always this moved by the terrible fate of Paillasse—I cannot help crying" explained the tenor.

"I understood at once", writes Chaliapine. "This singer who without doubt had no lack of talent, played his role badly simply because he shed not Paillasses's tears but his own, the tears of a man perhaps too sensitive for his own good. It was comic instead of tragic, because the tears of a tenor are of interest to nobody.

'Adaptation of the ideal means of expression for an artistic goal is the only way to create a harmonious and stable image, living its own life—no doubt through the actor, but independent of him. Through the actor-creator and independent of the actor-man."[2]

Later Chaliapine writes, "As I was singing the phrase I noticed that there were tears on my cheek. At first I paid no attention, thinking that they were the tears of Sousanine (the role I was playing), but in the next instant I noticed that in place of an agreeable vocal timbre, some sort of plaintive croak was issuing from my throat. I realized that it was Chaliapine crying, not Sousanine, and I instantly took hold of myself. 'My friend', said my inner critic, 'don't get too sentimental. Leave your Sousanine to his pain, and pay attention to singing and acting your best.' "[3]

When your 'expression' is derived from your internal tension, from your own personal reactions to the emotional content of the music you are playing instead of from the emotional content of the music itself, you as well run the risk of

---

[1] See also *Conception* in appendix III.

[2] Chaliapine, 116-117.

[3] Ibid., 119.

producing laughable instead of laudable pianistic results.

Static interference

Another issue related to emotions, or perhaps in this case to a background mental state, is a kind of static interference that tends to cloud the mind, most often when we most need clarity. It is related to the first category above, but instead of a physical disturbance this takes the form of a mental disturbance. The phenomenon is not triggered by 'feeling' an 'emotion', but rather is brought on by the effortfulness with which we approach a difficult musical or technical problem.

The practice of directed attention in meditation—observing something while your mind is clear of its normal stream of associative thought—can point the way towards solving this problem. Clearing the mind of associative thought is an extremely difficult task, but even a modicum of success here will tend to highlight the appalling lack of such a clear focus in our playing.

Whenever the music gets loud or intense, or necessitates a quick leap of some sort, our mind's first tendency is to succumb to the overwhelming nature of the experience. The effortfulness with which we approach the physical difficulty seems to make one's head fill up with cotton batten. Here it takes a great effort of will to maintain clarity of mental execution.

One of the root causes of this is a lack of familiarity with or mastery of our physical mechanism. As one gains increasing control over one's technique, one needs less effort to accomplish even difficult tasks. Beware, you may tend to maintain the initial effortfulness, that quality of trying even though it is now superfluous. Another insidious problem here is that audiences tend to *like* this feeling of trying. They respond to it; it gets their adrenaline juices going—they think something's happening!

They tend to think that this inner agitation indicates one is achieving something of musical value, when it is actually working against any such thing happening! It is a mistake to assume that any effort clouding the clarity of our perception is working for us. Check it out—can you catch the mental blackout which no doubt occurs just seconds before you make a blunder? Can you catch the genesis of that blackout, some sort of increased stress on your system triggered by a stressful technical situation in the music, which in turn leads to a 'trying' reaction?

Even if, having mastered a new ability, we do remember to lower the effort with which we employ it to the absolute minimum, the case often arises that there

is simply an awful lot going on, and it is difficult to keep track of it all! The more we can master this, the better performers we become.

Fear of feeling

A third category of problem also related to emotion and performance is of another order. One of my students possessed considerable expressive gifts and showed an exceptional affinity for Chopin. Yet despite repeated lessons aimed at her developing a really healthy, beautiful cantilena and opening up her sound, it had remained small. Even in the opening melody of Beethoven's Sonata in A flat major, Op. 110 she simply could not sing. Finally by my basically forcing her to use the 'whole arm as finger' technique, her sound eventually began to blossom. At this point I noticed a curious phenomenon: her arm was trembling—a small but continuous and almost out of control vibration. Finally the real nature of her situation dawned on me and we paused.

I told her, "I have always counted you among my most gifted students. Your Chopin has at times moved me to tears in a most genuine way. Powerful, emotionally almost searing in intensity, with a very profound understanding of its philosophical content. And yet your sound has remained small. I never realized why until now.

'These emotions you feel are so powerful that they can become even frightening. They can invade you, take you over, live in you, and the experience is so unsettling that you simply do not know how to handle it. And so you run. You play it safe, you don't touch *that*, don't really face it, because it is too overwhelming. But now because you feel you cannot *face* these emotions, your only alternative becomes to shut them out, clamp them down.

'You have a dilemma on your hands. By avoiding your greatest asset you turn it into your greatest problem. I have been working on technique with you, but even if you learn the techniques, your unresolved inner struggle will always override your technical knowledge. You will never be able to use the elements of musical and pianistic craft you are now acquiring until you realize and fully experience this truth: your capacity for strong emotion is not a character flaw but pure gold! If you only knew it! This is what will separate you from a hundred other pianists! This is what audiences crave. And yet you are running away from it!

'You may feel, if you really embark on this struggle, that you have opened a Pandora's box. That you are really and truly going crazy! But you must stick with it most courageously if you hold any hope of reaching the stage of true artistic

maturity I know is possible for you. I am with you 100 percent in this. I know how hard it will be. It will be tumultuous, destabilizing, disorienting, and frightening. But you must go through it and reach the other side, where you still feel these amazing emotions but now you have made them *yours*. You will have acknowledged them: their existence, their power and their importance. They will have become less frightening to you because you will have developed a working relationship with them. You honour them as your gold, your gift, and they in turn become little by little more your servant, less your torturer!"

This student had completely the opposite problem from the first discussed above. Instead of thinking she was feeling something when actually she felt nothing, she avoided feeling anything because she was actually feeling a very large and overwhelming something!

The way we happened upon it was interesting: when I forced her to play with the real sound the composition should have, she couldn't avoid feeling the emotions! A tangible experience of the true content of the work in sound—a powerful physico-audio experience—evoked the corresponding powerful emotions in her. She could no longer *not* feel them!

How many pianists could play big but don't, because unbeknownst to themselves, they are avoiding facing the huge, fascinating, compelling maelstrom of strong emotion which all humanity shares—the emotions that most certainly gave birth to these great works in the first place! How many play small not because they don't feel the emotions but because they daren't *face* them! A deeper, richer, more satisfying musical reality exists out there, or perhaps we should better say *in* there. By developing your sound, your strength, your musical craftsmanship, I hope you can come to know this reality ever more intimately and rewardingly.

APPENDIXES

APPENDIX I
EXCERPTS FROM *AWARENESS THROUGH MOVEMENT*: A THEORETICAL FRAMEWORK

In my forward I mention the necessity for a new path to pianistic perfection—there are many reasons why old draconian practices no longer suit our purpose. These passages from Moshe Feldenkrais' seminal book, *Awareness Through Movement*, present some of the background trains of thought that led me to formulate my general approach and my new style of keyboard exercises.

The difficulty of changing an earlier pattern

A man tends to regard his self- image as something bestowed upon him by nature, although it is, in fact, the result of his own experience. His appearance, voice, way of thinking... are all taken for granted as realities born within him whereas every important element in the individual's relationship to other people and to society is actually the result of extensive training... The arts of walking, speaking, reading are skills the individual accumulates over a period of many years; each of them depends on chance, and on the place and period of his birth. The acquisition of a second language is not as easy as that of the first, and the pronunciation of the newly learned language will impose itself on the second. *Every pattern of action that has become fully assimilated will* **interfere** *with the patterns of* **subsequent versions** *of that action* [bold, italics mine].

... The difficulties lie less in the learning of a new habit than in the *changing* of habits of body, feeling and mind from their estab-

lished patterns. What is meant here is not the simple substitution of one activity by another, but a change in the way an act is performed, a change in its whole dynamics so that the new method will be in every respect as good as or even better than the old.[1]

Thus we see that improving our technique is not as easy as it might seem. There's a double difficulty. This is why I hope that pedagogues will eventually incorporate the new patterns of movement engendered by my exercises into piano methods for beginners, that these 'movement templates' be learned in the easiest fashion—imprinted on the nice clean *tabula rasa* of fresh young musical minds!

There is no awareness of many parts of the body

A person who lies down on his back and tries to sense his entire body systematically—that is, turning his attention to every limb and part of the body in turn—finds that certain sections respond easily while others remain mute or dull and beyond the range of his awareness. The parts of the body that are easily defined in the awareness are those (such as the thumbs, fingers, lips) that serve man daily, while the parts that are dull or mute in his awareness play only an indirect in his life (such as the middle of the back or the back of the head between the ears) and are almost missing completely from his self-image when he is in action.[2]

My exercises are designed to wake up all the sleeping parts of your pianistic mechanism, so that *all* the physical parts of yourself and their functions are included in the range of your awareness, becoming a permanent part of your self-image.

A complete self-image is a rare and ideal state

A complete self-image would involve full awareness of all joints in the skeletal structure as well as of the entire surface of the body—at the back, the sides, between the legs and so on; this is

---

[1] Feldenkrais, 20.
[2] Ibid., 20-21.

an ideal condition and hence a rare one. We can all demonstrate to ourselves that everything we do is in accordance with the limits of our self-image and that this image is no more than a narrow sector of the ideal image.[3]

Did your investigations inspired by my text lead you to any conclusions in this regard? Did you discover, for instance the insidious collapsing of your second knuckle? Does it demonstrate at least one gap between your own self-image and the pianistic ideal?

Individuals act in accordance with their subjective image

The difference between image and reality may be as much as 300 percent and even more. Persons who normally have a sunken chest—flatter than it should be and too flat to serve them efficiently (to breathe effectively), are likely to indicate its depth as several times larger than it actually is if asked to do so with their eyes closed. The sunken chest appears right to them, because any expansion of the chest to normal dimensions feels to them as a deliberately puffed out chest would to another person.[4]

Again, when you play in such a way that consciously generates and maintains your hand structure, does it feel so different from your usual mode of playing as to unsettle and even disconcert you?

Systematic correction of the system is more useful than correction of single actions

From what has been said about the self-image, it emerges that systematic correction of the image will be a quicker and more efficient approach than the correction of single actions and errors in modes of behaviour, the incidence of which increases as we come to deal with smaller errors. The establishment of an initial more or less complete, although approximate, image will make it possible to improve the general dynamics instead of dealing with individual actions piecemeal. This second type of im-

---

[13] Ibid., 21.

[14] Ibid., 23.

provement may be likened to correcting playing on an instrument that is not properly tuned. Improving the general dynamics of the image becomes the equivalent of tuning the piano itself, as it is much easier to play correctly on an instrument that is in tune than on one that is not.[5]

Again, the implications are obvious: my exercises 'tune' your body—your mental and physical piano playing apparatus. Your entire 'pianist' self-image is improved, empowering you to better meet each individual pianistic challenge.

Later on in his book Feldenkrais makes the bold assertion that

Correction of movement is the best means for human self-improvement.

He gives several reasons—altogether they make a pretty convincing and comprehensive list:

1) The nervous system is occupied mainly with movement—thus when we engage the nervous system in *movement* we act on our *selves* in the most complete way.

2) We are more experienced at distinguishing qualities of movement than of feeling or thought

3) We have a richer experience of movement

4) The ability to move is important to self-value

5) *All* muscular activity is movement

6) Movements reflect the state of the nervous system. The muscles contract as a result of an unending series of impulses from the nervous system...Obviously neither position, expression or voice can be changed without a change in the nervous system that mobilizes the outward and visible changes. Thus, when we refer to muscular movement, we mean, in fact, the impulses of the nervous system that activate the muscles, which cannot function

---

[15] Ibid., 23-24.

without impulses to direct them. From this we may derive a conclusion that seems paradoxical at first sight: Improvement in action and movement will appear only after a prior change in the
brain and nervous system has occurred.

7) Movement is the basis of awareness

8) 'Hinges of habit': All behaviour is a complex of mobilized
muscles, sensing, feeling and thought. The motor cortex of the
brain lies just a few millimeters above the brain strata dealing
with associative processes. Owing to the close proximity to the
motor cortex of the brain structures dealing with thought and
feeling, and the tendency of processes in brain tissue to diffuse
and spread to neighboring tissues, a change in the motor cortex
will have parallel effects on thinking and feeling. A fundamental
change in the motor basis within any single integration pattern
will break up the cohesion of the whole and thereby leave thought
and feeling without anchorage in the patterns of their established
routines. In this condition, it is much easier to effect changes in
thinking and feeling, for the muscular part through which thinking and feeling reach our awareness has changed and no longer
expresses the patterns preciously familiar to us. Habit has lost its
chief support, that of the muscles, and has become more amenable to change.[6]

Crucial for us to note—the important thing is to hang on to the new, unfamiliar way of playing for that preliminary period when it doesn't seem to go
so well. This is because at first you are not only cultivating the new habit, but
also simultaneously fighting to eradicate the old. It takes time, but eventually
at a certain point that hesitated-ness literally dissolves—it's a very noticeable
phenomenon—this is a sign that the new habit has been assimilated to the
point where it is now the template by which all further variations on it are
measured.

Still later in his book, much of the preamble to Feldenkrais' actual ATM
lessons applies equally well to my exercises and approach.

---

[16] Ibid., 33-38.

The lessons are designed to improve ability, that is, to expand the boundaries of the possible, to turn the impossible into the possible, the difficult into the easy, and the easy into the elegant. Only those activities that are easy and pleasant will become a part of man's habitual life and serve him at all times. Actions that are hard to carry out, for which man must force himself to overcome his inner opposition, will never become a part of his normal daily life (read 'practice routine').

We should differentiate clearly between improvement of ability and sheer effort for its own sake. We should do better to direct our willpower *towards* improving our ability.

Ability and willpower

To the extent that ability increases, the need for conscious efforts of the will decreases. The effort required to increase ability provides sufficient and efficient exercise for our willpower. If you consider the matter carefully you will discover that most people of strong willpower (which they have trained for its own sake) are also people with relatively poor ability. People who know how to operate effectively do so without great preparation and without much fuss. Men of great willpower tend to apply too much force instead of using moderate forces more effectively.

If you rely mainly on your willpower, you will develop your ability to strain and become accustomed to applying an enormous amount of force to actions that can be carried out with much less energy, if it is properly directed and graduated.

Both these ways of operating usually achieve their objective, but the former may also cause considerable damage. Force that is not converted into movement does not simply disappear, but is dissipated into damage done to joints, muscles, and other sections of the body used to create the effort. Energy not converted into movement turns into heat within the system and causes changes that will require repair before the system can operate efficiently again.

Whatever we do well does not seem difficult to us. We may even venture to say that *movements we find difficult are not carried out correctly* (italics mine).

To understand movement we must feel, not strain

To learn we need time, attention and discrimination; to discriminate we must sense. This means that in order to learn we must sharpen our powers of sensing, and if we try to do most things by sheer force we shall achieve precisely the opposite of what we need.

Sharpened discrimination

"A fool cannot feel" said the Hebrew sages. If a man does not feel he cannot sense differences, and of course he will not be able to distinguish between one action and another. Without this ability to differentiate there can be no learning, and certainly no increase in the ability to learn. It is not a simple matter, for the human senses are linked to the stimuli that produce them so that discrimination is finest when the stimulus is smallest. More delicate and improved control of movement (something we assume desired by all pianists) is possible only through the increase of sensitivity, through a greater ability to sense differences.

The force of habit

We need a great deal of persistence and enough knowledge to enable us to move according to what we know rather than according to habit. If a person usually stands slouched, his pelvis is pushed too far forward and there will be far too great a curve in his back for good posture. If he then pushes his pelvis back and straightens his spine, the position will seem abnormal to him, and he will quickly return to his normal stance.

It is therefore impossible to change habit by relying on sensation alone. Some conscious mental effort must be made until the adjusted position [or new way of playing] ceases to feel abnormal

and becomes the new habit. It is much more difficult to change a habit than one might think, as all who have tried it know.

In changing our piano habits we have it one better, as the sound we are producing is an added spur to our maintaining the new habit. Love of that sound and the desire to keep producing it is an added motivation to effective learning.

Freeing an action of wasted energy

An efficient machine is one in which all the parts fit together accurately; all are properly oiled, with no grit or dirt between adjacent surfaces; where all the fuel used is turned into kinetic energy up to the thermodynamic limit; and where there is no noise or vibration, that is, no energy is wasted on useless movement that cuts down the effective operating power of the machine.

The exercises we are about to begin are intended to achieve just this, to gradually eliminate from one's mode of action all superfluous movements, everything that hampers, interferes with, or opposes movement.

In the systems of teaching generally accepted today emphasis is placed on achieving a certain aim at any price, without regard for the amount of disorganized and diffused effort that has gone into it. So long as the organs of thought, feeling, and control are not organized for action that is coordinated, continuous, smooth, and efficient—and therefore also pleasant—we are involving parts of the body indiscriminately, even if they are in no way required for this action or even interfere with it. One result is that we quite often perform an action and its opposite at the same time. Only mental effort can then make the part that is directed toward the goal overcome the other parts of the body operating to frustrate it. In this way, unfortunately, *willpower may tend to cover up an inability* to carry out the action properly. The right way is to learn to eliminate the efforts opposing the goal and to employ willpower only when a superhuman effort is required.

We shall come back to this point when the reader has proved it to himself through his own experience; he will then be able to progress along the desired road.

I like these last passages for many reasons. They betray Feldenkrais' background as a scientist and mechanical engineer—one of the big reasons I was drawn to his method rather than some of the other 'touchy-feely' fads that abound these days. Many of these sentences have their direct corollary in my text. For example, when he writes, *"No energy is wasted on useless movement that cuts down the effective operating power of the machine,"* read "Your classic arm movement out to the side may be hindering not helping you". For *"We are involving parts of the body indiscriminately, even if they are in no way required for this action or even interfere with it"*, read "Rising off the piano bench to produce a more impressive *forte* is totally counterproductive: all that lifting energy is not being used to produce sound". For *"we quite often perform an action and its opposite at the same time"*, read, "an up and down movement of the wrist on each note (to 'produce tone') is sure ruin your phrase line". And for *"Willpower may tend to cover up an inability"*, read "Banging is not an indication of too much strength but rather of weakness."

These passages also state in a nutshell the crux of the matter—here we have a clear expression of the underlying rationale for the development of my approach to piano technique. In short:

Define what is required from the piano in terms of music and sound.

Evaluate whether you are fulfilling these requirements. If not, what is missing from your mental and physical ability that prevents you from succeeding?

Acquire the abilities you need to fulfill your intentions in the most elegant, artistically complete way possible. Improve the functioning of your physical apparatus as a basis for improving your playing.

APPENDIX II
FELDENKRAIS AND THE MUSICIAN

With the increased incidence of music performance related injuries and the increasing achievement orientation of musicians leading to tense, inflexible playing, more pedagogues are beginning to explore movement education in relation to music performance. Disciplines such as the Alexander Technique (on the curriculum at Juilliard, the Guildhall School and the Royal Academy of Music in London) are increasingly popular, fostering better use of one's physical self.

Moshe Feldenkrais knew Matthias Alexander in the 1940s in London, and Alexander provided one crucial seed in the development of the Feldenkrais Method, espoused by such musicians as conductor Igor Markevich, guitarist Narciso Ypes (who maintained that Feldenkrais was personally responsible for the regeneration of his career), violinist Yehudi Menuhin and pianist Leon Fleisher, who has included Feldenkrais in Tanglewood's regular summer curriculum.

Where Alexander Technique improves function through directly addressing posture per se, Feldenkrais Method focuses more on the movement functions themselves that *generate* good posture. For instance, attention to the head-neck relationship generally only follows preliminary work on movement in and around the pelvic area, center for organization and power in the body. Feldenkrais Method cultivates the harmonious interaction of *all* parts of one's musculo-skeletal assembly, leading to a functionally oriented rather than an external, appearance-oriented postural improvement.

A sophisticated physical organization may look remarkably simple, easy and calm, but the easier it looks, probably the more difficult it is to achieve. An appropriately balanced quality of muscular-skeletal involvement at the piano must be largely supportive rather than active: well-intentioned but overly effortful attempts to involve the whole body in an activity can become counterproductive, causing more harm than good.

Feldenkrais Method avoids distracting the musician from musical concerns by providing a neutral, music-free environment for the training and improvement of one's movement habits. When one returns to one's instrument, analysis of each exact physical movement is replaced by the creation of a state of conscious readiness. The body itself is wiser, more intelligent: one realizes one's musical intentions more instinctively or reflexively because one is no longer inadvertently interfering with that process!

Besides its advantages in content, Feldenkrais Method offers a practical form of presentation for a music school setting. Awareness Through Movement group lessons are cost—as well as pedagogically—effective, while private Functional Integration sessions can address more severe cases such as tendonitis or carpal tunnel syndrome. These are movement rather than medically related problems, which is why Feldenkrais Method generally proves a more effective form of treatment.

APPENDIX III
THE PIANIST'S PROGRESS:
A MINI-AUTOBIOGRAPHY

(written 1993)

I was born musically talented yet had neither the mad internal desire nor the external surroundings that occasionally see the early development of outstanding ability. My piano teachers until university kept me interested but did not contribute much else. Mr. Cook told me to curl my fingers; I, failing to see why, couldn't be bothered, and that was the extent of my technical training.

Although the bulk of my technique was acquired later, my perceptual skills did develop well—I had a powerfully emotional, physically tangible response to wonderful music, and as my discrimination developed I became incessantly curious as to what separated great music making from the merely competent. Why did Ashkenazy thrill me to bits on one occasion yet bore me to tears on another? Could these radically differing qualities of performance be quantified, pinned down? This fascination, coupled with a dawning realization of the immense body of technical skills needed to play really well, led me to seek out teachers who might help me make up precious lost time, and perhaps offer some clues as to what constitutes transcendental piano playing.

My inquiry eventually led me to Phil Cohen, who had studied with Montreal pianistic doyenne Yvonne Hubert (a pupil of Alfred Cortot) alongside others such as Ronald Turini and Andre Laplante. Cohen's interest in the psychology and neuro-motor organization of performance led to his developing a unique pedagogical method. I first became acquainted with Cohen's principles while studying with two of his protégés, the first being composer-pianist Alan Belkin.

Alan Belkin : The Orchestrating Hand

Belkin was the first to show me the enormous world of orchestral sonority inherent in the piano. He could explain what he meant by 'play fortissimo but

don't bang', and showed me how to control and color my sound in many aspects to a startling degree. I still remember the thrill of the suddenly blossoming, magically three-dimensional sound obtained by 'pinging the pinkies' —voicing the top and the bottom—and my delight in seeing passagework, when played with true evenness, metamorphose into something sparkling, bubbling, exciting. It was here that I began to realize piano playing is to a large extent craftsmanship, involving much more than instinct, emotion and good intentions.

At this point in my academic studies I switched from the performance stream into theory, to grasp more fully Belkin's presentation of musical form and its inflection in performance. I studied voice and accompanied singers, in order to experience directly the singing quality I wanted to pull from the instrument. I studied composition: the pianist who thinks and perceives compositionally will more likely have a rich, three-dimensional sound.

Lauretta Milkman : The Choreographing Hand

Belkin eventually sent me on to Lauretta Milkman, who honed my physical approach to the keyboard even further. Laurie first acquainted me with many principles to be clarified and amplified later.

One thing she taught was a way of entering the keyboard that by appearances could be misinterpreted as a sort of 'arm weight' technique but which was actually an arm *function* technique: I learned how the particular organization of the arm's mass and muscular activity can have a radical effect on the sound. Rather than wrist position she taught wrist function: if I stopped at any point in a phrase could I be instantaneously at rest? Paradoxically, could I feel at rest even as I engaged in complex activity at the keyboard? 'Enter', 'rest', 'move through' and 'release': central themes of Laurie's keyboard etiquette.

This queer feeling of 'active resting' was achieved partly by something like a flip of the hand, wrist or forearm before entering a note or chord. This flip can be used to define both rhythmic and phrase structure.

Application III.1
WRIST II: THE HAND-FLIP 'CATCHING' TECHNIQUE

Try resting your hand on a flat surface like the desk in front of you. Begin to pull your hand away from the table: first your elbow begins to rise, then your wrist follows, and finally your hand slides along the surface and then leaves it. Just at the moment your fingers become free of the surface, return to it suddenly, as if you want to "catch" something that's on it with the heel of your hand. This movement is complicated to describe yet simple to do. The trick is, as the arm is going up the hand will follow: as the arm starts suddenly downwards the hand *continues* up, and only *after* it is above the wrist and fully extended will it be pulled in the opposite direction, following the wrist back down. It's like the Hawaiian hula dancers, that wavy motion of the hand and arm that seem paradoxically always together yet at the same time moving in opposite directions. This flip I call 'catching'.

When done properly—that is to say with true refinement and elegance, maintaining an exact balance between all opposing forces within the mechanism—it can free the fingers for truly independent, maximally effective movement. Most wonderful in all this is the resulting improvement in sound quality and musical expression. Aside from Laurie herself, Lublina Edlina, pianist with the Borodin Trio, provides a stellar example of this playing style.

As I became more aware of what could be achieved at the piano, I longed to hear true mastery of the instrument, the fantasy-filled, tasteful, enormously colorful and fluid playing of so many old pianists I knew only through recordings. Horowitz alone remained to be heard live, and hear him I did, enthralled! He also best exemplified the highly sophisticated organization that is the keystone of the Cohen philosophy.

Phil Cohen: The Mindful Hand

Philip Cohen's contribution to piano pedagogy has been twofold: a comprehensive analysis of the physical and perceptual organization of the master pianist, and the development of a method to effectively communicate much of this knowl-

edge to the student.

Cohen knows that the specific nature of a music's content, the very shape and character of its contour and inflection, is reflected in the physical movements of the performer. His approach is to draw attention to this correlation, improving music by directly addressing and modifying the physical habits involved in its expression. Much is summed up in this little nutshell: *Everything you do, sounds*. In playing, every movement no matter how small, and even each *sub-component* of a movement, will have its affect on the sound you're making.

Cohen's method is somewhat unique in its characteristic focus on the physical: not simply on relaxation, but on the exact balance between tension and relaxation, the exact path of movement of one's arm through space required to inflect a phrase shape and tone exactly as one desires. Through touch he communicates his ideas often more precisely and effectively than is possible through words, taking hold, moving, guiding one's arm, wrist, hand or finger, sometimes to the extent of literally 'playing' the player!

The playing of Cohen's students tends towards a noticeable sophistication of rhythm, depth of sound and musical integrity. My preliminary assimilation of his ideas with Belkin and Milkman perhaps facilitated the quantum leap in my abilities that took place when I experienced Cohen's cultivation of a Zen-like awareness, of 'mindful hands', directly.

This leap forward did not happen overnight. To use these transformative choreographic habits in performance effectively, there must be a period of internalization—they must become instinctive. You can't communicate with an audience when you're thinking about your elbow! The process of integrating what Cohen taught me continued long after my studies with him were finished—and continues to this day! I owe much to Phil Cohen for the germination of many ideas in this book.

Tom Plaunt: The Phraseful Hand

Tom Plaunt has a performer's instincts, intuitively sensing just the amount of exaggeration needed to have a phrase shape or voicing really touch the hearts of an audience. Tom cultivates an extravagant lyricism and luscious tone, focuses on pedaling, voicing, crescendo and decrescendo to suffuse his students' interpretations with expressive life. As I became familiar with the central concepts of his German training it was gratifying to see how radically differing logical trains of thought could lead to equally successful artistic results. But still eluding me was a

conceptual framework that could integrate all aspects of true mastery.

All my teachers to this point had noticed a sort of visceral tension that seemed to hinder my finger, hand and arm movements. It seemed that a more global exploration of physical organization was the best next step, so I turned to Feldenkrais Method, a discipline not related solely to piano, which investigates the essentials of the learning process itself.

Feldenkrais: The Mindful Body

Feldenkrais Method is specifically designed to develop superb physical organization, economy of movement, clarity of intention and mastery of execution: the very qualities exemplified by the master musician, dancer or athlete. Evolving from many illustrious predecessors such as judo, yoga, acupuncture, Zen meditation, Alexander Technique and Western neurophysiology, Feldenkrais Method practically and scientifically improves the actual neurological processes involved in learning

Throughout my four-year Feldenkrais practitioner training and since then as well, my posture has improved to the point where I have a stable, consistent and dependable stance at the piano. My sound has become bigger, more colorful and controlled. I sense more clearly when I am moving incorrectly, and I know better how to fix it.

Developed by Israeli physicist and judo master Moshe Feldenkrais in the mid-twentieth century, the method has a fourfold functional focus: *mechanical, muscular, neural* and *personal.*

But instead of beginning with mechanical training towards improvement of ability, Feldenkrais lessons or exercises use the body to first address neurological issues specifically to improve the functioning of the

    - *sensory-motor feedback loop* with which the body adjusts its movements, *receiving* information from the sensory nerves and *controlling* the muscles through the *motor* nerves.

    - This leads to the optimum balance of muscle *tonus* throughout the body, which in turn allows increased

    - *mechanical efficiency* in the system of levers and struts known as the skeleton.

    - All these three enhance the ease, *elegance and effectiveness* of one's movements, causing a tangible, concrete improvement of one's sense of

self as a person: a physical entity with perceptions, desires, intentions and abilities.

These foci are quite distinct from those of yoga, meditation or other related disciplines, and are achieved by increasing kinesthetic sensitivity through series of small, slow, easy, logically sequenced movements. In *Awareness Through Movement* (ATM) classes, students are guided through a movement series verbally, whereas in private *Functional Integration* (FI) lessons, the practitioner guides and senses manipulatively, tailoring movements to the student's specific problems.

The primary effect of Feldenkrais is not so much relaxation as a heightened physical readiness, a clear, focused energy, an increased awareness of *what* one is doing and *how* one is doing it. Now when I sit at the piano, the clarity of my physical organization ensures that no inadvertent muscle contraction or posture interferes with the fulfillment of my intentions.[1]

Though it proved to be a crucial element of my training, Feldenkrais alone could not bring me to the level of pianistic ability I sought. My quest was not over. I had always been attracted to the Russian school's healthy mastery of the instrument, so perhaps fate smiled on me the day I first heard Kemal Gekich play.

Kemal Gekich: The Masterful Hand

He reminds me of Horowitz in his quality of repose, of detached observation that nonetheless produces such a rich welter of sounds and colors. Most striking is the wonderful rhythmic vitality of his playing: his sound is virile, athletic, lithe, yet never heavy or unpleasant. His tremendous sense of pulse literally compels one forward through the music. In the playing of Kemal Gekich I finally found that magical, elusive synthesis: musical expression and transcendental technical execution: he seemed to possess all the qualities I had been seeking!

I have often marveled at the tremendously individual style of the great master pianists of the past. I have also wondered how to de-homogenize my own students' sound and have them create something truly personal which nonetheless respects the rules of true musicianship. Gekich's pedagogical framework (derived from the Russian tradition coupled with his own deep exploration of technique) combined with much of what I have previously learned, provides a body of

---

[1] For more on the applications of Feldenkrais Method in music pedagogy, see appendix II

knowledge whose globality can stimulate the evolution of each student's individual style.

Content

A thorough, thoughtful pedagogue, Gekich stresses a logical progression that begins with musical content. The litany of each lesson: what is a composition's emotional tone, its program, the meaning of each phrase or articulation? We feel that all music is programmatic, derived from human declamation, drama, ideas, emotions and abstractions. Interpretation is first of all the manifestation of music's content—its meaning. Although this idea is nothing new, the style of its implementation in Gekich's approach differs markedly from most of what I have seen in the West. How does one ensure that it 'tells a story'? If one has a clear conception of a music's meaning yet cannot *immediately* manifest it in performance, one must ask oneself 'Why?' and then turn one's attention to the practicalities of musicianship, to pianistic *craft*, to find the answers.

Good phrasing and expression without inherent meaning does not satisfy in the end. But if one has not first undertaken a composition's solid technical preparation there is no hope even for good phrasing and expression. Do not shortchange yourself: proper attention paid here does not sterilize one's playing, but ultimately frees one to realize fully one's musical conception and finally to play with true spontaneity.

Nuts and Bolts: Rhythm

The wonderful rhythmic integrity of Gekich's playing is no accident: effective rhythmic execution is the central pillar of a solid technical foundation. I may seem to belabor the obvious, yet very few pianists actually play with good rhythm, 100 percent. The execution of this seemingly simple task is actually difficult and complex, and its constituent parts bear detailed scrutiny:

Meter

Meter (the pattern of strong and weak beats delineated in a composition) is manifested in sound by *pulse* (as distinct from accent). Pulse should always be present, articulated and *felt* by the performer—however, the listener should not necessarily notice any accentual definition of pulse. If pulse is properly

defined, one merely hears a certain clarity, richness, excitement or color in the sound. The sound *lives*. Dynamic or agogic accents on the other hand are used to *highlight* structural or emotional content. One *should* draw the listener's attention to these—make sure they are noticed.

Pulse

The creation of healthy pulse involves slight stresses correlated to metrical structure. These stresses must not appear to disturb the even flow of attacks. However, to create an aesthetically pleasing illusion of true evenness, we must actually play unevenly! We must in fact articulate minuscule pauses—just big enough to exist—before every stressed note. Doing this

> - highlights the rhythmic structure, making it more visceral, larger than life,

> - counterbalances the tendency to rush by forcing one to really listen and control one's attack, and

> - allows one to sense immediately any excess effortfulness accumulated in the last group, and to adjust oneself accordingly.

Practice with a metronome may help establish a rudimentary sense of rhythmic regularity, but primarily it should serve only as a catalyst for the *internal* generation of healthy pulse. Far more effective than using the metronome is the overemphasis of metrical stresses in practice, while playing the intervening unaccented notes absolutely evenly and with about one tenth the effort normally expended. This must be done with a positively manic intensity of listening, and if done successfully has many beneficial side effects. For instance, it frees up the upper arm muscles that tend by overwork to inhibit free rhythmic flow, and allows the discovery of new, more subtle and efficient finger movements.

The character of these stresses is crucial: they must have the maximum mass possible with no sense of weight or pressing. The sound must be absolutely clean and sharp with no 'spread' or distortion, yet rich, not thin or pinched. This ensures that one's skeletal structure is used with maximum mechanical effectiveness: there is minimum energy loss through 'shear', the setting of one bone at an incorrect angle to another. With bones thus properly aligned, the muscles have no superfluous compensatory work to do and thus are free to maximally fulfill one's intentions.

Learning can be defined as the process of making distinctions: the heightened perception of hierarchical metrical levels engendered by this practice ensures that musical structure is learned with maximum kinesthetic richness and clarity.

Phrase Inflection

Phrase inflection is achieved through dynamic, articulate and agogic accentuation and through manipulation of the even flow of attacks (as this last occurs continually I keep it distinct from its subset, rubato).

Too often so-called 'musical' or expressive' rubato, heartbreakingly uniform or predictable, is not generated by the internal compositional structure but is rather imposed from without according to what happens to be in vogue at the time.

Only when one breaks habitual patterns of generic 'expressive' rhythmic manipulation and begins articulating the music's *internal* rhythmic structure, can the wonderful world of phrase inflection begin to be explored in a musically satisfying manner.

The playing of Rachmaninoff, a master of pulse and the dramatic accent, proves a peerless example. Like other masters, he tends to put all the notes under a phrase mark a little closer together in time, thus allowing a little space between phrases without forcing musical flow to a bumping halt. This is called 'breathing', and although I would again seem to belabor the obvious, the way he does it leaves us green with envy! Also, he inflects melodic contour through a tremendously precise and varied use of dramatic accentuation and discreet variations in tempo: these occur *within* the context of a cohesive pulse.

Sound

Listeners said that Rachmaninoff's sound was wonderful, and surely his phrase inflection was a prime element of this. But of course a wide dynamic range is also crucial in producing a great piano sound. There are two ways to increase one's total dynamic range: extend it either up or down! Extending it up requires increased strength and coordination.

Application III.2
STRUCTURAL FUNCTION XIII: 'GRAB AND SHAKE' TO REALLY JOIN WITH THE PIANO

Try this graphic way to discover the true upper limit of one's dynamic range. Grab a fistful of notes and attempt to shake the whole instrument like a dog shaking a bone. Can't do it?

> Step 1: Then close the piano, *push* on it as hard as you can. *Really* try to send it bursting through the wall into the next practice room (or your kitchen!) like a tank coming out of a barn. Notice how you mobilize *all* of yourself to do this, mentally, psychically, physically. The arms must be *almost* straight, *almost* locked at the elbows *but not quite totally.* You feel how each part of your body—torso, shoulder, upper arm, forearm, hand, all *couple* to each other supply but firmly.

> Step 2: Now grab the piano somewhere—on a grand, on that ridge just under the pinblock that is available to you when the fallboard is closed but the lid open. Take really firm hold of the instrument and *shake* it! *Move* it so it rocks on its casters! Ah, *now* you *can* achieve something!

> Step 3: Now open the fallboard again and see what you can do while grabbing two comfortable (not too wide spread, not too compact, something that complies to the natural position of the hand) five-note chords. I have had hilarious experiences with some of my more petite students who try this and it ends up looking like the *piano* is shaking *them*! However, with some determination and persistency, anyone larger than the average ten year old *can* do this!

Even if one can't even make the piano budge a millimeter, the attempt itself mobilizes one's forces, focuses one and gives a tangible, graphic impression of the feeling involved in producing a warm, resonant, rich and colorful fortissimo. Warning: finding this procedure difficult (or ludicrous!) may indicate the limitations not only of one's dynamic range but also of one's imagination!

Extending one's total dynamic range downwards needs delicacy and sensitivity: these must have a foundation of *control*. Paradoxically, the exercise above will

also aid your finding a finer, subtler *pianissimo*, by providing you with a secure foundation on which such control can be based.

Widening overall dynamic range leads to the next element of crucial importance: dynamic *discrimination*. It is not easy to produce even five distinct dynamic levels of piano sound. To do this *simultaneously* brings us to another principal concern of pianists, *voicing*. Voicing of course is everything in piano sound. No matter how much voicing we do, more is always possible and will almost always enhance the sound. This is the central issue in doing what the piano was intended to do: creating a whole orchestra of sounds. The accentuation practices mentioned earlier are effective here as well for maximum control of color and contrast in voicing.

Conception

These issues are just a few of the many one must address in honing pianistic and musical execution. But of overriding importance is conception. A fortissimo, staccato chord played angrily will sound completely different from exactly the same articulation played scherzando. The way in which a performer mobilizes himself, first in a feeling state and then in a physical state analogous to that, is the prime influence on his or her sound.

The exact transcription even of a composer's every note, phrase, dynamic, articulation and tempo indication cannot alone carry out his intentions. To create something of lasting value, musical sounds must express something of the intangible: another being's direct human experience.

Alchemy

Clearly, attention to the nuts and bolts is the largest part of a pianist's work. Though many are competent, why do so few transcend as a Horowitz, Rachmaninoff or even a Gekich? What process saw their tremendous natural gifts come to such full fruition?

Artistic striving gives rise to sophisticated physical organization—not vice versa

My initial fascination with Feldenkrais stemmed from the realization that artists such as Horowitz were doing something radically different from the normal, and these differences were perceptible in their physical organization. However, when told by David Dubal that he had the most wonderful nerv-

ous system in the world, Horowitz cackled with glee at the absurdity: "I'm a nervous system!"[2] Horowitz's quality of organization seems to be a result of whatever process he went through in order to play great, rather than a prerequisite for it. Obviously, Horowitz was first and foremost an artist, his primary concern was music, his exquisitely organized nervous system no more than a tool used in music's expression.

Physical ability only a tool for the artist

Feldenkrais Method as well is simply a valuable tool whose ultimate usefulness depends on many other factors. A pianist must be able to discriminate fine differences in physical movement—without a highly developed sensitivity he simply cannot play well. Even Glenn Gould, who said he would avoid all technical considerations in his teaching, clearly had thought about it in great detail (as his journals attest[3]), and in practice *did* work out his own highly idiosyncratic yet totally effective system. He *said* he wouldn't think about it because he knew that to avoid musical suicide, physical considerations must only be a response to musical ones.

Kemal Gekich never had a Feldenkrais lesson, never had a Cohen for a teacher. He describes his own work as an intuitive, trial and error process. After solving a particular technical problem he may notice that his hand moves differently or is shaped in a particular way, yet it is as if the hand learned on its own, the organism found its own way. He has a strong capacity to remember the newly learned organization and apply it elsewhere as needed.

He seems to be working out a conscious system on an unconscious level, respecting as he does the very nature of the process. A musician's art must grow not from technical concerns but rather be conceived in a world of fantasy and imagination, and be born of a burning desire to communicate something of that world through the medium of sound. One may have oodles of ability, intelligence, talent, aesthetic sense, dramatic flair, yet in the end it is a certain quality of intense desire that sees the greatest artists transcending the norm.

---

[112] David Dubal, *Evenings with Horowitz: A Personal Portrait* (Secaucus, N.J.: Carol Pub. Group, 1991).

[113] Otto Grindrich, *Glenn Gould: A Life and Variations* (New York: Random House, 1989).

Synthesis

Moshe Feldenkrais defined health as being able to fulfill one's unavowed dreams. For one such as I, who in the beginning lacked the burning desire and engaged intellect of a Gekich or Horowitz, Feldenkrais fostered a sense of health, not only of body but of spirit, which in the end empowered the tangible manifestation of this inner musician's unavowed dreams. Feldenkrais empowered me to activate my passion for music in a practical way.

Kemal Gekich, approaching the problem from the opposite direction, feels that if one plays well one will be healthy—one won't hurt oneself and won't need Feldenkrais either! He is right, of course. Moreover, when one considers the startling fact that proper execution of all aspects of rhythm as expounded by Gekich leads to the easy resolution of many problems of technical facility, one sees that the synthesis of the essential elements of these contrasting conceptual frameworks in the end can occur only in the context of pure music making.

The optimal physical organization cultivated through Feldenkrais-Cohen's choreographic concepts—these have been useful tools. It is appropriate that in their full, true integration into an artistic process they should fade into the background, sink into the unconscious, and thus manifest synthesis in the truest sense of the word.

Alan Fraser: The Activated Hand

As I work with students the world over, attempting to convey this conceptual framework in a practical way, I find their biggest immediate stumbling block is a simple lack of activity in the fingers and hand. For instance, although we feel that the fourth and fifth fingers are the weakest, in my experience it is the thumb and forefinger that are actually the most lax in the fulfillment of their duties. The most common flaw in legato playing is the failure to maintain support while moving to the thumb from one of the other fingers—most often the second—or back again. In some scores from my student days I even used to draw a little lobster claw to remind myself of the desired thumb-forefinger shape. However, this image is too rigid. Support must be derived from *active function* rather than through the dogged maintaining of a fixed position. The thumb-forefinger assembly is very strange: many students I've asked did not even realize that the thumb has three joints just like the other fingers, but that the third joint is nestled up against the wrist! Bringing the

third, uppermost joint of the thumb into play *opens up* that space between one and two. Maintaining this openness, feeling strength in that space, feeling it continually opening more and more, as if a balloon were continually expanding from within it, will empower this keystone of the hand's 'Russian arch' and improve overall functionality.

In addition to these aspects of the physical, stimulation of a pianist's imagination and desire provides the reason to wake their hands up. The resulting extra effort in the *right* place allows for freedom and ease, a well-deserved break from overexertion in all the supporting places, and leads to a new blossoming of both ability and spirit.

BIBLIOGRAPHY

Aide, William. *Starting from Porcupine*. Ottawa, Canada: Oberon Press, 1996.

Chaliapine, Fedor. *Ma Vie; traduit du Russe par Andre Pierre*. Paris: Albin Michel, 1932.

Cooke, James Francis. *Great Pianists on Piano Playing*. Philadelphia: Theo. Presser, 1913.

Dubal, David. *Evenings with Horowitz: A Personal Portrait*. Secaucus, N.J.: Carol Pub. Group, 1991.

————. *Horowitz Remembered*. New York: Schirmer Books, 1993.

Feldenkrais, Moshe. *Awareness Through Movement*. New York: Harper and Row, 1972.

Feynman, Richard. *Surely You`re Joking, Mr. Feynman!: Adventures of a Curious Character*. Edward Hutchings, ed. New York: W. W. Norton, 1997.

Gieseking, Walter, and Karl Leimer. *Piano Technique*. New York: Dover Publications, 1972.

Grindrich, Otto. *Glenn Gould: A Life and Variations*. New York: Random House, 1989.

Hoffman, Joseph. *Piano Playing with Piano Questions Answered*. New York: Dover Publications, 1976.

Horowitz, Joseph. *Conversations with Arrau*. New York: Knopf, 1982.

Kochevitsky, George. *The Art of Piano Playing, A Scientific Approach*. Evanston, Ill.: Summy-Birchard, 1967.

Matthay, Tobias. *The Visible and Invisible in Pianoforte Technique*. London: H. Milford, Oxford University Press, 1932.

Mohr, Franz with Edith Schaeffer. *My Life with the Great Pianists*. Grand Rapids, Mich.: Baker Books, 1996.

Neuhaus, Heinrich. *The Art of Piano Playing*. London: Barrie & Jenkins, 1986.

Ouspensky, P. D. *In Search of the Miraculous—Fragments of an Unknown Teaching*. Orlando: Harcourt and Brace, 1949.

Rosen, Charles. *The Classical Style*. New York: W. W. Norton & Co., 1972.

Schonberg, Harold. *Horowitz, His Life and Music*. New York: Simon & Schuster, 1992.

Schultz, Arnold. *The Riddle of the Pianist's Finger*. New York: Carl Fischer, 1936.

INDEX

abduction, of thumb, 72, 87-88

accent, agogic, 327-30, 342, 411, 412; arm vs. finger 283; as distinct from pulse, 410; dramatic, 412; dynamic, 304, 305, 310, 342, 411, 412; harmonic, 13; produced in wrong manner, 183; rhythmic, 16; risk of excessive, 127; unintended, 53, 249, 385

accompaniment, 17, 104, 126, 216, 220, 268, 324, 325, 332-33, 352, 353, 356

acoustic, playing a large, 67, 384-85

acoustics, science of, 18

action, finger, 43, 44, 141, 144, 146-48, 159, 168, 177, 229, 416

adduction, of thumb, 72

agogics, 220-21, 327-32, 342, 411, 412

Aide, William, 134-35

Alexander Technique, 2, 402, 408

arch, 75, 80; of the hand, 86, 102, 116, 246-48; in hand extension 102; Neuhaus leans on, 184; in the octave, 133, 260; Russian, 208-9, 281-82, 417; – support 125; thumb-fifth finger, 121, 102

arm, 25, 27, 44, 48, 71, 105, 133, 156, 248, 287, 297-98, 308-11, 332, 366, 401, 405-6; active, 253; basis for – freedom, 64-67, 84, 144-45; 'breathing' of, 66, 147, 229, 233-36, 257-58, 341; and contact with key, 337-38; differentiation from finger, 67, 116, 120, 141, 142, 273-77; facilitation of weight transfer, 93-94; in feather-legato, 184-85; in fingerstands, 57-58; fixation of, 38, 101, 144, 413; and grasping, 73-74; as guide, 237-40, 356; and hand, 156-60, 135, 145, 248; hidden involvement of – in playing, 145; internal activity of, 119, 136, 144, 161, 211, 283; involvement in tone production, 8, 24, 124-25, 180-81, 226, 389; isometric – wrestling, 162-63; and legato, 153, 243-45; looseness, 149, 156, 272, 278; normal position at rest, 253; over-effort, 8, 215, 252; passive vs. active, 135; as phraser 65, 174-76, 177-79, 183, 356, 407; position of, 37, 49, 117-18, 252; and rotation, 270; shaking of, 142, 306, stabilizing role, 11, 157, 178; sweep of, 126-29; swing of, 166-69; unified, 163; as whip, 109-10, 112-14, 163, 261-63; and wrist, 265

arm, upper, 11, 25, 27, 43, 119-20, 122, 136, 156, 158-60, 161, 163-65, 190, 211-13, 253, 283, 411, 413

200; loose, 109-10, 113, 265, 336; movement of, 265; negative consequences of its lateral motion, 190-91; as phrase machine, 177-79; in phrasing, 60-62, 158, 341-43, 401; – position, 59, 164-67, 405; stiffening, 38, 164, 260; and thumb, 199-200, 255, 416; transmission of forces through – , 165, 176-77

yin/yang, 344; leg, 55-6, 243; and finger, 60, 215-22

Ypes, Narciso, 402

Zen, 141, 407, 408

ABOUT THE AUTHOR

Born in Montreal in 1955, Canadian pianist Alan Fraser has made frequent appearances in recital and with orchestra on three continents, as well as numerous radio, television and CD recordings. He has bachelor's and master's degrees in theory and piano respectively from McGill University's Faculty of Music in Montreal (1980, 1987), as well as graduate diplomas in piano performance from Concordia University in Montreal (1984) and the Art Academy of the University of Novi Sad, Yugoslavia (1992). He completed a four-year professional training program in the Feldenkrais Method for neuromuscular re-education in 1992.

It was in Novi Sad that Alan Fraser began his longstanding collaboration with the virtuoso Kemal Gekich, as they pooled their ideas and shared their pedagogical expertise with many of Yugoslavia's top young pianists. There he also continued to pursue another of his passions, composing several choral and instrumental works. After a year's guest professorship in Wuhan, China (1999-2000), he has now returned to his professorship of piano and Feldenkrais at the Art Academy of Novi Sad. He divides his time between Novi Sad and Paris, France.